The U.S. Women's Movement in Global Perspective

People, Passions, and Power
Social Movements, Interest Organizations, and the Political Process
John C. Green, Series Editor

After the Boom edited by Stephen C. Craig and Stephen Earl Bennett
American Labor Unions in the Electoral Arena by Herbert B. Asher, Eric S.
  Heberlig, Randall B. Ripley, and Karen Snyder
Citizen Democracy, 2nd ed., by Stephen E. Frantzich
Coalitions across Borders edited by Joe Bandy and Jackie Smith
Cyberpolitics by Kevin A. Hill and John E. Hughes
Democracy's Moment edited by Ron Hayduk and Kevin Mattson
Gaia's Wager by Gary C. Bryner
Multiparty Politics in America edited by Paul S. Herrnson and John C.
  Green
Rage on the Right by Lane Crothers
Rethinking Social Movements edited by Jeff Goodwin and James M. Jasper
Social Movements and American Political Institutions edited by Anne N.
  Costain and Andrew S. McFarland
The Social Movement Society edited by David S. Meyer and Sidney Tarrow
The State of the Parties, 3rd ed., edited by John C. Green and Daniel M.
  Shea
The State of the Parties, 4th ed., edited by John C. Green and Rick D.
  Farmer
Teamsters and Turtles? edited by John C. Berg
Transnational Protest and Global Activism edited by Donatella della Porta
  and Sidney Tarrow
Waves of Protest edited by Jo Freeman and Victoria Johnson
The U.S. Women's Movement in Global Perspective edited by Lee Ann
  Banaszak

Forthcoming

The Art and Craft of Lobbying by Ronald G. Shaiko
Chimes of Freedom by Christine Kelly
The Gay and Lesbian Rights Movement by Steven H. Haeberle
Ralph Nader, the Greens, and the Crisis of American Politics by John C.
  Berg
Party Movements in the United States and Canada by Mildred A. Schwartz
The State of the Parties, 5th ed., edited by John C. Green and Daniel J. Coffey

The U.S. Women's Movement in Global Perspective

Edited by
Lee Ann Banaszak

ROWMAN & LITTLEFIELD PUBLISHERS, INC.
Lanham • Boulder • New York • Toronto • Oxford

ROWMAN & LITTLEFIELD PUBLISHERS, INC.

Published in the United States of America
by Rowman & Littlefield Publishers, Inc.
A wholly owned subsidiary of The Rowman & Littlefield Publishing Group, Inc.
4501 Forbes Boulevard, Suite 200, Lanham, Maryland 20706
www.rowmanlittlefield.com

P.O. Box 317, Oxford OX2 9RU, UK

British Library Cataloguing in Publication Information Available

Library of Congress Cataloging-in-Publication Data

The U.S. women's movement in global perspective / edited by Lee Ann Banaszak.
    p. cm. — (People, passions, and power)
  Includes bibliographical references and index.
  ISBN 0-7425-1931-7 (cloth : alk. paper) — ISBN 0-7425-1932-5 (pbk. : alk. paper)
  1. Feminism—United States. 2. Feminism—Cross-cultural studies. I. Title: US
women's movement in global perspective. II. Title: United States women's
movement in global perspective. III. Banaszak, Lee Ann, 1960- IV. Series.
HQ1410.U18 2005
  305.42'09—dc22

                                                                2005008346

Printed in the United States of America

∞™ The paper used in this publication meets the minimum requirements of
American National Standard for Information Sciences—Permanence of Paper
for Printed Library Materials, ANSI/NISO Z39.48-1992.

Contents

Tables

Acronyms

AAUW	American Association of University Women
ACLU	American Civil Liberties Union
ACT-UP	AIDS Coalition to Unleash Power
AD	Democratic Alliance (Alianza Democrática)
AFER	Alliance of Feminist Representatives
AIDS	Acquired Immune Deficiency Syndrome
BPW	Business and Professional Women
CAWP	Center for American Women and Politics
CCWI	Congressional Caucus for Women's Issues
CD	civil disobedience
CEDAW	Convention on the Elimination of All Forms of Discrimination against Women
CEM	Center for Women's Studies (Centro de Estudios de la Mujer)
CETA	Comprehensive Employment and Training Act
CPD	Congress of People's Deputies
CPS	Center for Policy Studies
C-R	consciousness-raising
CSW	Commission on the Status of Women
CWLU	Chicago Women's Liberation Union
DV	Domestic Violence [Law]
EEOC	Equal Employment Opportunity Commission
EEOL	Equal Employment Opportunity Law
EMILY	Early Money Is Like Yeast
ERA	Equal Rights Amendment
FIMA	Fusae Ichikawa Memorial Association

FMLA	Family and Medical Leave Act
FPA	family planning association
HUES	Hear Us Emerging Sisters
ICIWF	Information Center of the Independent Women's Forum
IFPA	Irish Family Planning Association
ILO	International Labor Organization
IPPF	International Planned Parenthood Federation
IREX	International Research & Exchange Board
IRLC	International Right to Life Committee
IRLF	International Right to Life Federation
ISEPP	Institute of Socio-Economic Population Problems
IWF	Independent Women's Forum
JAC	Joint Accountability Coalition
LA	Lesbian Avengers
LDP	Liberal Democratic Party
LOTOS	League for Emancipation from Societal Stereotypes
MCGS	Moscow Center for Gender Studies
MDP	Popular Democratic Movement (Movimiento Democrático Popular)
MPLV	Women for Life (Mujeres por la Vida)
MWR	Movement of Women of Russia
NAACP	National Association for the Advancement of Colored People
NARAL	National Abortion & Reproductive Rights Action League
NAWSA	National American Woman Suffrage Association
NGO	nongovernmental organization
NHS	National Health Service
NOW	National Organization for Women
NRLC	National Right to Life Committee
NSM	new social movement
NWEC	National Women's Education Center
NWP	National Woman's Party
NWPC	National Women's Political Caucus
NYC NOW	New York City [chapter of] National Organization for Women
PAC	political action committee
PCSW	Presidential Commission on the Status of Women
PETA	People for the Ethical Treatment of Animals
PLC	Pro-Life Campaign
PPFA	Planned Parenthood Federation of America
RM	resource mobilization
ROAMS	Reaching Out Across MovementS
SAFO	Free Association of Feminist Organizations (Svobodnaia Assotsiatsiia Feministskikh Organizatzii)

SDS	Students for a Democratic Society
SERNAM	National Women's Service (Servicio Nacional de la Mujer)
SMD	single-mandate district
SMO	social movement organization
SNCC	Student Nonviolent Coordinating Committee
SPUC	Society for the Protection of Unborn Children
STOP ERA	Stop Taking Our Privileges and Extra Responsibility Amendment
SWC	Soviet Women's Committee
UKFPA	United Kingdom Family Planning Association
UNDP	United Nations Development Project
USAID	United States Agency for International Development
US-NIS	United States-Newly Independent States
VAWA	Violence Against Women Act
WAC	Women's Action Coalition
WHAM	Women's Health Action Mobilization
WOR	Women of Russia
WPC	Women's Political Campaign
WUR	Women's Union of Russia
WWIN	Working Women's International Network
WWN	Working Women's Network

Preface

The students of my women and politics class are always fascinated with the topic of the women's movement in the United States and elsewhere. They know little about this piece of their own history, and what they do know is at best half-truths and vague ideas that confuse the women's movement with the rest of the sixties. They are surprised at the diversity of women's movements around the world and also at how issues, problems, and experiences seem to be repeated in very different cultural contexts. It is a joy to introduce these topics to them. Yet semester after semester, I found myself cobbling together readings from various sources to give students a sense of the U.S. women's movement within a larger world. The result was a set of readings that often made the classes feel disjointed. The initial motivation to edit this volume came from a desire to develop a book that would engage my students and provide a comparative perspective on the U.S. women's movement.

My other motivation for editing this volume came from a desire to unite the discussions on women's movements in the United States with analyses of women's movements in other countries. As a community, scholars of women's movements are split among a number of different subfields. Some in sociology speak mainly to others in the field of social movements, those in women's studies converse primarily with scholars of gender, and those in political science are often split by their focus on American politics or comparative politics (not to mention the group who speak largely to the international relations subfield). While in reality we are less divided than our subfield specialization might imply (we do after all meet at conferences and talk to each other informally), our scholarly work is spread over different venues, which usually reflect either an American, comparative, or women's studies focus.

My hope is that by looking at the women's movement in the United States in comparison with women's movements around the globe, I bring our voices together in a way that will excite students and incite further research. Nonetheless, there were many ways such a volume could be created, and the works collected here no doubt reflect my biases and opinions about the field. First, I believe in the importance of developing theoretical understandings of the U.S. women's movement, and so the chapters here move beyond the descriptive to analyze questions of why women's movements developed as they did in comparison both to other women's movements and to previous periods.

Second, the book represents a balance between works on the women's movement in the United States (part I) and pieces that compare the U.S. women's movement to other movements (part II). In choosing the pieces that went into part II, I gave preference to authors who compared across the usual regional boundaries that divide comparative scholars. Thus, although my own research focus has been on Western Europe and North America, I looked specifically for scholars who could draw new insights by drawing their comparisons from Latin America, Asia, and postcommunist countries. My hope is that such a different systems approach highlights both the commonalities in causal pathways across all women's movements (such as the importance of international networks of support) as well as the various ways important factors manifest themselves in different cultures or political systems.

Finally, many of the pieces here provide a feminist perspective on the nature of patriarchy and gender in society and how women's movements both exist in that context and seek to overcome it. In that sense, I hope that this volume contributes to our understanding of the gendered processes and institutions in which politics occurs. Yet, if the volume leans in a theoretical direction it is toward contributing to the larger field of social movement theory. As the introductory chapter suggests, the chapters in this volume draw their major concepts from that subfield, and it is my hope that they contribute to the larger debate in that area.

Acknowledgments

In putting this volume together, I have received inspiration and assistance from a number of different places. Without knowing it, Mary Katzenstein and Carol McClurg Mueller's (1987) volume on women's movements in the United States and Europe served as the initial inspiration for the idea that a theoretically relevant and contextually rich book could contribute meaningfully to both subfields. I thank them both for producing a work relevant even almost two decades later. Jennifer Knerr and John Green were instrumental in all of the phases in the book, from nudging me into action from a basic idea to providing sage advice. Most of all they were patient as life events slowed the progress of this book. The staff at Rowman & Littlefield were also especially helpful in moving the manuscript through the production process. In particular, Renee Legatt was quick and responsive as I dealt with the paperwork necessary for an edited volume of this sort, and Alden Perkins was instrumental in ushering the manuscript through the production process.

Several students contributed to the formation of the book: Tiffany Yanosky completed much of the library research necessary for chapter 1, and Claudiu Tufis and Hilary Ferrel helped in the formatting and printing of the manuscript. I am particularly grateful to the authors themselves, who dealt with my slowness as an editor and also provided many of the ideas that permeate the introductory and concluding chapters. A breakfast meeting with Lisa Baldez, Joyce Gelb, Carol Nechemias, and MaryAnn Barakso at the 2003 APSA meetings in San Francisco was particularly important to the development of the concluding chapter.

The last and biggest acknowledgment goes to my family. Isaac and Clara are now old enough to be cognizant of the fact that work sometimes intrudes into family life. Although they rightly give up family time only under protest, their sacrifices allowed this work to come to completion. More important, without them, none of this would be any fun. Most of all I thank Eric Plutzer, whose love and encouragement sustain me and whose willingness to take over the lion's share of child pickups and cooking has made this manuscript possible.

1

An Introduction to the U.S. Women's Movement in Global Perspective

Lee Ann Banaszak

1917, Washington, D.C. Four months after the United States declared war on Germany, women suffragists picket the White House wearing sashes in the suffrage colors of purple, white, and gold. They carry signs saying "Kaiser Wilson, Have You Forgotten Your Sympathy With the Poor Germans Because They Are Not Self-Governing? 20 Million Women Are Not Self-Governing/ Take The Beam Out Of Your Own Eye." Hecklers harass the women, striking them and tearing their clothes. The Washington police aid the hecklers, help to destroy the banners, and arrest the women. Many of the picketers are sentenced to prison. The prisoners engage in a hunger strike, demanding to be treated as political prisoners, and are force-fed by authorities (Ford 1991).

1980, Basel, Switzerland. The annual demonstration marking International Worker's Day is an important event that draws crowds every year. After lengthy negotiations, union leaders and Left politicians deny feminists' request that a woman finally be allowed to speak at the demonstration. At the demonstration, over two hundred feminists storm the podium, chanting: "Who are not allowed to speak? Women! Women! Who will speak anyway? Women! Women!" One of the feminists is slapped by a member of Parliament as several prominent socialist party and union leaders try to beat off the women advancing on the platform. In the end, feminist activists prevail, delivering speeches from the stage using bullhorns. From then on, demonstration organizers include women's movement leaders as speakers in the annual May Day celebration (OFRA Basel 1997).

1992, New York. Angered by a new talking Barbie that exclaims: "Math class is tough!" a group of feminists calling themselves the Barbie Liberation Organization switches the voice boxes of over three hundred dolls on sale at toy stores over the Christmas holidays. Publicity rises as girls receive Barbies for Christmas that say: "Eat lead, Cobra!" and a similar number of GI Joes that exclaim "Let's go shopping!" are sold. The ensuing media discussion focuses more on the humor of the action than on the sexual stereotyping of children's toys. Instructions for altering the toys are further distributed on the Internet (Firestone 1993; Barbie Liberation Organization n.d.).

Each of these stories chronicles the activities of feminists actively engaged in social change. Throughout the twentieth century and into the twenty-first, women in the United States and around the world have actively battled to achieve the same political and economic rights as men, to be free of violence, and to be raised in a society that does not impose limited roles for women. The stories above are spread throughout both space and time; two of the actions occurred in the United States although seventy-five years apart. The other took place a continent away but expressed demands similar to those of American feminists, who were also calling for political representation. Although of less renown, these actions were also some of the most flamboyant. Histories of the feminist movements in the United States (see, e.g., Carabillo, Meuli, and Csida 1993; Costain 1992; Ferree and Hess 1985; Freeman 1975; and Ryan 1992) and elsewhere (see among others Anderson 2000; Bystydzienski 1995; Dahlerup 1986; Kaplan 1992; Katzenstein and Mueller 1987; Lovenduski 1986a; Nelson and Chowdhury 1994; Threlfall 1996) have chronicled many such actions as well as others that were less dramatic but had even greater influence on government policy, individual attitudes, or social and economic systems.

To understand the actions described above, we need to ask larger questions about women's movements as a whole. What factors lead feminists to choose certain actions over others? What role have feminist organizations played in determining both what the women's movement does and what effect it has? How important are the actions of other political groups in determining what feminists do and what effect they have? When and how have feminists been able to affect public policy or create broader social change? In this book, we focus on the contemporary feminist movement, particularly in the United States, but also in other parts of the globe. We start with the rise of the second wave of the women's movement in the 1960s and follow feminist activism through the end of the 1990s, providing two types of analyses designed to address the questions above. First we utilize dynamic analyses, watching how the movement has changed over time and examining how previous historical events determine later ones. Second we compare the U.S. women's movement to other movements, focusing on their similarities and differences as well as the interaction between women's movements around the globe. Our understanding of how women have struggled to achieve both recognition as citizens and fair and equal treatment requires examining both the historical process by which movements develop and the larger factors that play a role in women's movements, not just in the United States but elsewhere.

The main premise of this book is that a combination of dynamic and comparative analyses is vital in understanding the causes and consequences of social movements. This idea is not new. In debates about the influence of political opportunities, social movement scholars have argued for this combination of methods. Initial discussions of the political opportunities that social movements faced had two different foci. Some authors favored a *political process* model—that is, analyzing how changes in the political context allow movements to emerge and influence their development (Costain 1992; McAdam 1982; Tarrow 1996). Other scholars took a decidedly comparative approach to political opportunities, comparing the different political environments of social movements. Most often, those examinations were static, comparing a single movement in different political environments (Kitschelt 1986; Kriesi et al. 1995). Increasingly, scholars have argued for both approaches (Tarrow 1996; McAdam, Tarrow, and Tilly 2001).

While not all social movement discussions have recognized the implications of utilizing dynamic versus comparative perspectives, the different methodological approaches generate slightly different research questions. For example, among those scholars who focus on organizational structure and resources, those interested in dynamics are drawn to the issue of organizational institutionalization (e.g., Meyer and Tarrow 1998a; Voss and Sherman 2000). On the other hand, debates about the effect of organizational resources on movement mobilization and outcomes have tended to rely on a more comparative perspective (Cress and Snow 1998; Gamson 1975). Similarly, as Johnston (2002, 66) notes, some scholars interested in ideational elements (such as the way movements frame discussions) have emphasized the framing process as the major theoretical issue. Others have highlighted the comparative study of framing (e.g., Ferree et al. 2002; Obershall 1996; Zdravomyslova 1996), focusing more on static differences between countries. Examinations of cultural effects on social movements have both compared different countries in a single time period (see, e.g., Jenson 1987) and examined cultural change over time (e.g., Rochon 1998).

In this book, we utilize both types of analyses to gain a stronger understanding of women's movements. This chapter lays the groundwork for the analyses that follow. I begin by placing the U.S. women's movement in historical context through a brief overview of the first wave of the feminist movement in the United States and its connection to the contemporary movement. In the next section, I discuss the theoretical concepts used to answer the questions framed above, most importantly mobilizing structures (also known as resource mobilization), political opportunities, and the ideational factors—frames, discourse, identity, and culture. The authors in this book use these concepts in various ways to explore changes in the U.S.

women's movement over time and to compare it to women's movements in other parts of the globe. The last section concludes by discussing how the chapters in this volume contribute to our understanding of women's movements.

THE FIRST WAVE OF THE U.S. WOMEN'S MOVEMENT

As the story of the suffragettes in World War I illustrates, the women's movement that arose in the United States in the late 1960s was not an isolated or novel movement. Rather, it continued a long history of women's activism, the start of which lies early in our nation's history. Individual women have always been a part of political life in the United States, but women's activism as a larger political force began in four movements starting in the early 1800s. First, women were major actors in moral reform, missionary, and charitable societies designed to help the poor and destitute (Scott 1991). Second, women were an important element in the temperance organizations of the 1820s, even as these were largely headed by men. Third, women were active participants in the growing antislavery movement. Finally, working women organized clubs beginning in the 1820s and 1830s to seek higher wages and better working conditions (Foner 1979).

After decades of work in these movements, women's advocacy in the mid-1850s began to concentrate more explicitly on women's rights. The earliest feminist campaigns centered on property and child custodial rights for married women; after New York extended property rights to married women in 1848, other states soon followed. Another early major issue was the education of women, which arose as local governments and private systems founded institutions of learning in the new republic. Emma Hart Willard (founder of Troy Academy for Women), Mary Mason Lyon (founder of Mount Holyoke Seminary), and a host of other women founded a network of female seminaries and colleges designed to provide systematic education for women. Finally, women also began to question their treatment as second-class citizens, particularly as a result of activism in other movements. In 1848, after observing women's exclusion at a World Abolitionist convention, Elizabeth Cady Stanton and Lucretia Mott organized the first women's rights convention in the United States in Seneca Falls, New York. Angelina and Sarah Grimke began speaking about rights for women after they were accosted for breaking gender norms by engaging in public speaking (Ryan 1992, 15).

Women's feminist activism took a turn at the close of the Civil War. While before the war most activism occurred through loose networks of women meeting largely at conventions (Banaszak 1996a; McCammon 2001) or within organizations dominated by men,[1] now women began to found their own formal organizations to pursue women's rights. For example, in 1867 feminists such as

Susan B. Anthony, Elizabeth Cady Stanton, and Lucy Stone joined forces with other antislavery supporters in the Equal Rights Association, which sought to gain equal rights both for African Americans and women. After extended campaigning in Kansas and elsewhere for legislation that would support this combined goal, the organization split into two factions—the American Woman Suffrage Association and the National Woman Suffrage Association—both focused even more explicitly on the right to vote.

These same years also saw the first significant adoption of women's voting rights, with women winning the suffrage in Wyoming Territory in 1869. Similarly, temperance activism now became focused first in large campaigns like the Women's Temperance Crusade of 1873–1874 and later in the form of the Women's Christian Temperance Union. While the previous temperance movement had been gender mixed, this new wave of activism was dominated by women, who argued that temperance was a means of protecting women in the home. Indeed, after 1879, the WCTU formally concentrated on "Home Protection," which was giving women the right to vote on questions related to liquor control.

But women's activism in the period between the Civil War and the Nineteenth Amendment was not solely focused on women's rights. Groups initially founded as literary clubs or reading groups soon branched out to issues about local communities. After the founding of the national General Federation of Women's Clubs in 1890, local organizations increasingly focused on issues of social reform such as child labor laws, public health, minimum wages, and pensions for destitute mothers (Scott 1991; Skocpol 1992). In addition, a number of different women's clubs also took on issues of government reform. The National Association of Colored Women's Clubs, founded in 1896, worked ceaselessly to promote civil and political rights for the entire African American community (Scott 1991). Settlement houses appeared in almost all of the large cities, many of these run by women. In addition, the first large national unions composed mainly of women began to organize (Flexner 1968). Building from the settlement houses designed to foster working-class neighborhoods, working women's clubs, and traditional unions seeking to extend unionization of occupations, women trade union leaders increasingly sought to organize women workers. Mary Kenney O'-Sullivan, for example, founded the Women's Trade Union League in 1903 with the aim of organizing women workers (Foner 1979).

Even as women's activism extended on many different fronts, the focus on women's rights concentrated more and more on the formal right to vote. In 1893, after nearly twenty-five years of divisions within the feminist movement, the two major woman suffrage organizations merged into the National American Woman Suffrage Association (NAWSA). The organization grew dramatically as the right to vote became the focus of more and more political battles. In the last decade of the nineteenth century, Colorado, Utah, and

Idaho enfranchised women voters, Colorado after a dramatic campaign by feminist activists. Increasingly, state legislatures considered women's voting rights legislation because of pressure from feminist organizations.

Women's activism for the vote took many different paths. In some periods, women focused on gaining the vote through conventional channels, using petitions, testimony before Congress and state legislatures, and eventually lobbying tactics to secure the vote. However, when these paths seemed blocked, women engaged in innovative and public forms of protest. Immediately after the Civil War, Elizabeth Cady Stanton ran for Congress, arguing that the Constitution did not prohibit women candidates. Between 1871 and 1872, approximately 150 women, including Susan B. Anthony, attempted to cast ballots in elections. In 1876, suffrage activists interrupted the Centennial Celebration of the Declaration of Independence to read the document calling for women's rights written at the Seneca Falls conference. In the last decade before the passage of the Nineteenth Amendment, suffrage activists engaged in increasingly large and visible suffrage parades. The largest were organized by Alice Paul and Lucy Burns, who went on to form the National Woman's Party (NWP; initially the Congressional Union) in 1914. It was the NWP that eventually organized the pickets of the White House described above. The feminists who had suffered jail time often went on national tours to encourage even more activism.

All of these actions increased pressure on the national and state governments to pass woman suffrage legislation. After the initial breakthrough in the West, other states also began to adopt woman suffrage. By 1920, the year that the Nineteenth Amendment was finally adopted, all of the Midwest states had some form of women's voting rights; two Southern states had adopted suffrage in primary elections, and even a few Eastern states (most notably New York) had enacted women's voting rights legislation. By 1919, suffrage organizations had grown to include over two million members (Park 1960, 12; Skocpol 1999), and in 1920 the Nineteenth Amendment was enshrined in the U.S. Constitution.

The years after women's enfranchisement proved, however, to be bad ones for women's organizing. The initial euphoria over the power of the vote soon gave way to a period of retrenchment. While women's organizations were crucial to the passage of the Sheppard-Towner Act providing social welfare for destitute mothers in 1921, by 1927 they were unable to halt a bill that eliminated this provision (Skocpol 1992). The two major suffrage organizations—the NWP and the NAWSA—split over whether protective legislation or an equal rights amendment would benefit women more (Banaszak 1996b; Ryan 1992). Moreover, the Red scares of the 1920s hurt many women's organizations as they were tied to Communist organizations through a "spider's web" of organizational connections (Banaszak 1996b; Foner 1979, 268–69).

Nonetheless, women's activism continued throughout the 1930s, 1940s, and 1950s. The League of Women Voters, the nonpartisan successor organization to the NAWSA, supported women candidates and encouraged women voters to serve as a force for progress. The NWP focused the bulk of its energies on pursuing an equal rights amendment but also encouraged women to run for elected office (Rupp and Taylor 1987). Women's professional organizations blossomed in the postsuffrage period with the founding of the National Business and Professional Women (1919) and the American Association of University Women (1921). These organizations pushed for equal opportunities for women even during the "doldrums" of the 1930s, 1940s, and 1950s.

Throughout this period, women continued to make gains in politics, albeit at a slow pace. Anderson (1996, 17) notes that by 1931, 146 women had been elected to state legislatures, and local women elected officials were relatively common. Women entered and became the backbone of political party organizations, slowly altering the nature of party politics and gaining a small measure of influence over party policy (Freeman 2000). The 1920s saw the first two women governors elected to office, and the 1930s saw the first woman elected to the U.S. Senate (Freeman 2000, 231; CAWP 2002a). By the time that the second wave of the U.S. women's movement began to mobilize, the number of women in Congress had been in the double digits for at least a decade (CAWP 2002b). While still a barely visible minority, women's presence in the political system prepared the way for what was to follow.

THE SECOND WAVE AND BEYOND

The story of the first wave illustrates the dramatic changes in women's movement organization, mobilization, and outcomes that occur over time. Central to that dynamic analysis is the concept of a wave—a period of intense mobilization and activism. The first wave of the U.S. women's movement arose within a social and political context that both encouraged activism and focused women's rights activism on particular issues. It ended in concrete legal gains for women, such as the Nineteenth Amendment, and in some changes in social norms for women. Although activism for women's rights diminished after 1920, it was by no means absent. Rather, feminist activism disappeared from public view (Rupp and Taylor 1987), and the political arena became much less hospitable to calls for additional rights for women (Skocpol 1992).

This book focuses on the rise and development of more recent waves of activism stemming from the contemporary women's movement—in Nancy Whittier's (chapter 3) view, a second wave of activism in the late 1960s and early 1970s and a third wave of activism in the 1990s. By focusing on how the U.S. feminist movement has changed over time, and by recognizing that the current movement is contingent on the historical events that occurred before, we gain a greater understanding of why the U.S. women's movement has developed in some ways but not others and has both gained great achievements and failed at others. By looking at the U.S. women's movement in comparison to other movements around the world we gain a better sense of how the U.S. women's movement is influenced by universal factors as well as by its own unique cultural, social, and political context. Finally, an examination of international feminist activism will show how U.S. feminists have engaged actively in conversation with feminists elsewhere, and how feminists cross national borders as they actively pursue social and political change in gender relations (Keck and Sikkink 1998a).

In this section, I highlight sets of concepts central to understanding the development of the contemporary movement and its effect on society and public policy: the resources and mobilizing structures of the movement, the opportunities provided by political context, and ideas, norms, and values that manifest themselves in the movement's collective identity and framing, as well as the culture and discourse that encompass movement events. A brief overview of each of these sets of concepts shows how each helps to illuminate issues of dynamic change within the movement and to account for similarities and differences across women's movements in various countries.

Resources and Mobilizing Structures

Social movement scholars have long realized that networks, organization, tactical choices, and the skills and resources available to movement activists influence whether movements will mobilize, how they develop, and what they achieve (see, e.g., McCarthy and Zald 1973, 1977; Oberschall 1973; Gamson 1975). At the beginning of a movement, as Freeman discusses in chapter 2, networks with other movements or with well-resourced individuals help determine whether movements actually arise (Snow, Zurcher, and Ekland-Olson 1980). A wide array of resources including community networks, material goods (or money), leaders, and information are necessary for movements to act, and initial movements may lack some or all of these resources (Cress and Snow 1998). For example, Nechemias (chapter 9) notes that the Russian feminist movement is almost completely dependent on the international community to support its efforts. Important resources may also be available to a movement internally, for example, as black churches served to mobilize the civil rights movement (McAdam 1982; Morris 1984). However, when movements acquire resources and skills from other movements or individuals, these external sources also alter the movements themselves (Jenkins and Perrow 1977; McCarthy and Zald 1977; Oberschall 1973). Regardless of whether resources come from movement participants or external sources, they are molded by their source, influencing—in both large and small ways—the receiving movement. For example, Jo Freeman's contribution (chapter 2)—a reprint of her 1973 *American Journal of Sociology* article "The Origins of the Women's Liberation Movement"—notes that the two branches of the movement arose among women with very different resources: professional women and political activists in the New Left. On the one hand, the actual number of women in postsecondary education and the proportion of women lawyers and other professionals—although small—increased throughout the 1940s, 1950s, and 1960s (Epstein 1993, 4; Ries and Stone 1992, 332).[2] On the other hand, the civil rights, student, and antiwar movements also trained a generation of feminist activists, creating networks of sympathetic activist women with skills in organizing and protest (Freeman, chapter 2; McAdam 1988). These two different sources for feminist activists at the beginning of the second wave influenced their expectations for the movement, their tactical choices, and the organizational forms they adopted.

Organizational forms or structures such as formal, hierarchical, centralized organizations with professional staff shape the activities of the organizations and the wider movement. Feminist theory suggests that women's movement structures should be informal, grassroots, nonhierarchical, and consensus driven (Ferguson 1984). These forms of organization permit the greatest amount of individual participation, avoid re-creating patriarchal structures within the movement, and give the greatest flexibility to the movement (Polletta 2002). Yet Freeman (1975) argues that consensus politics created other problems for the U.S. women's movement. Moreover, where feminists have sought to influence government policy, they have often found a need to build organizational forms that mirror traditional interest groups by hiring permanent staff members, developing formal national organizations, and creating hierarchical lines of accountability and decision making. A dynamic analysis of women's movements leads to larger debates about whether organizational structures become more hierarchical over time (McCarthy and Zald 1977; Meyer and Tarrow 1998a; Voss and Sherman 2000; Zald and Ash 1966). At issue is whether, regardless of the radical nature of the initial women's movement or its initial focus on nonhierarchical participatory organizational forms, the movement has been transformed into more formally organized, professional interest groups (Banaszak, Beckwith, and Rucht 2003a; Skocpol 2003).

Theories about resources and mobilizing structures also address issues of movement tactics, particularly how movement activists choose tactics and how tactical decisions are influenced by organizational structure and external resources (Bernstein 2001). Decisions about whether to take to the streets or to petition the government, for example, often relate to the organizational form of movement structures (hierarchical and professional structures are more likely to adopt conventional tactics) as well as the positions of allies. The choice of tactics becomes an important issue for the women's movement particularly as it faces different political opportunities. Which tactics work best in which situations and which tactics are available to the movement at that particular moment are factors that may lead movements to different decisions. Maryann Barakso (chapter 5), for example, finds that internal divisions and discussions over the appropriate action of the National Organization for Women (NOW) constrained the organization's ability to pursue reform tactics.

Finally, different branches of the movement may choose disparate organizational structures and tactics. This intramovement variation influences how women's movements develop and the degree of conflict or cooperation between these wings of the movement. Many chapters in this volume explore the connection between intramovement differences in tactics and organizational forms and the development of women's movements. Chapter 4, by Barbara Ryan, argues that regular cycles of intramovement cooperation and division arose in the course of the campaign for the Equal Rights Amendment (ERA). Barakso (chapter 5) finds that intramovement differences arise even within a single organization, NOW, while Whittier (chapter 3) finds both continuity and difference in organizing styles and tactics across the generations that make up the second and third wave. Finally, in a piece that provides many points of comparison, Robnett (chapter 7) shows how gender has split African American movements—creating an all-male national leadership that relies heavily on women to be the grassroots organizers.

The chapters here provide both static and dynamic analyses of resources and mobilizing structures. Barakso and Whittier utilize more dynamic approaches by examining developmental changes in the movement's structure or tactics. Together they provide a developmental overview of the U.S. women's movements from national membership organizations to local action groups. Ryan examines the fractionalization of the women's movement during the height of the ERA campaign and immediately afterward to determine how unifying issues influence the women's movement. The static analyses in this volume come largely from the comparative chapters: Gelb (chapter 10) finds that the Japanese women's movement was more fragmented and decentralized than its U.S. counterpart. Similarly, Nechemias (chapter 9) notes that the different experiences and resources of the Russian women under communism explain its different form of women's movement. By comparing the resource base of four local movements in the United States, Reger and Staggenborg (chapter 6) gain leverage on why local movement organizations get established. In many of these chapters, however, mobilizing structures and resources cannot be fully understood without examining the opportunities presented by the political context.

Political Opportunities

Social movement scholars recognize that whether a movement appears, how it develops, and what it achieves are all influenced by the political environment in which it operates. Scholars use the phrase *political opportunities*, which incorporate political rules and institutions (both formal and informal), historical events, and alliances or political coalitions, to refer to this environment. The choice of this term reflects the idea that the political environment of a social movement may encourage movement mobilization, development, and success by providing opportunities for action and mobilization. The counterargument holds as well: Sometimes the political environment constrains action or mobilization by limiting what a movement or potential movement can do. The elements included in the concept of political opportunities are many and varied (see McAdam 1996a). Changes in the electorate, varying rules about democratic institutions (such as the existence of initiative rights), the availability of allies like Left governments, the rise of countermovements, police brutality and repression, and unique historical events such as wars are some of the specific elements of political opportunity that have been identified as influencing the course of social movements (see Banaszak 1996a; della Porta 1995; McAdam 1982; Staggenborg 1991; Tarrow 1998; and others).

Expanding political opportunities are often identified as leading to the rise of the second wave of the women's movement. For one thing, the movement arose in a period ripe with political and social change. The issues of civil rights began to break into the American consciousness in the late 1950s with the Supreme Court's decision in *Brown v. the Board of Education* (1954) and the 1955 Montgomery bus boycott (McAdam 1982, 121). By the 1960s civil rights had blossomed into a major national issue. The election of John F. Kennedy in 1960 also had a clear impact on the women's movement, as his call for government activism at home and abroad, his apparent support for issues of social justice, and his connection to the Left provided an atmosphere that allowed many social movements to thrive. His creation of the Presidential Commission on the Status of Women in 1961 increased activism among women by documenting the inequities that they suffered in many aspects of life and by generating networks among professional women interested in advancing women's rights. Presidents Johnson and Nixon also created policies that advanced women. Johnson pushed through the Civil Rights Act, which created the Equal Employment Opportunity Commission, and Nixon created the Taskforce on Women's Rights and Responsibilities and encouraged women's appointment in government positions. But the most powerful events during the Nixon years occurred in other branches of government, with the 1972 Senate approval of the ERA and the 1973 Supreme Court decision *Roe v. Wade,* which established the right to an abortion without state intervention during the first trimester.

Political opportunities for the U.S. women's movement began to contract in the mid-1970s as both the ensuing ERA ratification campaign and the legalization of abortion mobilized opponents (Luker 1984; Ryan 1992; Staggenborg 1991). The National Right to Life Committee, formed in 1971, grew dramatically in the 1970s (Staggenborg 1991, 35). In the face of the ERA ratification campaign, Phyllis Schlafly's Stop ERA was founded in 1972 and Concerned Women for America in 1978. The rise of these and other "New Right" groups led to a fundamental realignment in the Republican Party as it sought to incorporate social conservatives into a winning electoral strategy. With the nomination of Ronald Reagan for president in 1979, the Republican Party, where some economically conservative feminist women had remained, became less hospitable to feminists (Freeman 1987; Wolbrecht 2000). The Republican administrations of Reagan and Bush, in contrast to that of Nixon, were hostile to the concerns and philosophies of feminists. On the other hand, the Democratic Party increasingly aligned with feminists. At century's end, the rift between the two political parties widened, leaving issues of feminism awash in a highly politicized atmosphere where support for a political agenda depended much on the composition of Congress and the White House.

The dynamics of political opportunities are taken up in Jo Reger and Suzanne Staggenborg's chapter examining local chapters of NOW (chapter 6) as well as in Carol Nechemias's chapter comparing the Russian and U.S. women's movements (chapter 9). Both chapters combine comparative and dynamic analyses of political opportunities. Reger and Staggenborg compare four different local chapters in the United States, examining their initial formation and their ability to maintain themselves over time. Continuity and change in structure follow from the local political environment as well as the relationship between local chapters and the national organization. Carol Nechemias's chapter on the U.S. and Russian women's movements incorporates both comparative and dynamic analyses by examining Russian feminist activism across the dramatically changing political environment of a country moving from a one-party Communist state through a transition to democracy at the same time as it compares the U.S. and Russian movements. Nechemias notes that although the U.S. and Russian movements share a similar international and historical context, the differences in political opportunities and culture (see below) create stark differences in ideology, action, and mobilization. The result is a divided Russian movement, with the strong women's organizations focused on traditional women's issues such as family and motherhood and the radical feminist wing weak and dependent.

Two comparative pieces in this volume utilizing static comparisons also highlight how differences in political opportunities can influence women's movements. Joyce Gelb's chapter (chapter 10), focusing explicitly on the differences in political opportunities that faced the U.S. and Japanese women's movements, argues that the post–World War II Japanese party system created little space for women. The result is a women's movement in Japan that has largely worked outside of the existing party system, with housewife organizations making the largest gains in local politics and women politicians running as ordinary housewives gaining much of women's representation. Lisa Baldez and Celeste Montoya's analysis of the U.S. and Chilean women's movements (chapter 8) emphasizes how the political environment can heighten awareness of gender differences and thereby encourage the development of women's movements. In their chapter, two very different political environments—Chile's repressive military government and the Democratic Party under John F. Kennedy—bring issues of gender to the fore and create the circumstances that allow women to frame issues in a way that allows broad-based coalition building.

International Opportunities

Political opportunities may also come from outside a nation's borders: from actions and events in other countries, from international organizations and transnational networks, or from other aspects of the international political context (Imig and Tarrow 2001a; Keck and Sikkink 1998a; Marx and McAdam 1996; Smith, Chatfield, and Pagnucco 1997). Even within the first wave, political events outside the United States had visible and concrete effects on the development of the U.S. women's movement. World War I played a large role in determining the form and tenure of the protest by the NWP highlighted above (Lunardini 1986). Even the Russian Revolution and the Cold War affected the women's movement as accusations of ties to Communist organizations in the late 1920s and early 1930s (Banaszak 1996b) and again in the 1940s and 1950s (Rupp and Taylor 1987, 139–44) reduced the movement's legitimacy among potential allies and the wider public; delegitimized other potential alliances, tactics, and goals; and led to greater divisions among women's organizations.

As Keck and Sikkink (1998a) argue, the international context also encourages social movement mobilization by providing a community of external organizations and activists that encourage activism and push for concrete changes. Early U.S. suffrage activists had always maintained connections to activists in other countries, but in the late nineteenth century this international network of women created transnational organizations such as the International Council of Women and the International Woman Suffrage Alliance (later the International Alliance of Women), founded to coordinate suffrage activism (Rupp 1997).[3] Between the two world wars, additional feminist organizations like Equal Rights International and the World Women's Party organized as well (Stienstra 1994, 66). These international groups served multiple purposes: They were a source of solidarity, a resource of information and ideas to individual movements,[4] and an opportunity to engage in symbolic politics (Keck and Sikkink 1998a, 51–58). Other international organizations have also provided a forum for women's movement activists to interact. Both the League of Nations and, later, the United Nations (UN) offered opportunities for women's organizations to develop cross-national ties as well as to elaborate legal standards on the rights of women (Galey 1995; Stienstra 1994). However, the power of international connections among women expanded dramatically after the UN declared 1975 International Women's Year. Activists at the nongovernmental forum at the Mexico City conference (as well as at later UN conferences) used the meeting to build solidarity across borders, exchange information about tactics and issues, and organize common campaigns with other like-minded organizations (Moghadam 2000). Other international and regional conferences supplemented UN-sponsored meetings and provided more frequent opportunities for transnational and international activism (Stienstra 1994).

The influence of transnational activism on national women's movements is demonstrated throughout part 2 of this book. Carol Nechemias (chapter 9) argues, for example, that international women's activism influenced the development of the Russian women's movement in both positive and negative ways. The standards set by the UN conferences were instrumental in bringing pressure on the Japanese government to change its policy, according to Joyce Gelb (chapter 10). Rohlinger and Meyer (chapter 11) argue that international organizations can supply important resources to their national affiliates, as, for example, when the International Planned Parenthood Federation furnishes money, materials, and professional assistance to the Irish Federation of Planned Parenthood.

Opportunities and Culture

One major point of discussion among social movement scholars has been whether political opportunities always have an immediate effect on social movements. In particular, in recent years scholars have argued that social movements do not always take advantage of all available political opportunities (Banaszak 1996a; Sawyers and Meyer 1999). Banaszak (1996a), for example, argues that the cultural context of social movements leads them to pay attention to some tactical choices and to overlook others, regardless of the objective political opportunities or resources at hand. Belinda Robnett (chapter 7) argues that issues of gender have created such missed opportunities among African Americans; cultural views of the role of black women have bifurcated African American movements and reduced their ability to respond to political opportunities. Such arguments suggest that the cultural context and the ideological framing of individual movements are as important as their political environment.

The World of Ideation: Identity, Culture, Discourse, and Framing

In addition to the political environment and movements' organizations and resources, social movement scholars have recognized that the content and context of ideas, values, and norms influence how social movements act, what they can achieve, and ultimately how they develop (Banaszak 1996a; Bernstein 1997; Benford and Snow 2000; Snow and Benford 1992; Snow et al. 1986; Swidler 1986).

Cultural arguments have tended to focus on how wider beliefs, rituals, and language place limits on social movements (Johnston and Klandermans 1995).[5] Some authors (see, e.g., Jenson 1987) have argued that certain social movements are virtually impossible in some cultural contexts. Nechemias (chapter 9), for example, finds that the gender ideology of Russia creates an inhospitable culture for feminist organizations like those in the United States. Such arguments place culture as an opportunity structure (although not political) that may constrain or encourage certain movements (see also Gamson and Meyer 1996). Others have tied culture to action, arguing that strategies represent cultural constructs but that there are multiple choices to be made in any cultural context (Banaszak 1996a; Swidler 1986; Tilly 1978). Increasingly, discussions of culture recognize the multiple levels of culture and how they interact. Banaszak (1996a) argues for the existence of movement subcultures that can challenge societal culture. Barakso (chapter 5) espouses this view when she observes that there has been an enduring political culture within NOW, which determines its institutional structure and tactical decisions. The international women's movement also influences the culture of national movements. In the case of the U.S. women's movement, international interactions altered the ideology and voices that appeared on the national scene. International experiences reinforced those voices that challenged the lack of diversity in the initial women's movement and increased the degree to which U.S. women became cognizant of their dominant and often negative role in the international system (Keck and Sikkink 1998a).

If culture forms part of a movement's context, framing represents the movement's (or its opponent's) ability to actively produce ideas and meaning (Benford and Snow 2000; Snow and Benford 1992; Snow et al. 1986). Within a wide and variable culture, social movements or specific movement organizations choose the way they frame themselves, their actions, and their goals. Those choices are contingent upon both internal factors, such as the need to maintain or build a collective identity (as described in the next paragraph), and external considerations, such as concerns about the most effective way to sway the public, key government actors, or allies. As the movement, countermovements, the state, and other actors present frames, a discourse emerges that reflects culture and influences future frames. Baldez and Montoya (chapter 8), for example, contend that both the Chilean and the

U.S. women's movements framed issues in ways that reflected underlying national cultures. In Chile this resulted in frames emphasizing women's traditional concerns, while the U.S. movement utilized frames of equality. Framing occurs within a path dependent discourse, which means other actors, such as the government or countermovements, influence the potential frames a movement can choose (Benford and Snow 2000; Snow and Benford 1992). Rohlinger and Meyer (chapter 11), for example, find that international organizations can affect the frames of their national affiliates if there is interaction between the national and international organizations.

A third ideational element that is central to understanding social movements is collective identity. Collective identity is the symbolic work that creates solidarity among movement activists and creates boundaries between the movement and other societal groups. Movements try to foster collective identity because it is vital to transforming individual supporters into committed activists (Bernstein 1997; Melucci 1988). However, movements are not always able to completely control their collective identity. Society may appropriate or alter a movement's identity (e.g., Friedman and McAdam 1992), and battles over collective identity may foster intramovement divisions rather than create movement solidarity (Gamson 1997; Ryan 1992).

The dynamics of identity, frames, discourse, and culture come more to the fore in the contributions by Mary Ann Barakso, Belinda Robnett, and Nancy Whittier. Both Barakso (chapter 5) and Whittier (chapter 3) argue for a combination of continuity and change in the evolution of the women's movement over time. Maryann Barakso, focusing on the national office of NOW, examines how the organization adapts its actions to its stated goals. Barakso notes that the goals of national NOW have remained important to the organization and its members, forming the basis for collective identity and action over time. Yet she notes that critical events, such as the Clinton sex scandal, make it difficult to translate the frames that the organization has developed into actions. Her story is one of the resiliency of principles in the face of differing political opportunities. Nancy Whittier focuses on continuity and change in the radical wing of the women's movement. She also notes continuity in organizational form even as independent generations arise out of different cultural and political contexts. The political context of the group, which influences its collective definition, creates the largest differences among political generations. Belinda Robnett's examination of gender differences among African Americans (chapter 7) also demonstrates the unintended consequences of cultural change. In her chapter, the U.S. women's movement's penetration of culture creates, in part, divisions within the African American movement after the 1960s. Robnett contrasts the failure of African Americans to mobilize with women's movement mobilization against antiabortion countermovements and argues that gender differences divided African Americans, causing them to miss a political opportunity.

Comparative analyses of culture and framing dominate the chapters by Carol Nechemias and Deana Rohlinger and David S. Meyer (chapter 11). Rohlinger and Meyer examine the framing of abortion by pro-life and pro-choice organizations in the United States, Great Britain, and Ireland as well as by the international affiliated organizations. Pro-choice organizations had frames that varied more by national political context and culture, but when the national organizations had strong ties to their international affiliates they also shared more similarities in their frames. Nechemias also emphasizes the importance of national culture, arguing that the Russian women's movement is constrained by Russian traditions as well as the now discredited Soviet emphasis on the woman worker.

In all, mobilizing structures, political opportunities, and ideational elements provide the tools necessary to gain a comprehensive understanding of the women's movement in the United States and around the globe. Yet what lessons do these chapters teach us about women's movements and social movements more generally?

LESSONS FROM ANALYZING THE U.S. WOMEN'S MOVEMENTS IN SPACE AND TIME

The dynamic and global perspectives of these contributions intersect in multiple ways. However, I would like to highlight five themes inherent in many of the pieces in this volume. While these themes are not unknown to the study of social movements, they remain ideas that are only occasionally examined in the social movement literature. The works here underscore the importance of each of these arguments for understanding the development of social movements.

1. *The three major sets of concepts in social movement research are not completely independent but causally intersect each other in complex ways.* While social movement scholars have tended to utilize resource mobilization, political opportunities, and culture/framing as separate factors, several of these chapters find that political opportunities and culture influence the resources available to the movement. For example, in exploring the development of local movements, Reger and Staggenborg note that political opportunities at the national level intersect with local leadership as causes of organizational form. Local leadership operates in the context of a strong national organization differently than it does in a weak one, and national organizations' influence on local chapters depends in part on the affinity of local leadership to national NOW. Similarly, Robnett argues that the lack of a strong African American movement is due as much to the culture of gender roles within the African American community as it is to the leadership of the movement, which places men in national leadership positions and women

as the major actors at the grassroots. The effect of gender culture on the movement is related to the leadership structure. In both chapters, the concepts interact to create surprising results. These interactive effects are found in many of the other chapters in this volume (see, for example, Barakso and Rohlinger and Meyer).

2. *Cultural norms about gender play an important role in the emergence of social movements (not just the women's movement).* Classic discussions of the emergence of the U.S. women's movement have focused first and foremost on the resources and political opportunities available to the movement (see Freeman 1975 and chapter 2 in this volume; Costain 1992; Ferree and Hess 1985; Ryan 1992). However, once one moves beyond a single focus on the United States or in comparison with West European countries, differences in gender norms come more to the fore. The comparative chapters in this volume—especially the pieces by Baldez and Montoya and Nechemias—highlight the role that different gender norms play in the emergence and character of the movement. Nechemias notes that Soviet ideology did not challenge the essentialism of motherhood, and that traditional religious institutions and ideologies expanded during the process of democratization. These gender norms limit the emergence of counterparts to Western feminism even in a context where such groups receive preference in gaining external resources. Baldez and Montoya note that gender norms of women as outside party lines allowed women to unify across ideological differences in the 1980s. In both cases, gender norms and the ability of the movement to mold them to organize effectively determine whether mobilization can occur. Robnett (chapter 7 in this volume and 1997) indicates that gender norms influenced the civil rights movement and the lack of African American mobilization in later years. Her work and that of others (see, e.g., Beckwith 1996 and McCammon, Campbell, and Granberg 2001) indicates that attention to the culture of gender norms is an inherent part of understanding mobilization in any movement.[6]

3. *Intramovement dynamics are very important to social movements; however, divisions within a movement can mask considerable continuity.* Analyses of feminist movements both in the United States and in a comparative perspective have long understood the existence of multiple feminisms and that the strength of various strands varies over time. If this volume differs from other analyses of the women's movement, it is in emphasizing an underlying stability in the change wrought by these intramovement dynamics. That is brought home perhaps most forcefully by Ryan, who concludes that cycles of cooperation and division exist alongside more traditional cycles of protest based on mobilization and decline.[7] Whittier argues for a more static continuity when she counters women's movement scholars' arguments about the death of radical feminism. In her work, there is continuity in the existence of radical feminism and also within each cohort; change occurs as each cohort

is molded by specific critical events. Focusing on the other wing of the women's movement, Barakso notes stability in NOW both as an organization and as a set of founding principles, even as political opportunities—in the form of a difficult political environment and challenging critical events—have been an impetus for change. Thus, even while the movement changes with different critical events, there is also considerable underlying stability of ideology and goals.

4. *Social movements are path dependent; the timing and character of critical events are vital to understanding the strength, collective identity, and tactics of movements.* While many of these critical events are categorized under the label of political opportunities, the general hypotheses about political opportunities are not sufficient to deal with the problems of path dependence. In this volume, many contributors argue that it is not just the existence of events as opportunities or constraints, but their occurrence at a particular point in the movement's development or in conjunction with other events, that determines their role in influencing the women's movement. Freeman, for example, notes the incredible mobilizing power that Betty Friedan's (1963) book, *The Feminine Mystique,* had on the women's movement. Although certainly influenced by the same social and economic context that fostered the women's movement, the book predated most second wave activity and increased attention to the issue of the status of women. The timing of the book's publication made it a very important tool for mobilizing women into the movement. Similarly, Whittier sees critical events as influencing the identity of feminists as they enter the movement; each cohort defines itself in reaction to the events that surround its mobilization. Thus, she finds that the Acquired Immune Deficiency Syndrome (AIDS) epidemic influences third wave feminists' views of feminist identity, allies, and appropriate tactics.

For many women's movements outside the United States, the timing and character of democratic transitions are important critical events that mobilize women's movements. The democratic transitions of Chile and Russia discussed by Baldez and Montoya and Nechemias both mobilized women, but the character of these transitions differed in ways that had a significant impact on the movements. The transition toward democracy in Chile largely ignored women's issues, but the divisive nature of the opposition provided an opportunity for women to unify the opposition and mobilize women into the movement. In Russia, the transition included calls for returning women to their traditional roles as mothers. Although women were also mobilized by the democratic transition, particularly to defend their rights to employment, they were also divided by the degree to which they continued to expound an essential connection to motherhood. The two contrasting chapters suggest that the role of gender ideology and partisan divisions in democratic transitions may influence the role that these play in mobilizing women's movements.

5. *Movements can only be understood by examining activism at multiple levels: Transnational, national, and local activism all interact in the course of any social movement.* Increasingly, social movement scholars and feminist scholars have moved beyond focusing on national movements to recognizing the importance of transnational activism. The contributions in this volume continue this trend but imply a much more complex world of multiple layers of activism. Transnational activism not only exists as an important element of the women's movement but is interwoven with national and local activism. Moreover, national movements are also interwoven with local movements. The result is a multilayered feminist movement with the actions and strategies of one layer influencing the others. Gelb argues that international feminism has provided Japanese feminists with an additional forum for pressuring the Japanese government. Rohlinger and Meyer also find a link between international/transnational and national feminism but argue that national contexts continue to dominate feminist mobilization. Two contributions suggest that discussions of local activism must be added to the analysis of national and transnational activism. Nechemias notes that the international women's movement influenced the development of local feminist organizations in Russia (particularly in Moscow and St. Petersburg), both by serving as a source of ideas, which Russian feminists mobilized both for and against, and by providing resources. Reger and Staggenborg's chapter discusses the interaction of national and local mobilization and organization. The national organization of NOW is affected by some local chapters more than others, and the development of some local chapters is also influenced by national activism. But Reger and Staggenborg also argue that the relationship between the levels changes over time and is contingent on local contexts. All in all, the research in this volume suggests that analyses of the women's movement (and other social movements) need to consider all three levels of activism in understanding the development of movement ideas, actions, and success.

PLAN OF THE BOOK

This chapter has set the stage for the analyses that follow by providing the historical context of the contemporary women's movement, introducing the social movement concepts used to explain the development of women's movements, and highlighting the main themes of the book. Reflecting the major premise of the importance of both dynamic and comparative studies of women's movements, the book is broken into two sections. The first part of the book focuses on the women's movement in the United States, providing a dynamic analysis both by chapters that examine specific periods of the movement's development (Freeman and Ryan) and through individual chapters that undertake longitudinal comparisons (Whittier; Reger and Staggenborg; and Barakso). The second section of the book provides comparative insights into the U.S. women's movement through a comparison to other movements (Robnett) and to women's movements in other parts of the globe (Baldez and Montoya; Nechemias; Gelb; and Rohlinger and Meyer). The concluding chapter uses the insights from both sections to discuss the future of the women's movement.

NOTES

1. The exception to this rule was the wide range of charitable organizations mostly organized under the auspices of churches.

2. African American women were largely excluded from these social changes. In 1957 only 3 percent of black women over twenty-five years of age had completed four years of college, half the percent of white women. Although African American women's labor force participation exceeded that of their white counterparts, Epstein (1993, 14–15) notes that the combined barriers against women and blacks kept African American women out of most professions.

3. Still later, women peace activists organized the International Committee of Women for Permanent Peace, which later became the Women's International League for Peace and Freedom.

4. Indeed, even money flowed between different national movements. After the adoption of the vote in the United States, NAWSA used its remaining funds to aid suffrage organizations in other countries (Catt 1929).

5. As Swidler (1986, 273) notes, there are extensive debates over the meaning of culture. In this chapter, I follow her lead in focusing on the "symbolic forms" that capture people's experiences and understandings.

6. Indeed, while gender is of primary interest to this volume, the culture of class and race/ethnicity is equally important to understanding mobilization of any movement.

7. Ryan's concept differs from the cycle of radicalization and moderation inherent in the cycle of protest literature.

Part I

THE WOMEN'S MOVEMENT IN THE UNITED STATES

2

The Origins of the Women's Liberation Movement[1]

Jo Freeman

Editor's Note: The following piece was originally published in the *American Journal of Sociology* in 1973. Jo Freeman's "The Origins of the Women's Liberation Movement" is one of the most compelling and theoretically relevant discussions of the rise of the second wave of the women's movement. Thirty years after the piece was originally published, it not only provides one of the best descriptions of the period, but it identifies factors crucial to the development of the movement that have withstood the critical test of time. Nonetheless, in the intervening three decades since the piece was published, some significant changes in the social movement literature have occurred. Although Freeman begins by noting the dearth of research on how movements are constructed, social scientists have spent a great deal of effort studying the issue and many of the central concepts that we now use to analyze social movements—political opportunities and framing for example—developed in response to these issues. On the other hand, the collective behavior ideas that Freeman criticizes at the beginning of the piece have largely been abandoned by social movement scholars. Yet, Freeman's focus on networks, critical events, and ideas in the development of the U.S. women's movement presages the central concepts of resources, political opportunities and frames that came later. As such, her work serves as a keystone to other authors in this volume.

The emergence in the last few years of a feminist movement caught most thoughtful observers by surprise. Women had "come a long way," had they not? What could they want to be liberated from? The new movement generated much speculation about the sources of female discontent and why it was articulated at this particular time. But these speculators usually asked the wrong questions. Most attempts to analyze the sources of social strain have had to conclude with Ferriss (1971, p. 1) that, "from the close perspective of 1970, events of the past decade provide evidence of no compelling cause of the rise of the new feminist movement." His examination of time-series data over the previous 20 years did not reveal any significant changes in socio-economic variables which could account for the emergence of a women's movement at the time it was created. From such strain indicators, one could surmise that any time in the last two decades was as conducive as any other to movement formation.

I

The sociological literature is not of much help: the study of social movements "has been a neglected area of sociology" (Killian 1964, p. 426), and, within that field, virtually no theorists have dealt with movement origins. The *causes* of social movements have been analyzed (Gurr 1970; Davies 1962), and the *motivations* of participants have been investigated (Toch 1965; Cantril 1941; Hoffer 1951; Adorno et al. 1950; but the mechanisms of "how" a movement is constructed have received scant attention.[2] As Dahrendorf (1959, p. 64) commented, "The sociologist is generally interested not so much in the origin of social phenomena as in their spread and rise to wider significance." This interest is derived from an emphasis on cultural processes rather than on people as the major dynamic of social change (Killian 1964, p. 426). Consequently, even the "natural history" theorists have delineated the stages of development in a way that is too vague to tell us much about how movements actually start (Dawson and Gettys 1929, pp. 787–803; Lowi 1971, P. 39; Blumer 1951; King 1956), and a theory as comprehensive as Smelser's (1963) is postulated on too abstract a level to be of microsociological value (for a good critique, see Currie and Skolnick 1970).

Part of the problem results from extreme confusion about what a social movement really is. Movements are rarely studied as distinct social phenomena but are usually subsumed under one of two theoretical traditions: that of "collective behavior" (see, especially, Smelser 1963; Lang and Lang 1961; Turner and Killian 1957) and that of interest-group and party formation (Heberle 1951; King 1956; Lowi 1971). The former emphasizes the spontaneous aspects of a movement; and the latter, the structured ones. Yet movements are neither fully collective behavior nor incipient interest groups except in the broadest sense of these terms. Rather, they contain essential elements of both. It is "the dual imperative of spontaneity and organization [that] . . . sets them apart from pressure groups and other types of voluntary associations, which lack their spontaneity, and from mass behavior, which is altogether devoid of even the rudiments of organization" (Lang and Lang 1961, p. 497).

Recognizing with Heberle (1951, p. 8) that "movements *as such* are not organized groups," it is still the structured aspects which are more amenable to study, if not always the most salient. Turner and Killian (1957, p. 307) have argued that it is when "members of a public who share a common position concerning the issue at hand supplement their informal person-to-person discussion with some organization to promote their convictions more effectively and insure more sustained activity, a social movement is incipient" (see also Killian 1964, p. 426). Such organization(s) and other core groups of a movement not only determine much of its conscious policy but serve as foci for its values and activities. Just as it has been argued that society as a whole has a cultural and structural "center" about which most members of the society are more or less "peripheral" (Shils 1970), so, too, can a social movement be conceived of as having a center and a periphery. An investigation into a movement's origins must be concerned with the microstructural preconditions for the emergence of such a movement center. From where do the people come who make up the initial, organizing cadre of a movement? How do they come together, and how do they come to share a similar view of the world in circumstances which compel them to political action? In what ways does the nature of the original center affect the future development of the movement?

II

Most movements have very inconspicuous beginnings. The significant elements of their origins are usually forgotten or distorted by the time a trained observer seeks to trace them out, making retroactive analyses difficult. Thus, a detailed investigation of a single movement at the time it is forming can add much to what little is known about movement origins. Such an examination cannot uncover all of the conditions and ingredients of movement formation, but it can aptly illustrate both weaknesses in the theoretical literature and new directions for research. During the formative period of the women's liberation movement, I had many opportunities to observe, log, and interview most of the principals involved in the early movement.[3] The descriptive material in Section III is based on that data. This analysis, supplemented by five other origin studies made by me, would support the following three propositions:

Proposition 1: The need for a preexisting communications network or infrastructure within the social base of a movement is a primary prerequisite for "spontaneous" activity. Masses alone don't form movements, however discontented they may be. Groups of previously unorganized individuals may spontaneously form into small local associations—usually along the lines of informal social networks—in response to a specific strain or crisis, but, if they are not linked in some manner, the protest does not become generalized: it remains a local irritant or dissolves completely. If a movement is to spread rapidly, the communications network must already exist. If only the rudiments of one exist, movement formation requires a high input of "organizing" activity.

Proposition 2: Not just any communications network will do. It must be a network that is *co-optable* to the new ideas of the incipient inovement.[4] To be co-optable, it must be composed of like-minded people whose background, experiences, or location in the social structure make them receptive to the ideas of a specific new movement.

Proposition 3: Given the existence of a co-optable communications network, or at least the rudimentary development of a potential one, and a situation of strain, one or more precipitants are required. Here, two distinct patterns emerge that often overlap. In one, a crisis galvanizes the network into spontaneous action in a new direction. In the other, one or more persons begin organizing a new organization or disseminating a new idea. For spontaneous action to occur, the communications network must be well formed or the initial protest will not survive the incipient stage. If it is not well formed, organizing efforts must occur; that is, one or more persons must specifically attempt to construct a movement. To be successful, organizers must be skilled and must have a fertile field in which to work. If no communications network already exists, there must at least be emerging spontaneous groups which are acutely attuned to the issue, albeit uncoordinated. To sum up, if a co-optable communications network is already established, a crisis is all that is necessary to galvanize it. If it is rudimentary, an organizing cadre of one or more persons is necessary. Such a cadre is superfluous if the former conditions fully exist, but it is essential if they do not.

Before examining these propositions in detail, let us look at the structure and origins of the women's liberation movement.

III

The women's liberation movement manifests itself in an almost infinite variety of groups, styles, and organizations. Yet, this diversity has sprung from only two distinct origins whose numerous offspring remain clustered largely around these two sources. The two branches are often called "reform" and "radical," or, as the sole authoritative book on the movement describes them, "women's rights" and "women's liberation" (Hole and Levine 1971). Unfortunately, these terms actually tell us very little, since feminists do not fit into the traditional Left/Right spectrum. In fact, if an ideological typography were possible, it would show minimal consistency with any other characteristic. Structure and style rather than ideology more accurately differentiate the two branches, and, even here, there has been much borrowing on both sides.

I prefer simpler designations: the first of the branches will be referred to as the older branch of the movement, partly because it began first and partly because the median age of its activists is higher. It contains numerous organizations, including the lobbyist group (Women's Equity Action League), a legal foundation (Human Rights for Women), over 20 caucuses in professional organizations, and separate organizations of women in the professions and other occupations. Its most prominent "core group" is the National Organization for Women (NOW), which was also the first to be formed.

While the written programs and aims of the older branch span a wide spectrum, their activities tend to be concentrated on legal and economic problems. These groups are primarily made up of women—and men—who work, and they are substantially concerned with the problems of working women. The style of organization of the older branch tends to be traditionally formal, with elected officers, boards of directors, bylaws, and the other trappings of democratic procedure. All started as top-down national organizations, lacking in a mass base. Some have subsequently developed a mass base, some have not yet done so, and others do not want to.

Conversely, the younger branch consists of innumerable small groups—engaged in a variety of activities—whose contact with each other is, at best, tenuous. Contrary to popular myth, it did not begin on the campus nor was it started by the Students for a Democratic Society (SDS). However, its activators were, to be trite, on the other side of the generation gap. While few were students, all were "under 30" and had received their political education as participants or concerned observers of the social action projects of the last decade. Many came direct from New Left and civil rights organizations. Others had attended various courses on women in the multitude of free universities springing up around the country during those years.

The expansion of these groups has appeared more amoebic than organized, because the younger branch of the movement prides itself on its lack of organization. From its radical roots, it inherited the idea that structures were always conservative and confining, and leaders, isolated and elitist. Thus, eschewing structure and damning the idea of leadership, it has carried the concept of "everyone doing her own thing" to the point where communication is haphazard and coordination is almost nonexistent. The thousands of sister chapters around the country are virtually independent of each other, linked only by numerous underground papers, journals, newsletters, and cross-country travelers. A national conference was held over Thanksgiving in 1968 but, although considered successful, has not yet been repeated. Before the 1968 conference, the movement did not have the sense of national unity which emerged after the conference. Since then, young feminists have made no attempt to call another national conference. There have been a few regional conferences, but no permanent consequences resulted. At most, some cities have a coordinating committee which attempts to maintain communication among local groups and to channel newcomers into appropriate ones, but these committees have no power over any group's activities, let alone its ideas. Even local activists do not know how big the movement is in their own city. While it cannot be said to have no organization at all, this branch of the movement has informally adopted a general policy of "structurelessness."

Despite a lack of a formal policy encouraging it, there is a great deal of homogeneity within the younger branch of the movement. Like the older branch, it tends to be predominantly white, middle class, and college educated. But it is much more homogeneous and, unlike the older branch, has been unable to diversify.

This is largely because most small groups tend to form among friendship networks. Most groups have no requirements for membership (other than female sex), no dues, no written and agreed-upon structure, and no elected leaders. Because of this lack of structure, it is often easier for an individual to form a new group than to find and join an older one. This encourages group formation but discourages individual diversification. Even contacts among groups tend to be along friendship lines.

In general, the different style and organization of the two branches was largely derived from the different kind of political education and experiences of each group of women. Women of the older branch were trained in and had used the traditional forms of political action, while the younger branch has inherited the loose, flexible, person-oriented attitude of the youth and student movements. The different structures that have evolved from these two distinctly different kinds of experience have, in turn, largely determined the strategy of the two branches, irrespective of any conscious intentions of their participants. These different structures and strategies have each posed different problems and possibilities. Intra-movement differences are often perceived by the participants as conflicting, but it is their essential complementarity which has been one of the strengths of the movement.

Despite the multitude of differences, there are very strong similarities in the way the two branches came into being. These similarities serve to illuminate some of the microsociological factors involved in movement formation. The forces which led to NOW's formation were first set in motion in 1961 when President Kennedy established the President's Commission on the Status of Women at the behest of Esther Peterson,[5] to be chaired by Eleanor Roosevelt. Operating under a broad mandate, its 1963 report (American Women) and subsequent committee publications documented just how thoroughly women are still denied many rights and opportunities. The most concrete response to the activity of the president's commission was the eventual establishment of 50 state commissions to do similar research on a state level. These commissions were often urged by politically active women and were composed primarily of women. Nonetheless, many believe the main stimulus behind their formation was the alleged view of the governors that the commissions were excellent opportunities to pay political debts without giving women more influential positions.

The activity of the federal and state commissions laid the groundwork for the future movement in three significant ways: (1) it brought together many knowledgeable, politically active women who otherwise would not have worked together around matters of direct concern to women; (2) the investigations unearthed ample evidence of women's unequal status, especially their legal and economic difficulties, in the process convincing many previously uninterested women that something should be done; (3) the reports created a climate of expectations that something would be done. The women of the federal and state commissions who were exposed to these influences exchanged visits, correspondence, and staff and met with each other at an annual commission convention. Thus, they were in a position to share and mutually reinforce their growing awareness and concern over women's issues. These commissions thus created an embryonic communications network among people with similar concerns.

During this time, two other events of significance occurred. The first was the publication of Betty Friedan's (1963) book, *The Feminine Mystique.* An immediate best seller, it stimulated many women to question the status quo and some to suggest to Friedan that a new organization be formed to attack their problems. The second event was the addition of "sex" to Title VII of the 1964 Civil Rights Act. Many men thought the "sex" provision was a joke (Bird 1968, chap. 1). The Equal Employment Opportunity Commission (EEOC) certainly treated it as one and refused to adequately enforce it. The first EEOC executive director even stated publicly that the provision was a "fluke" that was "conceived out of wedlock" (Edelsberg 1965). But, within the EEOC, there was a "prowoman" coterie which argued that "sex" would be taken more seriously if there were "some sort of NAACP for women" to put pressure on the government. As government employees, they couldn't organize such a group, but they spoke privately with those whom they thought might be able to do so. One who shared their views was Rep. Martha Griffiths of Michigan. She blasted the EEOC's attitude in a June 20, 1966 speech on the House floor (Griffiths 1966) declaring that the agency had "started out by casting disrespect and ridicule on the law" but that their "wholly negative attitude had changed—for the worse."

On June 30, 1966, these three strands of incipient feminism were knotted together to form NOW. The occasion was the last day of the Third National Conference of Commissions on the Status of Women, ironically titled "Targets for Action." The participants had all received copies of Rep. Griffith's remarks. The opportunity came with a refusal by conference officials to bring to the floor a proposed resolution that urged the EEOC to give equal enforcement to the sex provision of Title VII as was given to the race provision. Despite the fact that these state commissions were not federal agencies, officials replied that one government agency could not be allowed to pressure another. The small group of women who had desired the resolution had met the night before in Friedan's hotel room to discuss the possibility of a civil rights organization for women. Not convinced of its need, they chose instead to propose the resolution. When the resolution was vetoed, the women held a whispered conversation over lunch and agreed to form an action organization "to bring women into full participation in the mainstream of American society now, assuming all the privileges and responsibilities thereof in truly equal partnership with men." The name NOW was coined by Friedan, who was at the conference researching her second book. Before the day was over, 28 women paid $5.00 each to join (Friedan 1967).

By the time the organizing conference was held the following October 29–30, over 300 men and women had become charter members. It is impossible to do a breakdown on the composition of the charter membership, but one of the first officers and board is possible. Such a breakdown accurately reflected NOW's origins. Friedan was president, two former EEOC commissioners were vice-presidents, a representative of the United Auto Workers Women's Committee was secretary-treasurer, and there were seven past and present members of the State Commissions on the Status of Women on the 20–member board. Of the charter members, 126 were Wisconsin residents— and Wisconsin had the most active state commission. Occupationally, the board and officers were primarily from the professions, labor, government, and the communications industry. Of these, only those from labor had any experience in organizing, and they resigned a year later in a dispute over support of the Equal Rights Amendment. Instead of organizational expertise, what the early NOW members had was media experience, and it was here that their early efforts were aimed.

As a result, NOW often gave the impression of being larger than it was. It was highly successful in getting publicity, much less so in bringing about concrete changes or organizing itself. Thus, it was not until 1969, when several national news media simultaneously decided to do major stories on the women's liberation movement, that NOW's membership increased significantly. Even today, there are only 8,000 members, and the chapters are still in an incipient stage of development.

In the meantime, unaware of and unknown to NOW, the EEOC, or to the state commissions, younger women began forming their own movement. Here, too, the groundwork had been laid some years before. Social action projects of recent years had attracted many women, who were quickly shunted into traditional roles and faced with the self-evident contradiction of working in a "freedom movement" without being very free. No single "youth movement" activity or organization is responsible for the younger branch of the women's liberation movement; together they created a "radical community" in which like-minded people continually interacted with each other. This community consisted largely of those who had participated in one or more of the many protest activities of the sixties and had established its own ethos and its own institutions. Thus, the women in it thought of themselves as "movement people" and had incorporated the adjective "radical" into their personal identities. The values of their radical identity and the style to which they had been trained by their movement participation directed them to approach most problems as political ones which could be solved by organizing. What remained was to translate their individual feelings of "unfreedom" into a collective consciousness. Thus, the radical community provided not only the necessary network of communication; its radical ideas formed the framework of analysis which "explained" the dismal situation in which radical women found themselves.

Papers had been circulated on women,[6] and temporary women's caucuses had been held as early as 1964, when Stokely Carmichael made his infamous remark that "the only position for women in SNCC is prone." But it was not until late 1967 and 1968 that the groups developed a determined, if cautious, continuity and began to consciously expand themselves. At least five groups in five different cities (Chicago, Toronto, Detroit, Seattle, and Gainesville, Florida) formed spontaneously, independent of each other. They came at a very auspicious moment. The year 1967 was the one in which the blacks kicked the whites out of the civil rights movement, student power had been discredited by SDS, and the organized New Left was on the wane. Only draft-resistance activities were on the increase, and this movement more than any other exemplified the social inequities of the sexes. Men could resist the draft; women could only counsel resistance.

What was significant about this point in time was that there was a lack of available opportunities for political work. Some women fit well into the "secondary role" of draft counseling. Many did not. For years, their complaints of unfair treatment had been ignored by movement men with the dictum that those things could wait until after the revolution. Now these movement women found time on their hands, but the men would still not listen.

A typical example was the event which precipitated the formation of the Chicago group, the first independent group in this country. At the August 1967 National Conference for New Politics convention, a women's caucus met for days but was told its resolution wasn't significant enough to merit a floor discussion. By threatening to tie up the convention with procedural motions, the women succeeded in having their statement tacked to the end of the agenda. It was never discussed. The chair refused to recognize any of the many women standing by the microphone, their hands straining upward. When he instead called on someone to speak on "the forgotten American, the American Indian," five women rushed the podium to demand an explanation.

But the chairman just patted one of them on the head (literally) and told her, "Cool down little girl. We have more important things to talk about than women's problems."

The "little girl" was Shulamith Firestone, future author of *The Dialectic of Sex* (1971), and she didn't cool down. Instead, she joined with another Chicago woman, who had been trying to organize a women's group that summer, to call a meeting of those women who had half-heartedly attended the summer meetings. Telling their stories to those women, they stimulated sufficient rage to carry the group for three months, and by that time it was a permanent institution.

Another somewhat similar event occurred in Seattle the following winter. At the University of Washington, an SDS organizer was explaining to a large meeting how white college youth established rapport with the poor whites with whom they were working. "He noted that sometimes after analyzing societal ills, the men shared leisure time by 'balling a chick together.' He pointed out that such activities did much to enhance the political consciousness of the poor white youth. A woman in the audience asked, 'And what did it do for the consciousness of the chick?'" (Hole and Levine 1971, p. 120). After the meeting, a handful of enraged women formed Seattle's first group.

Groups subsequent to the initial five were largely organized rather than emerging spontaneously out of recent events. In particular, the Chicago group was responsible for the creation of many new groups in that city and elsewhere and started the first national newsletter. The 1968 conference was organized by the Washington D.C. group from resources provided by the Center for Policy Studies (CPS), a radical research organization. Using CPS facilities, this group subsequently became a main literature-distribution center. Although New York groups organized early and were featured in the 1969–70 media blitz, New York was not a source of early organizers.[7]

Unlike NOW, the women in the first groups had had years of experience as local-level organizers. They did not have the resources, or the desire, to form a national organization, but they knew how to utilize the infrastructure of the radical community, the underground press, and the free universities to disseminate ideas on women's liberation. Chicago, as a center of New Left activity, had the largest number of politically conscious organizers. Many traveled widely to Left conferences and demonstrations, and most used the opportunity to talk with other women about the new movement. In spite of public derision by radical men, or perhaps because of it, young women steadily formed new groups around the country.

Initially, the new movement found it hard to organize on the campus, but, as a major congregating area of women and, in particular, of women with political awareness, campus women's liberation groups eventually became ubiquitous. While the younger branch of the movement never formed any organization larger or more extensive than a city-wide coordinating committee, it would be fair to say that it has a larger "participationship" than NOW and the other older branch organizations. While the members of the older branch knew how to use the media and how to form national structures, the women of the younger branch were skilled in local community organizing.

IV

From this description, there appear to be four essential elements contributing to the emergence of the women's liberation movement in the mid-sixties: (1) the growth of a preexisting communications network which was (2) co-optable to the ideas of the new movement; (3) a series of crises that galvanized into action people involved in this network, and/or (4) subsequent organizing effort to weld the spontaneous groups together into a movement. To further understand these factors, let us examine them in detail with reference to other relevant studies.

1. Both the Commissions on the Status of Women and the "radical community" created a communications network through which those women initially interested in creating an organization could easily reach others. Such a network had not previously existed among women. Historically tied to the family and isolated from their own kind, women are perhaps the most organizationally underdeveloped social category in Western civilization. By 1950, the 19th-century organizations which had been the basis of the suffrage movement—the Women's Trade Union League, the General Federation of Women's Clubs, the Women's Christian Temperance Union, the National American Women's Suffrage Association—were all either dead or a pale shadow of their former selves. The closest exception was the National Women's Party (NWP), which has remained dedicated to feminist concerns since its inception in 1916. However, since 1923, it has been essentially a lobbying group for the Equal Rights Amendment. The NWP, having always believed that a small group of women concentrating their efforts in the right places was more effective than a mass appeal, was not appalled that, as late as 1969, even the majority of avowed feminists in this country had never heard of the NWP or the ERA.

References to the salience of a preexisting communications network appear frequently in the case studies of social movements, but it has been given little attention in the theoretical literature. It is essentially contrary to the mass-society theory which "for many . . . is . . . the most pertinent and comprehensive statement of the genesis of modern mass movements" (Pinard 1968, p. 682). This theory hypothesizes that those most likely to join a mass movement are those who are atomized and isolated from "a structure of groups intermediate between the family and the nation" (Kornhauser 1959, p. 93). However, the lack of such intermediate structures among women has proved more of a hindrance than a help in movement formation. Even today, it is those women who are most atomized, the housewives, who are least likely to join a feminist group.

The most serious attack on mass-society theory was made by Pinard (1971) in his study of the Social Credit Party of Quebec. He concluded that intermediate structures exerted *mobilizing* as well as restraining effects on individuals' participation in social movements because they formed communications networks that assisted in the rapid spread of new ideas. "When strains are severe and widespread," he contended, "a new movement is more likely to meet its early success among the more strongly integrated citizens" (Pinard 1971, p. 192).

Other evidence also attests to the role of previously organized networks in the rise and spread of a social movement. According to Buck (1920, pp. 43–44), the Grange established a degree of organization among American farmers in the 19th century which greatly facilitated the spread of future farmers' protests. In Saskatchewan, Lipset (1959) has asserted, "The rapid acceptance of new ideas and movements . . . can be attributed mainly to the high degree of organization. . . . The role of the social structure of the western wheat belt in facilitating the rise of new movements has never been sufficiently appreciated by historians and sociologists. Repeated challenges and crises forced the western farmers to create many more community institutions . . . than are necessary in a more stable area. These groups in turn provided a structural basis for immediate action in critical situations. [Therefore] though it was a new radical party, the C.C.F. did not have to build up an organization from scratch." More recently, the civil rights movement was built upon the infrastructure of the Southern black church (King 1958), and early SDS organizers made ready use of the National Student Association (Kissinger and Ross 1968, p. 16).

Indirect evidence of the essential role of formal and informal communications networks is found in diffusion theory, which emphasizes the importance of personal interaction rather than impersonal media communication in the spread of ideas (Rogers 1962; Lionberger 1960), and in Coleman's (1957) investigations of prior organizations in the initial development of conflict.

Such preexisting communications networks appear to be not merely valuable but prerequisites, as one study on "The Failure of an Incipient Social Movement" (Jackson, Peterson, Bull, Monsen, and Richmond 1960) made quite clear. In 1957, a potential tax-protest movement in Los Angeles generated considerable interest and public notice for a little over a month but was dead within a year. According to the authors, its failure to sustain itself beyond initial spontaneous protest was largely due to "the lack of a pre-existing network of communications linking those groups of citizens most likely to support the movement" (Jackson et al. 1960, p. 40). They said (p. 37) that "if a movement is to grow rapidly, it cannot rely upon its own network of communication, but must capitalize on networks already in existence."

The development of the women's liberation movement highlights the salience of such a network precisely because the conditions for a movement existed *before* a network came into being, but the movement didn't exist until afterward. Socioeconomic strain did not change for women significantly during a 20-year period. It was as great in 1955 as in 1965. What changed was the organizational situation. It was not until a communications network developed among like-minded people beyond local boundaries that the movement could emerge and develop past the point of occasional, spontaneous uprising.

2. However, not just any network would do; it had to be one which was co-optable by the incipient movement because it linked like-minded people likely to be predisposed to the new ideas of the movement. The 180,000-member Federation of Business and Professional Women's (BPW) Clubs would appear to be a likely base for a new feminist movement but in fact was unable to assume this role. It had steadily lobbied for legislation of importance to women, yet as late as "1966 BPW rejected a number of suggestions that it redefine . . . goals and tactics and become a kind of 'NAACP for women' . . . out of fear of being labeled 'feminist'" (Hole and Levine 1971, p. 81). While its membership has become a recruiting ground for feminism, it could not initially overcome the ideological barrier to a new type of political action.

On the other hand, the women of the President's and State Commissions on the Status of Women and the feminist coterie of the EEOC were co-optable, largely because their immersion into the facts of female status and the details of sex-discrimination cases made them very conscious of the need for change. Likewise, the young women of the "radical community" lived in an atmosphere of questioning, confrontation, and change. They absorbed an ideology of "freedom" and "liberation" far more potent than any latent "antifeminism" might have been. The repeated contradictions between these ideas and the actions of their male colleagues created a compulsion for action which only required an opportunity to erupt. This was provided by the "vacuum of political activity" of 1967–68.

The nature of co-optability is much more difficult to elucidate. Heretofore, it has been dealt with only tangentially. Pinard (1971, p. 186) noted the necessity for groups to "*possess* or *develop* an ideology or simply subjective interests congruent with that of a new movement" for them to "act as mobilizing rather than restraining agents toward that movement" but did not further explore what affected the "primary group climate." More illumination is provided by the diffusion of innovation studies which point out the necessity for new ideas to fit in with already-established norms for changes to happen easily. Furthermore, a social system which has as a value "innovativeness" itself (as the radical community did) will more rapidly adopt ideas than one which looks upon the habitual performance of traditional practices as the ideal (as most organized women's groups did in the fifties). Usually, as Lionberger (1960, p. 91) points out, "people act in terms of past experience and knowledge." People who have had similar experiences are likely to share similar perceptions of a situation and to mutually reinforce those perceptions as well as their subsequent interpretation.

A co-optable network, therefore, is one whose members have had common experiences which predispose them to be receptive to the particular new ideas of the incipient movement and who are not faced with structural or ideological barriers to action. If the new movement as an "innovation" can interpret these experiences and perceptions in ways that point out channels for social action, then participation in social movement becomes the logical thing to do.

3. As our examples have illustrated, these similar perceptions must be translated into action. This is the role of the "crisis." For women of the older branch of the movement, the impetus to organize was the refusal of the EEOC to enforce the sex provision of Title VII, precipitated by the concomitant refusal of federal officials at the conference to allow a supportive resolution. For younger women, there were a series of minor crises. Such precipitating events are common to most movements. They serve to crystallize and focus discontent. From their own experiences, directly and concretely, people feel the need for change in a situation that allows for an exchange of feelings with others, mutual validation, and a subsequent reinforcement of innovative interpretation. Perception of an immediate need for change is a major factor in predisposing people to accept new ideas (Rogers 1962, p. 280). Nothing makes desire for change more acute than a crisis. If the strain is great enough, such a crisis need not be a major one; it need only embody symbolically collective discontent.

4. However, a crisis will only catalyze a well-formed communications network. If such networks are only embryonically developed or only partially co-optable, the potentially active individuals in them must be linked together by someone. As Jackson et al. (1960, p. 37) stated, "Some protest may persist where the source of trouble is constantly present. But interest ordinarily cannot be maintained unless there is a welding of spontaneous groups into some stable organization." In other words, people must be organized. Social movements do not simply occur.

The role of the organizer in movement formation is another neglected aspect of the theoretical literature. There has been great concern with leadership, but the two roles are distinct and not always performed by the same individual. In the early stages of a movement, it is the organizer much more than any "leader" who is important, and such an individual or cadre must often operate behind the scenes.[8] Certainly, the "organizing cadre" that young women in the radical community came to be was key to the growth of that branch of the women's liberation movement, despite the fact that no "leaders" were produced (and were actively discouraged). The existence of many leaders but no organizers in the older branch of the women's liberation movement and its subsequent slow development would tend to substantiate this hypothesis.

The crucial function of the organizer has been explored indirectly in other areas of sociology. Rogers (1962) devotes many pages to the "change agent" who, while he does not necessarily weld a group together or "construct" a movement, does do many of the same things for agricultural innovation that an organizer does for political change. Mass-society theory makes reference to the "agitator" but fails to do so in any kind of truly informative way. A study of farmer's movements indicates that many core organizations were organized by a single individual before the spontaneous aspects of the movement predominated. Further, many other core groups were subsidized by older organizations, federal and state governments, and even by local businessmen (Salisbury 1969, p. 13). These organizations often served as training centers for organizers and sources of material support to aid in the formation of new interest groups and movements.

Similarly, the civil rights movement provided the training for many another movement's organizers, including the young women of the women's liberation movement. It would appear that the art of "constructing" a social movement is something that requires considerable skill and experience. Even in the supposedly spontaneous social movement, the professional is more valuable than the amateur.

V

The ultimate results of such "construction" are not independent of their origins. In fact, the attitudes and styles of a movement's initiators often have an effect which lasts longer than they do. Those women and men who formed NOW, and its subsequent sister organizations, created a national structure prepared to use the legal, political, and media institutions of our country. This it has done. The EEOC has changed many of its prejudicial attitudes toward women in its recent rulings. Numerous lawsuits have been filed under the sex provision of Title VII of the Civil Rights Act. The Equal Rights Amendment has passed Congress. Complaints have been filed against over 400 colleges and universities, as well as many businesses, charging violation of Executive Order 11246 amended by 11375, which prohibits sex discrimination by all holders of federal contracts. Articles on feminism have appeared in virtually every national news medium, and women's liberation has become a household word.

These groups have and continue to function primarily as pressure groups within the limits of traditional political activity. Consequently, their actual membership remains small. Diversification of the older branch of the movement has been largely along occupational lines and primarily within the professions. Activity has stressed using the tools for change provided by the system, however limited these may be. Short-range goals are emphasized, and no attempt has been made to place them within a broader ideological framework.

Initially, this structure hampered the development of older branch organizations. NOW suffered three splits between 1967 and 1968. As the only action organization concerned with women's rights, it had attracted many different kinds of people with many different views on what and how to proceed. With only a national structure and, at that point, no local base, it was difficult for individuals to pursue their particular concern on a local level; they had to persuade the whole organization to support them. Given NOW's top-down structure and limited resources, this placed severe limits on diversity and, in turn, severe strains on the organization. Additional difficulties for local chapters were created by a lack of organizers to develop new chapters and the lack of a program into which they could fit. NOW's initiators were very high-powered women who lacked the time or patience for the slow, unglamorous, and tedious work of putting together a mass organization. Chapter development had to wait for the national media to attract women to the organization or the considerable physical mobility of contemporary women to bring proponents into new territory. Locally, women had to find some common concern around which to organize. Unlike that of New York, which had easy access to the national media and many people skilled at using it, the other chapters had difficulty developing programs not dependent on the media. Since the national program consisted almost exclusively of support of legal cases or federal lobbying, the regional chapters could not easily fit into that either. Eventually, connections were made; and, in the last year, national task forces have begun to correlate with local efforts so that individual projects can combine a national thrust with instrumentation on the local level. After initial difficulties, NOW and the other older branch organizations are thriving at this point because they are able to effectively use the institutional tools which our society provides for social and political change. Yet, these groups are also limited by these tools to the rather narrow arenas within which they are designed to operate. The nature of these arenas and the particular skills they require for participation already limit both the kind of women who can effectively work in older branch groups and the activities they can undertake. When their scope is exhausted, it remains to be seen whether organizations such as NOW will wither, institutionalize themselves as traditional pressure groups, or show the imagination to develop new lines for action.

The younger branch has had an entirely different history and faces different prospects. It was able to expand rapidly in the beginning because it could capitalize on the infrastructure of organizations and media of the New Left and because its initiators were skilled in local community organizing. Since the prime unit was the small group and no need for national cooperation was perceived, multitudinous splits increased its strength rather than drained its resources. Such fission was often "friendly" in nature and, even when not, served to bring ever-increasing numbers of women under the movement's umbrella.

Unfortunately, these masses of new women lacked the organizing skills of the initiators, and, because the idea of "leadership" and "organization" were in disrepute, they made no attempt to acquire them. They did not want to deal with traditional political institutions and abjured all traditional political skills. Consequently, the growth of the movement institutions did not go beyond the local level, and they were often inadequate to handle the accelerating influx of new people into the movement. Although these small groups were diverse in kind and responsible to no one for their focus, their nature determined both the structure and the strategy of the movement. One result has been a very broad-based creative movement to which individuals can relate pretty much as they desire with no concern for orthodoxy or doctrine. This branch has been the major source of new feminist ideas and activities. It has developed several ideological perspectives, much of the terminology of the movement, an amazing number of publications and "counter-institutions," numerous new issues, and even new techniques for social change. The emphasis of this branch has been on personal change as a means to understand the kind of political change desired. The primary instrument has been the consciousness-raising rap group which has sought to change women's very identities as well as their attitudes.

Nonetheless, this loose structure is flexible only within certain limits, and the movement has not yet shown the propensity to transcend them. While rap groups have been excellent techniques for changing individual attitudes, they have not been very successful in dealing with social institutions. Their loose, informal structure encourages participation in discussion, and their supportive atmosphere elicits personal insight; but neither is very efficient in handling specific tasks. While they have been of fundamental value to the development of the movement, they also lead to a certain kind of political impotency. It is virtually impossible to coordinate a national action, or even a local one, assuming there could be any agreement on issues around which to coordinate one.

Individual rap groups tend to flounder when their numbers have exhausted the virtues of consciousness-raising and decide they want to do something more concrete. The problem is that most groups are unwilling to change their structure when they change their tasks. They have accepted the ideology of "structurelessness" without realizing its limitations.

The resurgence of feminism tapped a major source of female energy, but the younger branch has not yet been able to channel it. Some women are able to create their own local-action projects, such as study groups, abortion counseling centers, bookstores, etc. Most are not, and the movement provides no coordinated or structured means of fitting into existing projects. Instead, such women either are recruited into NOW and other national organizations or drop out. New groups form and dissolve at an accelerating rate, creating a good deal of consciousness and very little action. The result is that most of the movement is proliferating underground. It often seems mired in introspection, but it is in fact creating a vast reservoir of conscious feminist sentiment which only awaits an appropriate opportunity for action.

In sum, the current status of the women's movement can be said to be structurally very much like it was in its incipient stages. That section which I have called the older branch remains attached to using the tools the system provides, while the younger branch simply proliferates horizontally, without creating new structures to handle new tasks.

NOTES

1. I would like to thank Richard Albares and Florence Levinsohn for having read and criticized earlier versions of this paper.

2. "A consciously directed and organized movement cannot be explained merely in terms of the psychological disposition or motivation of people, or in terms of a diffusion of an ideology. Explanations of this sort have a deceptive plausibility, but overlook the fact that *a movement has to be constructed* and has to carve out a career in what is practically always an opposed, resistant or at least indifferent world" (Blumer 1957: 147; italics mine).

3. As a founder and participant in the younger branch of the Chicago women's liberation movement from 1967 through 1969 and editor of the first (at that time, only) national newsletter, I was able, through extensive correspondence and interviews, to keep a record of how each group around the country first started, where the organizers got the idea from, who they had talked to, what conferences were held and who attended, the political affiliations (or lack of them) of the first members, etc. Although I was a member of Chicago NOW, information on the origins of it and the other older branch organizations comes entirely through ex post facto interviews of the principals and examination of early papers in preparation for my dissertation on the women's liberation movement. Most of my informants requested that their contribution remain confidential.

4. The only use of this significant word appears rather incidentally in Turner (1964: 123).

5. Then director of the Women's Bureau.

6. "A Kind of Memo," by Hayden and King (1966: 35) circulated in the fall of 1965 (and eventually published), was the first such paper.

7. The movement in New York has been more diverse than other cities and has made many major ideological contributions, but, contrary to popular belief, it did not begin in New York. In putting together their stories, the news media, concentrated as they are in New York, rarely looked past the Hudson for their information. This eastern bias is exemplified by the fact that, although the younger branch of the movement has no national organization and abjures leadership, all but one of those women designated by the press as movement leaders live in New York.

8. The nature and function of these two roles was most clearly evident in the Townsend old-age movement of the thirties. Townsend was the "charismatic" leader, but the movement was organized by his partner, real estate promoter Robert Clements. Townsend himself acknowledges that, without Clement's help, the movement would never have gone beyond the idea stage (see Holzman 1963).

3

From the Second to the Third Wave: Continuity and Change in Grassroots Feminism

Nancy Whittier

A vibrant local group organizes candlelight marches; performs street theater; protests against right-wing activists; lobbies against antigay legislation; and produces T-shirts, posters, and pamphlets.

- The group sings folk songs at demonstrations./*The group eats fire at demonstrations.*
- The group is made up primarily of women in their twenties, with long hair and flannel shirts./*The group is made up primarily of women in their twenties, with multiple body piercings, dressed in black.*
- The group promotes cervical self-examination in which women learn to locate their cervixes and assess their health with the assistance of other group members./*The group promotes sexual awareness and liberation through the dissemination of women-produced pornography and classes in masturbation techniques.*
- The group distinguishes itself from previous movements of the Left, which it sees as male-dominated./*The group distinguishes itself from previous women's movements, which it sees as white-dominated, sex-phobic, and promoting an essentialist model of gender.*
- The group is opposed by a well-organized and well-funded conservative movement that emphasizes the challenge to women's traditional roles in the family./*The group is opposed by a well-organized and well-funded conservative movement that emphasizes the rising tide of immorality led by lesbians and gay men who seek to recruit children to their lifestyle.*
- The group receives funding directly and indirectly through federal and state grants, subsidized workers through the Comprehensive Employment

and Training Act (CETA) program, foundation monies, and contracts or fees for service provision./*The group receives no funding from federal coffers, as funding for activist and even social service groups or subsidies for the unemployed is minimal; it does not engage in service provision itself. While it supports shelters for battered women and rape crisis services, it argues that these should be extended to transgendered people and to women battered or raped by other women, rather than promoting the idea that women are universally victimized by men, which it sees as reinforcing essentialist notions of gender. Its monies, such as they are, come from individual donations or independent feminist foundations.*

- The word *feminist* has negative connotations, and few feminist goals have been achieved./*The word* feminist *has negative connotations, yet popular discourse and opinion about issues such as rape, battering, women's employment, and political equality reflect feminist stances.*

The first passage could describe any period of active grassroots feminist organizing that has occurred continuously since the late 1960s. The following pairs of statements, however, illustrate the stylistic, tactical, and contextual changes that separate second and third wave grassroots feminism. In this chapter I outline the development of this branch of feminist organizing, which Jo Freeman (1975) calls the "younger branch," and which has also been termed radical, grassroots, lesbian, or cultural feminism. I refer to it primarily as "grassroots" feminism, because the other terms were claimed primarily by activists of specific historical moments. This strand of the women's movement is distinguished by its reliance on nonbureaucratic, usually local organizations; an emphasis on cultural- and identity-based modes of organizing alongside more conventional engagement with the state; a strong presence of politicized lesbians and other sexual minorities; and an affinity for antinormative and dramatic tactics and self-presentation. Over more than three decades of existence, grassroots feminism has changed dramatically, but there are connections and commonalities across its phases. Feminism as a whole, and grassroots feminism in particular, began to move from a second to a third wave in the late 1980s; the consolidation of a distinct third wave perspective was complete by the mid-1990s. Meanwhile, however, individuals, organizations, and mobilizing patterns of the second wave continued alongside third wave mobilization.

The collective identity, goals, tactics, and organizations of the grassroots women's movement have changed because of both internal movement dynamics and external contexts. I use the concept of political generations to conceptualize the intersection of internal identities and processes with external opportunities and culture. A political generation is made up of individuals who are politicized at the same time and place and as a result develop a shared *collective identity*, which is a distinct group definition and perspective on the world and on social movements (Whittier 1995, 1997; Klatch 1999; Mannheim 1952). In the women's movement, changes in cultural norms about gender and gender inequality mean that activists at different times have different perspectives about the nature of the problem and its solutions, as Banaszak points out in chapter 1. Further, critical events such as legislation (e.g., the Defense of Marriage Act), court decisions (e.g., *Roe v. Wade*), egregious and publicized cases of sexism (e.g., hearings on sexual harassment in the military), and other influential movements (e.g., ACT-UP) shape both activists' points of view and the direction of the movement. Political generations form in response to these conditions. They are different from chronological or biological generations because they form at varying intervals, with new political generations emerging as conditions change. A political generation need not be made up of age-mates but may contain people of different ages who became politicized at the same time, under the same circumstances. Further, members of political generations may vary among themselves in more small-scale ways as a result of changes in the internal movement and environmental contexts that shape somewhat different perspectives for members coming of age at different points. These "micro-cohorts" may form as often as every one or two years during periods of rapid movement change (usually during movement peaks). Micro-cohorts that form during one wave of a social movement, such as the second wave of the women's movement, share a basic common perspective that connects them and distinguishes them from those micro-cohorts that form during a different wave of the movement, such as the third wave of the women's movement.

My perspective draws on recent social movement theory that emphasizes the connections between movements' internal dynamics, including their collective identities, organizational structures, interactions, and frames, and their external contexts, including political opportunities and mainstream culture (McAdam, Tarrow, and Tilly 1996; Meyer, Whittier, and Robnett 2002; Whittier 2002). As Banaszak discusses in chapter 1, movement resources and organizations, cultures and identities, and political opportunities influence each other and combine to shape the directions of social movements. In the sections that follow, I analyze the shifting forms of grassroots feminism, showing how changes in collective identity, mobilization, and external contexts intersected, and highlighting the role of political generations in those changes. I discuss four phases of grassroots feminist activism, two within the second wave (emergence and growth/institutionalization) and two within the third wave (anti-identity politics and third wave feminism). The discussion is based on my own research on various forms of feminist activism (Taylor and Whittier 1992; Whittier 1995, 1997, 2000, 2001), additional primary source materials on third wave activism (mainly published and Web-based documents), and secondary sources.

THE SECOND WAVE

Emergence (Late 1960s–Early 1970s)[1]

Radical feminism emerged in the late 1960s, as women coming out of the New Left formed consciousness-raising groups in which they discussed the political roots of their individual circumstances, developed groundbreaking theory about women's oppression, and mobilized to challenge the structures and cultures that maintained that oppression. Jo Freeman discusses the origins of this branch of the movement in her 1973 article, reprinted as chapter 2 of this volume. As they realized the depth and breadth of gender inequalities that many women had previously taken for granted, these activists organized first within New Left groups, then quickly outside them. Within a year or two, consciousness-raising groups were meeting in virtually every part of the country, calling themselves the women's liberation movement, and their members began organizing political actions aimed at changing the conditions that they saw as limiting women's lives. These groups tended to be relatively small, local, and collectivist in structure, in conscious response to both the New Left ideal of a beloved community in which all members were connected and valued and the Left's failure to live up to that ideal because of the dominance of articulate male theoreticians and the invisibility and silencing of women (Rosen 2000; Evans 1979; Whittier 1995; Brownmiller 1999; Freeman 1975; Cassell 1977; Taylor, Whittier, and Pelak 2001).

The first years of women's liberation have been the subject of numerous scholarly and activist accounts. The by-now-familiar story distinguishes what Jo Freeman (1975) termed "younger," "small-groups," or "women's liberation" feminists from feminists who organized in larger, bureaucratic organizations oriented toward changing legislation and public policy, although the distinctions between these two wings were far from clear-cut (Boles 1991; Reger 2002a; Ferree and Hess 1994). While most studies focus on the East and West Coasts (particularly New York City and Berkeley) (e.g., Rosen 2000; Cassell 1977; Echols 1989; Ryan 1992), women's liberation groups grew all around the country and developed influential perspectives and projects on issues ranging from media, rape, abortion, health, work and unionization, to sexuality (see Freeman 1975; Sealander and Smith 1986; Strobel 1995; Kaplan 1995; Whittier 1995; Ezekiel 2002). The earliest women's liberation activists shared experiences in the New Left; virtually all of them had been involved in some way with the antiwar, student, and civil rights movements, many with SDS. As a result, their conceptualization of inequality and oppression was shaped by the class and race analyses of SDS, and they emphasized capitalist and imperialist domination, analogizing from class to gender to argue that women made up a subordinate "sex-class." Many of their early actions aimed at illuminating the gender dimensions of women's status in Vietnam, for example, or the double oppression of African American women at the hands of white employers, or the rights of women on welfare. Yet they also shared a sense of anger at the New Left for marginalizing women and women's issues and a desire to forge an autonomous women's movement (Rosen 2000; Whittier 1995; Evans 1979). The open discussion and heady atmosphere of consciousness-raising groups led them to politicize new issues, such as sexual experiences and expectations, the objectification of women's bodies, access to improved birth control, abortion, and women's responsibility for housework and child-raising.

They forged a collective identity out of these shared experiences, conversations, and their initial activism. Collective identities define a group in politicized terms, define activists' own position in society, frame relevant issues, and shape tactics, which aim to express the group's view of itself and the world (Melucci 1989; Taylor and Whittier 1992; Whittier 1995). The first cohort of activists called themselves "women's liberationists," drawing on the terminology of the New Left, and they emphasized women's oppression based on economic, sexual, and relational issues. They saw themselves as revolutionaries, fueled both by anger at their treatment by the larger society and their brothers on the Left and by the prevailing political climate that saw revolution as possible, indeed imminent, and rejected incremental change and compromise. Although they drew on resources from their New Left ties, as Jo Freeman describes, they organized autonomously. They did not seek funding from foundations or government, rarely engaged directly with those institutions, and saw themselves as mounting a guerrilla challenge from outside, swaying opinion and winning allies by dramatizing and publicizing the problems that women faced under sexism. Their actions included "zaps" in which small groups did things like pouring glue on *Playboy* magazines in newsstands, tossing bras and other symbols of femininity into "freedom trash cans" at the Miss America Pageant, holding a "child-in" in which women students brought their children to class in protest over lack of childcare facilities, or protesting lack of equal athletic facilities by sitting in in a men's sauna or marching into a men's locker room (Rosen 2000; Morgan 1978; Whittier 1995).

A political generations approach suggests that movements and collective identities take the forms they do because of individuals' experiences at a particular moment in time (Mannheim 1952; Whittier 1995, 1997; Klatch 1999). This political generation was formed by participants' experiences coming of age in a prefeminist culture, becoming politicized in the New Left, and raising feminist issues in a context that provided little external support initially. While there were some well-placed women in the federal Women's Bureau who would later provide some support to the more bureaucratically structured feminist organizations (Gelb and Palley 1996; Costain 1992), women's liberationists did not see them as allies. In fact, because activists were more likely to target forms of oppression in daily life, they had little direct contact with the state except as an abstract oppressor or an agent of police repression. In addition, the ridicule that feminist demands faced in the larger culture shaped early activists' sense that they were embarking on a radical new venture (as they were) and their collective identity as brave revolutionaries.

As a result, activists who first came to women's liberation during this period formed a sense of themselves and their movement that differed from those who entered later. In other words, they formed a distinct micro-cohort (and marked the beginning of a new political generation that differed from the micro-cohorts of the first wave and interwave abeyance period). Elsewhere I've called this micro-cohort "initiators" because they sparked the movement, and to highlight their sense of themselves as striking out where no woman had gone before (Whittier 1995, 1997).[2] As the movement grew and changed, later entrants began to reconceptualize it, and themselves, as women and as feminists.

Growth and Institutionalization (1970s)

Initiators' early efforts quickly brought in a large number of new recruits, who joined consciousness-raising groups, participated in actions, and founded new organizations. Their experience differed from that of initiators because of two main factors. First, they were not beginning a brand new movement but entering one that already existed, although they did radically expand and change it. Many of those who entered only a few years after the first micro-cohort did not have much previous activist experience and therefore were first politicized in the women's movement rather than the larger Left. As a result, they defined themselves less by reference to the mixed-sex New Left—either its particular perspectives or its sexism—and focused more on defining women's issues from their own point of view. Second, the larger culture had already begun to be more familiar with feminist ideas, and there were some allies within the state. As a result, both the kinds of activism that these activists engaged in, and their collective identity, differed from their predecessors'. Elsewhere I've called the micro-cohorts that formed during this period "founders"—the first entrants who were the "founding mothers" of numerous organizations—and "joiners"—those whose numbers swelled the new organizations and who helped to establish numerous other institutions that were influential in the following years (Whittier 1995, 1997).[3]

The new recruits focused on founding organizations that included consciousness-raising; developing classes on women's experiences (leading to the establishment of women's studies at colleges and universities); challenging rape through self-defense training, public education, and assistance to raped women; training women in nontraditional skills such as car repair; feminist bookstores; health clinics; and spaces for meetings and cultural events. Many of these groups thrived, and within a few years there were visible feminist organizations and institutions in most major cities, college towns, and many other locations around the country. The most visible, and ubiquitous, were antirape organizations, women's studies programs, and feminist bookstores, which also served as gathering places and clearinghouses for information about movement activities. In addition to these local organizations, national organizations developed, including feminist publishing houses, recording companies, and conferences and festivals (Whittier 1995; Matthews 1995; Staggenborg 1998; Echols 1989). During this period, many local and national organizations associated with what Freeman calls the "older" wing also were influential, including the National Organization for Women (NOW) and the National Abortion and Reproductive Rights Action League (NARAL). Although these organizations are not the focus of my account, they were an important part of the context for the radical feminist groups, adding to their sense of operating in a more friendly world.

The first wave of organizations mostly focused on serving women and providing an infrastructure for a community of feminists in which participants could find support and hone political perspectives, and from which they could mount protests and other actions. Fairly quickly, however, many groups began interacting with the very institutions that they opposed, usually beginning as adversaries, but often developing working relationships. For example, feminist antirape groups initially taught self-defense and rape prevention classes to women and provided crisis hotlines for women who had been raped. In Columbus, Ohio, these activists began monitoring the (usually dismal) treatment that rape victims received in the hospitals, courts, and mental health centers. In response, they began offering training to medical, therapeutic, and law enforcement agencies, often through paid contracts (Whittier 1995). Antirape groups in Los Angeles followed a similar pattern (Matthews 1995). Such work provided the groups with much-needed funds as well as direct influence over institutions, and did in fact produce substantial change in how rape cases are dealt with in court and how rape victims are treated by police and medical staff when they make a report. Battered women's shelters and women's health clinics followed a similar path from autonomous feminist organization to service provision with external funding (Reinelt 1995). In many cases, by the late 1980s these groups' functions had been absorbed by the institutions that they targeted, as hospitals sponsored rape crisis hotlines, health centers were bought out by nonfeminist groups, and self-defense training for children became part of the curriculum of local school districts (Taylor 1996; Whittier 1995). At the same time, many organizations that were not amenable to external control, mostly those that didn't provide services, also expanded and thrived. A women's movement community grew during these years, with feminist musicians and artists, coffeehouses and bookstores, much writing published by feminist presses, and a dense network of friendships and activist collaborations (Taylor and Whittier 1992; Whittier 1995;

Staggenborg 1998; Taylor, Whittier, and Pelak 2001). In other words, the grassroots women's movement became institutionalized simultaneously within dominant institutions and in an autonomous alternative community.

These years have been discussed by various scholars, who interpret the developments quite differently. Several have labeled the mid-1970s and later an era of "cultural feminism," arguing that the movement turned away from political aims and tactics toward the establishment of a largely apolitical subculture (Ryan 1992; Echols 1989). Others have argued that this cultural turn remained political, both because activists continued to mount external protests and because the establishment of alternative institutions allowed them to sustain themselves, their collective identity, and a membership base from which to mobilize (Whittier 1995; Taylor and Rupp 1993). There is general agreement, however, that this period marked a heyday of feminist collective identity, in which many activists and organizations promoted a sense of sisterhood or solidarity among women and the idea that shared identity as women provided the basis for shared political commitments (Taylor and Whittier 1992; Ryan 2001a; Echols 1989). A strong lesbian presence in the movement helped to shape the idea that women's connections to other women were to be celebrated as a form of resistance to a system that devalued women. Such "identity politics" were not unique to the women's movement but motivated activism by African Americans, Latino/as, Native Americans, lesbians and gay men, and even right-wing Christians during this period. Powerful collective identities intensified activists' sense of commitment and connection to each other and to a movement even as they also idealized those connections and discouraged dissent and difference.

The collective identity formed by these activists differed from that of the very earliest activists. Although the first activists, too, had reveled in their new connections to each other and had attempted to form autonomous spaces apart from male domination (Rosen 2000), they had not developed the elaborate women's culture or sense of shared subjectivity that emerged during the movement's peak. The micro-cohorts that spurred the movement's growth and institutionalization emphasized women's solidarity and the importance of women's spaces and autonomy from men partly because they saw women as different and better than men, less violent and more caring and nurturing (Taylor and Whittier 1992).[4] A growing lesbian presence in the movement, and the growth of lesbian feminism as an ideological strand nationally, heightened the emphasis on women's community and contributed to a decrease in concern with sexism in personal or intimate interactions with men (Myron and Bunch 1975; Radicalesbians 1987; Taylor and Rupp 1993; Whittier 1995).

Activists in this micro-cohort understood themselves and the movement in the ways they did because of both internal and external factors. The movement context they experienced was very different from that of their predecessors, since they became politicized when the women's movement was rising, and without much contact with the mixed-sex Left. They thus thought of themselves as radical feminists first and saw their ties to other women and a movement on behalf of women as primary. Because the movement was growing and, for a while, experiencing one success after another, participants felt optimistic about achieving sweeping feminist transformations. The external environment, while never exactly friendly to feminists, was more supportive during this period than earlier or later. Abortion was legalized in 1973, shifting the movement's focus—at least temporarily—away from reproductive rights toward other issues. Radical feminist organizations in many cities received foundation funding for projects on rape, child sexual abuse, battering, and feminist psychotherapy, to name a few. Some even received federal grants, and many made use of the CETA program, which funded public service jobs for the unemployed, to hire paid staff (Matthews 1995; Whittier 1995, 2001; Taylor 1996; Reinelt 1995). Federal and state funding for community mental health programs, community centers, women's studies, work training programs for women and minorities, and even women's sports all helped to support feminist activism in those arenas. At the same time, allies to the movement were entering elected office and, equally influential, entering the federal and state bureaucracies that administered public policy, and provided tangible support and encouragement to activists (Gelb and Palley 1996; Boles 1991). Further growth in feminist organizations such as NOW, NARAL, and state-level groups provided another source of external support. Beginning with Reagan's election to the presidency in 1980, however, external funding began to dry up; rising conservatism, the defeat of the ERA in 1982, the rise and growing success of the antiabortion movement, and the strength of the well-organized religious Right further entrenched external hostility to feminism (Whittier 1995; Blanchard 1994; Marshall 1995).

Because most of the initial grassroots feminist organizations were informally structured or sprang up around particular issues, they were not as long-lived as more highly structured or bureaucratic organizations formed by other feminists. But they spawned other groups, and the activist network and movement community they organized persisted and served as a staging-ground for a variety of organizations and actions (Whittier 1995; Meyer and Whittier 1994; Taylor and Rupp 1993). Thus the movement survived over the years. By the early 1980s, however, many of the grassroots, autonomous organizations had folded. Those that survived either could be sustained by internal resources from membership or sales, such as bookstores or recording labels, or had institutionalized and relied on external funding for service provision, such as rape crisis centers and battered women's shelters. Those organizations that did survive did so in the holding pattern that Taylor (1989a) calls abeyance: Few new recruits entered and much of activist energies was concentrated on maintaining their organizations, services, and commitments in the face of external hostility (Whittier 1997). This lull lasted from approximately the early or mid-1980s until the late 1980s, when activism by radical, grassroots women began to resurge again. This time, however, it took quite a different form; despite ties with preexisting organizations, the incoming activists founded their own groups and shifted the movement in different directions.

THE THIRD WAVE

The Politics of Anti-Identity (Late 1980s-Early 1990s)

The idea of a "third wave" of feminism, qualitatively different from the "second wave" of the 1960s and 1970s, emerged among activists and scholars in the late 1980s. Activism by younger women appeared to be on the upswing and was taking different forms from the radical feminism of the preceding decades. After several years when there were virtually no visible activist groups made up of younger feminists, in the late 1980s women in their twenties became active and visible, organizing around sexual identity, abortion rights, and Acquired Immune Deficiency Syndrome (AIDS). Lesbians were particularly influential during this period, as they had been from the late 1970s on, and they took the movement and the meaning of politicized sexuality in new directions.

Much of the upsurge in activism came from lesbian and bisexual women, who were integral to new AIDS and queer movements. As AIDS became more visible and more devastating, not only did government leaders neglect the issue, but antigay forces used the issue to denounce all gay men and lesbians as dangerous disease carriers. In response, lesbians began to work alongside gay men in large numbers, staffing AIDS service organizations and participating in the activist group AIDS Coalition to Unleash Power (ACT-UP), a decentralized organization that used street theater and direct action to target government and medical neglect of AIDS and its underlying homophobia (Shepard 2002). Even longtime lesbian feminist activists from earlier political generations reported feeling a new connection and identification with gay men (Whittier 1995). For women coming of age during this period, an alliance with gay men seemed natural, and they came to see themselves as part of a group bound together by shared sexual identity.

Yet they rejected the notion of sexual identity as fixed or essential and distanced themselves from the second wave idea that women were intrinsically different from—and better than—men. Instead, their alliances with gay men emphasized a commonality based on exclusion from institutional heterosexuality that overrode any distinctions of gender. Shortly after the emergence of ACT-UP, some members founded the new group Queer Nation to focus specifically on issues of sexuality. Queer Nation, like ACT-UP, was a radically decentralized group that had chapters in numerous cities, only loosely tied to one another. The groups both used dramatic tactics, including visual art campaigns with posters and stickers with slogans such as "Men: Use a Condom or Beat It," and "Read My Lips" (with a picture of two women or two men kissing), theatrical demonstrations such as kiss-ins in shopping malls, and direct actions such as traffic stoppages (Shepard 2002). The new "queer" politics argued that exclusion and difference bound together members of various sexual minorities, including gay men, lesbians, bisexuals, transsexuals, and even people who practiced non-normative forms of male-female sex. The distinctions among these groups were less important, and perhaps more fluid, than lesbian feminists had argued, with their vision of women's bonds with each other as the basis for a new society.

In practice, as women and people of color within the groups pointed out, queer politics often did reproduce the identities and hierarchies of the larger society, marginalizing less privileged groups. Although women and lesbians formed separate caucuses within the groups as a result, they did not abandon the claim to a fluid, less essentialized anti-identity politics (Morgan 2002). Inherent in this was a rejection of the "identity politics" of second wave feminism. Activists and authors argued that any claim to a fixed or essential identity reinforced existing hierarchies, even when that identity was used as a basis for opposition. In the eyes of these activists, if feminists mobilized women by calling on their peacefulness, sense of difference from a dominant male culture, and connections to other women, they were reinforcing the cultural justifications for women's oppression. In addition, queer politics fostered an approach to identity and sexuality that emphasized disruption and that sought to find the "queer" within heterosexual contexts, calling into question both heterosexual and homosexual categories, in contrast to lesbian feminists who had demonized the heterosexual (even as they suggested that women could choose to become lesbian) (Taylor and Whittier 1992; Walters 1996). Their critique, echoed by scholars who were inspired by the new queer activism, proved extremely influential in both feminist theory and activism (see, e.g., Butler 1990, 1997; Ryan 2001a; Heywood and Drake 1997a).

At the same time, the new wave of lesbian feminists saw sexual practice as a form of revolt in itself and argued for freeing sexual norms from limits and prescriptions promulgated not only by dominant culture, but by the women's movement itself. The well-publicized "sex wars" of the early 1980s brought out a conflict between feminists who argued that sexuality was an arena of risk for women, in which even apparently consensual sexual relationships could in fact play out hierarchies and inequalities, and those who argued that sexuality in any form was a source of power for women and ought not to be censored or repressed. In this vein, butch-fem roles, sado-masochism, and even heterosexual intercourse were rehabilitated, even celebrated, by proponents (Snitow et al. 1983; Vance 1984). As younger women came of age after the sex wars, they were exposed to the "pro-sex" point of view in community groups, movement publications, and women's studies classes, and many of them took the perspective for granted (Raymond 1997; Walker 1995b). Consequently, the late 1980s saw an upsurge in openness about sexual behaviors and a reclaiming of some of the trappings of traditional femininity. Young women of various sexual identities argued that they could choose to wear short skirts, makeup, or high heels in a playful way that was about decoration and satire, rather than conformity to patriarchy. By the mid-1990s, this would develop into a full-blown embrace of "girlie culture" as some segments of the next micro-cohort took it one step further (Baumgardner and Richards 2000).

Other younger feminists besides queer activists also became visible in the early 1990s. Naomi Wolf published her best seller, *The Beauty Myth*, in 1991, and gained extensive media coverage of her attempt to promote a feminist analysis of beauty to a new generation of women. Also in the early 1990s, the Riot Grrrl movement emerged. Linking feminist politics, punk rock music, and confrontative styles, they "scrawled *slut* on their stomachs, screamed from stages and pages of fanzines about incest, rape, being queer, and being in love . . . influencing countless girls and showing them feminism" (Baumgardner and Richards 2000, 133). Their style and culture influenced the growing anti-identity feminism of young women.

Despite these changes, not all feminist activism at the grassroots was discontinuous with what had gone before. Many of the major organizations, including service provision groups, feminist bookstores, and women's studies programs, survived and remained influential (Taylor, Whittier, and Pelak 2001). External events, particularly Supreme Court decisions allowing increased restrictions on abortion, brought scores of younger activists into existing feminist organizations such as NARAL and NOW. Massive demonstrations for abortion rights in 1989 and 1992 brought young and veteran activists alike to Washington, D.C. Many of the persisting organizations provided some continuity by socializing incoming activists (Reger 2002a). Women's studies programs, for example, institutionalized the process of instructing students about the nature of gender and the history of feminist organizing. NOW held special training sessions for "young feminists," attempting with mixed success to train a new generation of activists and to encourage activism on particular issues. Its first Young Feminist Conference, held in Akron in 1991, brought seven hundred attendees. The conference, however, was organized primarily by second wave feminists, with smaller numbers of young feminist organizers; it, and other later such conferences, were not without generational conflict (Dill 1989). While NOW was not closely associated with radical feminist activism during the 1970s, by the late 1980s the distinction between branches of the women's movement had diminished as veterans of radical feminist activism joined more mainstream groups increasingly in the 1980s (Boles 1991; Ferree and Hess 1994; Whittier 1995). In addition, large organizations such as NOW often served as an entry point for incoming women who later entered more grassroots-oriented groups, because they were the most visible surviving feminist organizations (Reger 2002a).

The revolt against identity politics fostered by queer activists was influential in these broader feminist activities as well. Particularly, younger activists within some campus feminist groups and established organizations like NOW began to criticize what they saw as gender essentialism. They argued that the differences among women outweighed their similarities and began to break down the distinction between women and men that led to the separatist stances of the earlier years. This was only to increase as the next cohort of activists formed closer ties with a growing movement of transgender people (Lynn 2001).

The collective identity of this micro-cohort was shaped by several factors. First, the social movement context had changed drastically, largely as a result of AIDS and the growing collaboration with gay men. Second, debates within the women's movement, in the form of the sex wars, produced a rethinking of what it meant to be a woman and a lesbian that then shaped the perspective of the incoming cohort of activists. Third, the external environment remained hostile, but escalating antigay rhetoric made organizing around sexuality particularly salient; gains by the antiabortion movement similarly prioritized that issue. More funding was available for AIDS work than any other issue, which further solidified connections with gay men as those organizations thrived and pulled in activists. Finally, and perhaps most important, women who came of age in the late 1980s and early 1990s had lived their entire lives under the influence of second wave feminism. As a result, they took for granted many of the gains made by the women's movement. Their sense of themselves as women—and of their grievances—was necessarily different because their objective circumstances were different. Many also saw feminism as the province of their mother's generation and were reluctant to affiliate with it. Instead, they moved in new directions, called themselves queer activists or third wave feminists, and began to forge a new movement. By the mid-1990s, these trends had increased and another micro-cohort emerged.

Third Wave Feminism (Mid-1990s–Early 2000s)

While the term "third wave feminism" emerged in the late 1980s, it was not until nearly a decade later that the movement had changed and solidified sufficiently to be considered a new movement wave. Even then, the organizations and activists of the second wave remained active and influential, and the divide between the two generations was far from complete. There were, however, markedly new directions and new syntheses of existing trends. These extended anti-identity politics to incorporate a greater focus on intersections of race and gender, sexual fluidity, and challenging the gender dichotomy partly through increased organizing around transgender issues. These new directions often proved flash points for generational conflict (Lynn 2001). The conflict was exacerbated by the generation gap that existed between the cohorts who had entered the movement prior to the 1980s and those who entered in the late-1980s and after. Generation gaps emerge when there is a period of time when a new cohort does not enter an organization (McNeil and Thompson 1971; Whittier 1997, 771). Because few activists joined grassroots feminist organizations during the early and mid-1980s, the changes in collective identity were not continuous but had a gap of several years; consequently, earlier and later entrants had fewer overlapping networks and relationships.

According to Baumgardner and Richards, Rebecca Walker first used the term "third wave" in a 1992 *Ms. Magazine* article, declaring "I am not a postfeminism feminist. I am the Third Wave" (quoted in Baumgardner and Richards 2000, 77). The phrase cropped up with increasing frequency in the early 1990s. A voter registration drive in 1992 that mobilized student activists around the country was sponsored by Third Wave Direct Action (a precursor to the Third Wave Foundation). Several influential anthologies were published in the mid-1990s under the "third wave" rubric, further solidifying the sense that there was a new direction in feminism (Findlen 1995; Walker 1995a; Heywood and Drake 1997a). Media coverage increased as well (Baumgardner and Richards 2000, 79).

New organizations emerged at both local and national levels to advocate for a third wave approach. Nationally, a group called Third Wave Direct Action formed in 1992, founded by Rebecca Walker (daughter of feminist author Alice Walker) and Shannon Liss. Its first project was a national voter registration drive called "Freedom Summer '92," in which young activists traveled around the country registering more than twenty thousand voters (Third Wave Foundation 2002a). Based in New York City, the organization grew steadily and began substantial fund-raising. It held film festivals and talks about issues including funding for the arts, education reform, affirmative action, and reproductive rights, as well as a series of intergenerational events including second and third wave feminists. It formed a separate Third Wave Fund in 1995, but the two groups merged into the Third Wave Foundation in 1996, and had grown to five thousand members and a $300,000 annual budget by the early 2000s (Baumgardner and Richards 2000, 271; Third Wave Foundation 2002a). The group had dual foci: raising money by encouraging philanthropy among younger women and those interested in feminism and fostering activism on particular issues at the grassroots. For a fledgling foundation, Third Wave was quite successful, raising over $300,000 in 1999, granting more than $100,000 in 2000, and building an endowment that was re-portedly over $350,000 by the end of 2000 (Labaton 2000). Grants went to several areas: reproductive rights, including "the training of new abortion providers, increasing access to reproductive healthcare services in under-served areas, and reproductive healthcare education . . . [and] emergency grants for abortion procedures"; organizing and advocacy by and for young women; and scholarship grants to students who are also activists, particularly "young women of color who prioritize social justice and the work done in the spirit of justice and equality over academic performance, and who integrate social justice into all areas of their lives" (Third Wave Foundation 2002b).

While the bulk of its activities were centered in New York, Third Wave or-ganized various forms of outreach to local activists, including chapters in San Francisco and Madison, Wisconsin (Third Wave Foundation 2002a). For ex-ample, the group started a "public action campaign" it called "I Spy Sexism," encouraging women to send postcards to individuals or organizations that discriminate against women. They designed the campaign not just to pres-sure offenders but to encourage women to notice the "day-to-day" sexism around them. In 2000, a delegation from the group called "Third Wave ROAMS (Reaching Out Across MovementS)" made a tour of the Southeast, meeting local activist groups and participating in local protest. The newslet-ter explained that ROAMS aimed "to spread the word about Third Wave, to find out what issues people were working on, to distribute our grant appli-cations throughout a region of the country that is undeserved [sic] by the philanthropic community, and to network progressive young feminist ac-tivists with each other. . . . This trip was about something much larger than Third Wave—it was about movement-building" (Labaton 2000). The trip started with a note of continuity, however, as the activists spent a training weekend at the long-lived activist school the Highlander Center. A second ROAMS tour focused on the Pacific Northwest (*ROAMS Newsletter* 2000).

The Third Wave Foundation was national but shared important character-istics with grassroots feminism, primarily its emphasis on nonhierarchical re-lationships among participants; focus on fostering local action; and goals that addressed institutional, cultural, and individual change. The activities of lo-cal chapters of Third Wave in Madison, Wisconsin, and the San Francisco Bay Area illustrate this. In Madison, for example, the chapter reported working with activists in other movements, including NOW's Young Feminist Task Force and the Wisconsin Greens; one action protested tampons with dioxin by giving out dioxin-free tampons and sending "the 'bad' tampons back to their manufacturers with letters expressing our desire for a healthier bleach-ing process." The group also reported doing consciousness-raising, working on legislation mandating insurance coverage of contraceptives, and consid-ering projects such as "a baby-sitting service for local low-income single mothers, collaboration with a local union for women of color, and work with the campus' retention plan for diverse students" (Westberg 2001). The New York chapter sponsored a reading on International Women's Day on pay inequity (Cella 2001). It is notable that these activities differ little from the list of activities of many second wave feminist groups at colleges and universities during the 1970s. In fact, Third Wave is distinguished by its attempt to engage younger women in working on many issues that are long-standing second wave feminist issues. At the same time, there is a strong allegiance to younger women, with grants going to young feminist organizations, framing issues of reproductive rights as the territory of young women; for example, a newsletter story about endometriosis framed the issue as relevant to the third wave by explaining that "there are many stories of young women whose bodies and lives have been affected by endometriosis" (Zollicoffer 2000). While this is accurate, endometriosis affects women of all ages; as with other issues, the organization framed a more universally relevant issue as a young women's issue. Reger (2002c) argues, in fact, that although third wave feminism "shifts the definitional foundation of feminism" to emphasize women's power, third wavers "at the same time draw upon tactics, ideologies, and organizational structures of the second wave."

Media efforts also distinguished the third wave (Baumgardner and Richards 2000). These included zines such as *Bust* and *Bitch*, mainstream magazines such as *Sassy* and *Jane*, independent mass-market efforts such as *HUES* (*Hear Us Emerging Sisters*), and efforts to influence or produce media coverage. The short-lived magazine *HUES*, for example, promoted a multiracial, sexually diverse feminism by and for young women, and was quite influential at the grassroots, spreading through word of mouth as much as conventional newsstand sales. The magazine's founders report that they "wanted to see multiculturalism finally done right in a women's movement. It wasn't about handholding and singing cheesy songs. And we weren't trying to pimp 'diversity' as a cover-up for token representation. . . . Rather, we were looking for a forum wherein women of different cultures and classes could come together without losing our identities" (Edut et al. 1997, 93). (Note that their statement rests on implicit criticism of how earlier feminists had "done" multiculturalism [Lynn 2001].) These media efforts merged advocacy for long-standing feminist issues (abortion rights, broad standards of beauty, sexual self-determination) with an advocacy of playful adoption of parts of traditional femininity (makeup, for example), open sexual expressiveness, and a reclaiming of the term "girl." Baumgardner and Richards call this "girlie feminism," but the term obscures the degree to which this approach also advocated the political and policy goals of its feminist foremothers.

Attention to intersectionality, or the relationships among gender, race, class, and sexuality, is one of the distinguishing characteristics of the third wave, which is less inclined to organize a "women's movement" per se, and more inclined to build coalitions among women and men of different groups

(Lynn 2001; Heywood and Drake 1997b). Some of the significant organizations, such as the Third Wave Foundation, are multicultural in their staffs and
boards of directors. For example, thirteen out of twenty-seven members of
the 2002 Third Wave Board of Directors are women of color, and the white
members generally also identify themselves by ethnic origin, making whiteness visible rather than the reference category (e.g., "Liz Zale is a 31-year-old
white lesbian activist") (Third Wave Foundation 2002c). Media outlets like
HUES magazine depicted the multicultural strand of the movement, and the
anthologies of personal narratives that serve as this movement's public face
are all thoroughly multicultural (Findlen 1995, 2001; Walker 1995a). As a result, third wave feminist organizing is distinguished by the connections and
coalitions it makes to other movements. The Third Wave Foundation
newsletter covered the School of the Americas, protest around the shooting
of Amadou Diallo by the police, and prison reform, as well as feminist activism by African American women (in, for example, the group Black Grrl
Revolution). Despite these influential multicultural strands, however, in practice, much of the movement was not clearly more multiracial and multicultural than its predecessor (Lynn 2001); both waves were heavily white, educated movements that made significant coalitions with women of color and
working-class women, and feminist organizing and theorizing by women of
color certainly predates the third wave (Heywood and Drake 1997a; Roth
2003). However, activism in the late 1990s and after *was* distinct in its reluc-
tance to generalize about women or make claims on women's similarity as
the basis for solidarity.

In fact, some third wave activists challenged even the idea of women as a
meaningful category. Building on queer theory and poststructuralist approaches to gender, they argued that gender is highly fluid and not dichoto-
mous (Butler 1990). This approach was heavily influenced by academic theories of gender, but it is also indebted to organizing by transgender activists.
Many third wave activists saw transgender organizing as part of their movement, arguing that overthrowing a binary gender system is the central goal
(Lynn 2001; Wilchins 1997; Califia 1997). This often marks a point of dis-
agreement between second and third wave feminists. For example, at a national conference, longtime second wave feminist activists disagreed vehemently with a third wave panelist who argued that the freedom to shift
gender, including access to surgery and the ability to live as a member of either or neither gender, regardless of birth, were central feminist issues.[5] In-
corporating transgender issues has concrete implications for daily practice;
activists can no longer refer to their members and supporters unproblemati-
cally as "women"; people identifying as men must be included in organizations, goals, and constructions of collective identity (including, of course, fe-
male-to-male transgendered people); and sexual identity categories become
more fluid following the gender categories they rest on.

Rebecca Walker argues that contradiction and messiness characterize third wave feminism, in contrast to what she sees as a more simplistic form of feminism that went before: "Constantly measuring up to some cohesive fully down-for-the-feminist-cause identity without contradictions and messiness . . . is not a fun or easy task" (Walker 1995a, xxi). Indeed, criticism of identity politics was central to the third wave and built directly on the anti-identity politics of the late 1980s and early 1990s. Although third wave grassroots feminism is diverse in sexual identity, it is in many senses a "queer" movement because of this approach to identity.

At the grassroots, the Lesbian Avengers (LA) took over where Queer Nation left off. Founded in 1993 in New York City, the Avengers initially defined themselves as "a direct action group using grass-roots activism to fight for lesbian survival and visibility. Our purpose is to identify and promote lesbian issues and perspectives while empowering lesbians to become experienced organizers who can participate in political rebellion" (Schulman 1994, 290). By 2002, web pages for the New York and Chicago chapters quoted from the *Lesbian Avengers Handbook* to define themselves as "a direct-action group focusing on issues vital to lesbian survival and visibility" (Lesbian Avengers 2002). The group grew rapidly in its first years, with more than twenty chapters by 1994 (Schulman 1994, 313). By 2002, the group still had a number of local chapters, mostly in major cities such as Chicago and San Francisco; these chapters continued to use the handbook for action as written in 1994. The chapters were only loosely affiliated with each other and held no power over each other; there was no national organization. Chapters did, however, share information, such as a manual for planning actions. Lesbian Avengers chapters in many cities sponsored "Dyke Marches" before the annual lesbian and gay pride marches (Schulman 1994, 311). The Dyke Marches feature a celebratory, militant style, including fire-eating by Avengers, topless women, and enthusiastic chanting. In addition, the Lesbian Avengers became involved in fighting local antigay initiatives in the mid-1990s, traveling to Maine to assist in organizing there. Following a loss in Maine when the antigay ballot initiative passed, the Avengers formed what they called a "Freedom Ride," traveling around New England to publicize the Maine battle, organize more LA chapters, and create pressure for a federal antidiscrimination bill (Schulman 1994, 316).

The combination of a legislative focus, usually associated with "liberal feminism," and direct action grassroots tactics, usually associated with "radical feminism," shows how third wave grassroots feminism transcends that distinction. Certainly, LA members sometimes clashed with local activists working against antigay ballot initiatives when they advocated coming out and emphasizing lesbian and gay rights rather than general nondiscrimination (Schulman 1994, 313–19). But LA never considered ballot or legislative goals to be reformist, and they continued to push for coalition with "assimilationist" activists. At the same time, their logo, a bomb with a lit fuse, conveyed their direct action style. The collective identity of LA is nicely summarized in a document from the group's early years that lists the "Top 10 Avenger Qualities." These include, in order, "access to resources (xerox machine), good dancer, pro sex, fighting spirit, righteous anger, fearlessness, informed, no big ego, leadership, and compassion" (Schulman 1994, 296). We see here many of the elements of third wave organizing, including the emphasis on sexuality and the combination of serious politics with playfulness and fun.

In sum, then, third wave collective identity saw gender and feminism as connected with race, class, and sexuality; included transgender issues; and combined militant tactics with playfulness. Like second wave feminists, third wave feminists understood their individual experiences in political terms, as shaped by the intersections of sexism, racism, and other oppressions. They also emphasized the importance of their own cultures and the struggles of integrating feminism with commitment to cultures of origin. (For examples of such narratives, see selections in Findlen 1995 and Walker 1995a). Third wave activism was characterized by grassroots organizing outside the established large women's movement organizations, evolving approaches to sexual identity as a central feminist issue, and varying uses of militant tactics and radical ideologies.

Third wave feminists developed as a distinct political generation because of their internal and external contexts. Because they came of age after many of the goals of the 1960s and 1970s women's movement had been achieved, it is not surprising that they focused on different issues. By 1992, with the election of Bill Clinton to the presidency, they also faced a more favorable political climate than any of their predecessors. Under Clinton and sympathetic appointees, feminist activists of both generations gained access to decision makers, funding, and a sense of possibility. Although policy changes under Clinton went against feminists at least as often as they went for them (witness the Welfare Reform Act, the "don't ask, don't tell" policy on gays in the military, and the antigay Defense of Marriage Act), feminists' sense of being beleaguered or under siege was replaced by a sense of efficacy. Further, the economic boom of much of the 1990s made fund-raising much easier and enabled the emergence of groups like the Third Wave Foundation.

In addition to a different external context, activists in the third wave also came of age in a different movement context. The influence of ACT-UP and Queer Nation on the emerging politics of anti-identity cannot be overestimated, as with the influence of the transgender movement (Lynn 2001). Second wave feminism also exerted a strong influence on third wave activism, despite third wave activists' attempts to differentiate themselves. Heywood and Drake (1997a, 3) argue that growing up with multiple, contradictory versions of feminism—feminists focused on equity within the current power structures, feminists focused on transforming society more generally, feminists focused on documenting and ending women's oppression, "black feminism, women-of-color feminism, working-class feminism, pro-sex feminism"—is part of what shaped third wavers' embrace of contradiction. In addition, women who came of age in the 1980s or 1990s did so in a world that reflected many feminist changes and embraced much of feminist discourse, yet dismissed the women's movement as irrelevant and mocked any critique of the operation of sexism in daily life (such as men's opening doors for women, standards of conventional feminine attractiveness, and nonsexist language) as "political correctness." This, too, promotes a certain tolerance of ambiguity and contradiction and fosters activists' embrace of some gender conventions, such as the ironic use of hyperfeminine presentations of self by some activists (Walker 1995b). Despite the influence of second wave feminism on the new political generation of activists, however, there were substantial conflicts between the two groups.

GENERATIONAL CONFLICTS BETWEEN SECOND AND THIRD WAVE

As a new political generation coalesced, conflicts and differences grew between second and third wave feminist generations. Second wave feminists often wrote as if there were no third wave, as if younger women remained apolitical or "postfeminist," or simply as if they were not part of the women's movement, as when Susan Brownmiller referred to young feminists in *Time* magazine by declaring, "These are not movement people" (quoted in Baumgardner and Richards 2000, 227). This was exacerbated by the elevation to media stardom of a few young women who wrote significant challenges to feminist tenets under the rubric of feminism. Most notable among these was Katie Roiphe, who criticized feminist focus on violence against women and the very notion of date rape in her book *The Morning After*. While her work was opposed by feminists of all ages, longtime feminists sometimes used her age as the basis for dismissing all young feminists as "postfeminist" or "antifeminist," at the same time as the media held her up as a representative of the new feminist approach (Baumgardner and Richards 2000, chap. 7).

For example, in 1997 longtime feminist activist and author Phyllis Chesler published *Letters to a Young Feminist*. The book, which might have sought intergenerational dialogue, was written as if young feminists knew nothing of second wave issues and approaches, and as if there were no autonomous organizing by younger feminists. As the reviewer in the *New York Times Book Review* wrote, "*Letters to a Young Feminist* is Chesler's attempt to pass [on] . . . wisdom. . . . But she proceeds to share this information without considering the possibility that if the movement ever is resurrected, its goals and tactics might differ significantly from those of its earlier incarnation" (quoted in Baumgardner and Richards 2000, 225). The review of the book in the feminist newspaper *off our backs*, written by longtime contributor and second wave feminist Carol Anne Douglas, also contained no reference to third wave activists or to the responses of younger women to the book. Baumgardner and Richards argue that young feminists are mostly invited to serve as token representatives on public panels dominated by second wave feminists and are often excluded from the planning for projects designed to reach out to younger women, such as an ad campaign run by the Pro-Choice Public Education Project (Baumgardner and Richards 2000, 223).

At the same time, third wave activists often wrongly assume that second wave feminists did not engage with issues that now seem crucial, such as race or sexuality (Roth 2003; Lynn 2001; B. Smith 1998), or that the directions of the third wave are new insights. In a foreword to Rebecca Walker's third wave anthology, *To Be Real*, Gloria Steinem wrote that, when she reads third wave critiques that call for attention to race and class, point out difficulties in the notion of universal sisterhood, or integrate sexuality into political action, she feels "like a sitting dog being told to sit" (Steinem 1995). Two third wave activists who worked at the largely second wave publication *Ms. Magazine* and at other established feminist organizations reported that

> we have spent most of our time acting as intergenerational mediators: [explaining that] "Gloria Steinem is really cool and interested in what younger feminists are up to. She's actually not a dinosaur." "[Third wave author] Elizabeth Wurtzel's work is smart and original. . . ." "Ms isn't just for asexual fifty-year old women." "You should get [third waver] Strawberry Saroyan . . . to write that story." "There have always been black women in the movement—and the movement has always been more diverse than the mainstream." (Baumgardner and Richards 2000, 220)

Despite these generational gaps and conflicts, there is extensive overlap, cooperation, and mutual influence between second and third wave activists. This is made possible by the unique position of the contemporary women's movement: A large cohort of second wave activists and their organizations remain mobilized at the same time that a distinct cohort of third wave activists, with their new organizations and issues, are mobilizing. With both waves operating simultaneously, there are unique opportunities for cross-fertilization. The Third Wave Foundation, for example, has hosted intergenerational dinners with second wave feminists, and the annual Young Women's Day of Action is organized by both young feminists and second wave activist Marlene Fried (Eighth Annual National Young Women's Day of Action 2002; Baumgardner and Richards 2000, 231).[6] NOW continued to sponsor its Young Feminist conferences, with a Young Feminist Summit on violence in 1995 and a Young Feminist Skill-Building Summit in 1997. Although some attendees complained of a patronizing air and lack of input from young feminists into the content of the conferences (let alone into NOW's organizational policy), the conferences nevertheless served as an important link between second and third wave feminisms (NOW Foundation 2002). Finally, because in some locales third wave activists engage in protest and consciousness-raising that are very similar to those of the second wave (around rape and domestic violence, women's health, the impact of beauty standards, sexual self-determination, and male domination in academia), they continue to find inspiration and support from second wave writings and individuals (Reger 2002c).

CONCLUSION

The United States, like much of the rest of the world, has experienced enormous changes in gender and women's status in response to the women's movement. The activists who wrought these changes were themselves formed by the obstacles they faced and the goals they envisioned. Their collective identities, views of each other, demands for social change, and definitions of feminism were therefore shaped by their social locations and differed between political generations. In response to feminist successes, changes in political opportunities and mainstream culture, and generational dynamics within the movement, the women's movement at the grassroots has changed significantly over the past four decades. Yet it has remained vital precisely *because* it has changed. The presence of multiple cohorts of activists working on different issues makes for a particularly broad-based and effective movement. Diversity in organizational structure and goals means that there are organizations positioned to take advantage of various openings in political opportunities, and diversity in collective identity and framing means that there are rhetorics that are potentially persuasive to various constituencies and targets.

Like other long-lived challenges, the contemporary form of the women's movement is shaped by both generational conflicts and continuities between second and third wave feminists. Its future form will likewise be a product of the intersections of changing external contexts, the influence of ongoing women's movement organizations, and the new political generations that emerge as a result. Incoming feminists in the mid-2000s face renewed hostility in political opportunities, with a conservative president, a country at war, and a crackdown on domestic dissidence. The form that a fourth wave of feminism takes, then, will doubtless diverge from previous waves. Yet we would expect activists to draw on resources from preexisting feminist organizations and networks, political opportunities provided by supportive government officials and feminist public policy gains, and frames and identities based in discourses about gender that have been irrevocably shaped by the women's movement. If the women's movement is to survive as a viable challenge to gender inequality in the 2000s, it will do so by continuing to change.

NOTES

1. Dates are approximate because of variation in periodicization in different parts of the country.

2. Of course, they were not the first feminists, nor even the first to raise the issues they raised. See Weigand (2001), Robnett (1997), Rupp and Taylor (1987), and Gabin (1990).

3. I discuss these two micro-cohorts together here because they are sufficiently similar, because the founders only covered two years or so, and because the crucial development in the movement—its expansion and institutionalization—was a direct outgrowth of the actions of both groups.

4. These strands were not absent from the movement's initiators, however, who were also critical of male New Leftists' violence and focus on confrontational politics (Rosen 2000).

5. Agents of Social Change Conference, Sophia Smith Collection, Smith College, Northampton, Massachusetts, September 2000.

6. The Young Women's Day of Action is an annual event that focuses on reproductive rights and brings together activists to network and strategize, "plac[ing] reproductive and sexual freedom in the context of larger goals: racial justice, economic justice, an end to punitive immigration and welfare policies, the right to exist as lesbian, gay, bisexual, and transgendered people, accessible health care, freedom from violence, and quality education."

4

Political Activism and Discursive Politics in the ERA Campaign

Barbara Ryan

In the year 2000, the beginning of a new century, I was asked to give a presentation at my university for Accepted Students' Day. I suggested a slide show on the Equal Rights Amendment[1] (ERA) Campaign, a wonderful visual documentary of the years 1975–1982 from the state of Illinois, where I was an activist and researcher of this dynamic period in the contemporary women's movement.

The organizer of the day's events, he must have been twenty-five, no older than thirty, reported back to me a few days later that the committee was looking for something more current, something that people would be interested in today. It was suggested that I give a presentation on my time in India where I had recently spent a semester as a Fulbright Scholar. I did that and it was fine. India is a fascinating country and I was happy to share my experience there.

But I kept returning to his words about the ERA. It rankled me, particularly when he said that he doubted most people would even know what the ERA was and added, unnecessarily, that he had never heard of it. How could those years of activism be missing from his, and others', knowledge? All that effort, the idealistic fervor, innovative actions, and joy really—the fun of it— as well as the disappointments. It was glorious and it was wearing. But, as we frequently reminded ourselves, we were making history.

What is history if it is not recorded, written down, and passed on to future generations? Although many books have been written about this phase of the women's movement, they are fast becoming dated,[2] not in the sense that they are no longer accurate but that they are less likely today to be used in college classes or read by the general reader. It is time for an updated work on women's movements in the United States and other countries. I am pleased to have the opportunity to reintroduce this chapter of feminist social

activism in a new millennium book. Even though the ERA did not pass, that
activism was not in vain. We were making history, and this collection of readings helps keep that history alive.

THE ERA CAMPAIGN

The meaning and importance of diversity in feminist organizing is an area of
study that promises to increase our understanding of how social movements
encourage unified efforts for change and, also, how they fail to overcome
differences to achieve common goals. The women's movement in the United
States consists of a multigroup structure with extensive variance in leadership style, group organization, and types of activism. With these characteristics, the movement lends itself to comparative analysis of diverse groups:
whether they can work together for the same goal, what they need to do for
this to happen, and how different groups undermine or promote joint efforts
for social movement success.

In the formative years of the contemporary women's movement, researchers described the various groups as coexisting with antagonistic relations (Carden 1974; Hole and Levine 1971; Redstockings of the Women's Liberation Movement 1978; Ryan 1989), whereas in the late 1970s to early 1980s
feminist groups were characterized as interacting in a complementary rather
than competitive way (Chafetz and Dworkin 1986; Ferree and Hess 1985;
Ryan 1992; Taylor 1989b). However, by the mid-1980s and 1990s the movement once again was divided, this time along the lines of identity politics
(Franzen 1993; Kessler-Harris 1992; Leidner 1991; McKay 1993; Ryan 1997,
2001a; Whisman 1993; Women of Color Association 1991). Thus, it is the
middle period that provides a view of a transformed movement, when various forms of feminist activism converged around the ERA Campaign. This
brief history raises questions of how and why a fluctuating pattern of factionalism and cooperation in intramovement group relations occurs, particularly in relation to different activist orientations and leadership styles.

The campaign for the ERA is a good case study to examine these questions
since there were many types of groups involved, which employed diverse
tactics. In the final years of the campaign (1980–1982), two distinct sectors of
the movement had emerged: the mass movement sector representing a structured political form of activism, and the small group sector that concentrated
on direct action forms of activism.

In the spring of 1982, activists converged on the Illinois state capital to
push for passage of the ERA. The mass movement sector was represented by
the National Organization for Women (NOW), the foremost structured political group organizing the ERA Campaign. Two interrelated groups, A Group
of Women and A Grassroots Group of Second Class Citizens, represented the
small group direct action sector. In this chapter I employ a comparative

analysis of activism during the ERA Campaign by these groups. Identifying characteristics of different leadership styles contributes to an analysis of the underlying rationale of multiple organizing efforts. Therefore, leaders from each of these sectors, Eleanor Smeal and Sonia Johnson, are compared for contrasting leadership styles.

Focusing on these sectors during a limited period also allows for concrete analysis of what happens to diverse groups after a unifying issue is no longer an organizing goal. Thus, by looking at the ERA Campaign and the post-ERA period, factors can be identified that enhance or discourage continuing activism when ideologies (or parts of ideologies) diverge. In other words, what did these leaders and groups do after the drama of the ERA drive was over, and how is their post-ERA involvement related to the choices they made in activist orientation during the earlier period?

Data for this study are drawn from interviews with feminist activists, movement publications, newspaper accounts, and participant observation of feminist groups from different sectors of the U.S. women's movement.[3] Two interacting theoretical frameworks underlie this work. The first is resource mobilization (RM), a perspective centered on the ways social movements mobilize resources, including people, money, media attention, power, and influence. The second is new social movement (NSM) theory, a framework for looking at why individuals get involved. Resource mobilization defines social movements as purposeful activity that acquires, uses, and organizes resources to achieve goals. The mobilization process is analyzed by looking at the effects of the interactions among the various movement groups, oppositional forces, and the social environment (Zald and McCarthy 1979).[4] New social movement theory focuses on the *meaning* people place on their activism. Accordingly, a focus on *meaning* foreshadows ideology, theory, identity, connectedness, community, self-esteem, and group enhancement as important areas of research for understanding social movement participation.[5]

The first section of this chapter compares the types of activism utilized by activists in NOW and A Group of Women/Grassroots Group in the ERA Campaign. From these data, the second section derives two forms of social movement practice: political activism and discursive politics. The next section examines these groups, their leaders, their particular forms of activism, and new issues and divisions that emerged in the post-ERA years. Finally, the outcomes of different activist directions for the future attainment of feminist goals are discussed.

THE ERA CAMPAIGN: A MERGING OF POLITICS AND CIVIL DISOBEDIENCE

The Equal Rights Amendment was written and introduced into Congress in 1923, and every year after that, with a predictable pattern of languishing in committee. With the reemergence of an energized women's movement in the late 1960s, interest in the ERA flourished. The contemporary women's movement achieved two significant victories in the early 1970s: congressional passage of the ERA and the Supreme Court decision in *Roe v. Wade,* which legalized abortion. In reaction, Stop ERA, the antiabortion movement; The Heritage Foundation, the "profamily" movement; and The Eagle Forum were formed.[6] By the mid-1970s these groups and their offspring constituted an antifeminist/New Right coalition supported by the Mormon Church, fundamentalist churches, the Catholic Church, the John Birch Society, corporate leaders, and political conservatives in general. An economic recession after 1973 led to further growth in conservative opposition.

At the same time that antifeminist groups were proliferating, feminist groups were dissolving amid factionalism. In 1975 the NOW elected new leadership and instituted structural change. Eleanor (Ellie) Smeal became president of NOW, and under her leadership the organization began to focus on state passage of the ERA. Smeal, a political scientist, wanted to build a movement large enough for politicians to take seriously. With two years left for ratification, she took the position that this was a historic moment and, even when Congress granted a three-and-a-half-year extension, the "historic moment" appeal was still persuasive.

NOW used the ERA to mobilize, growing from 35,000 members and a $500,000 budget to 250,000 members and a budget of $13 million by 1982. By the end of the ERA Campaign the organization was raising a million dollars a month[7] and was identifying itself as a politically oriented group that organized people across the country, including coalition formations, to do the political work necessary for passage of the ERA. This political work included lobbying politicians, working in campaigns to get pro-ERA activists (men and women) elected, educating the general public through newspaper coverage of marches, public speaking, traveling through unratified states (Indiana, where they were successful, and Illinois, where they were not) in ERA caravans, taking part in radio talk shows, and speaking at meetings hosted by local chapters of Business and Professional Women (BPW) and American Association of University Women (AAUW).

The ERA became a symbol of women's equality and a highly successful mobilization tool. Unfortunately, the symbolic value of ERA also contributed to the antifeminist forces. Both factions gained adherents; however, feminist activism—unlike antifeminism—was handicapped by a political climate in the country that was moving in an increasingly conservative direction.

The political process was not working—the ERA was stalled with three states short of ratification—yet NOW and other politically focused groups held to their strategies. Within this vacuum, small unaffiliated groups began to emerge. These groups used confrontational direct action methods and nonviolent civil disobedience (CD). The major force behind this direction was Sonia Johnson, a fifth generation Mormon who was excommunicated from the Mormon Church for forming Mormons for ERA. In the early 1980s she organized women into a "spiritual mission" that inspired street theater, sit-ins, chain-ins, civil disobedience, and a thirty-seven-day fast.[8]

ERA had passed both houses of Congress and twenty-two states in the first year, the thirty-five states that did pass the amendment represented 70 percent of the population, and opinion polls reflected 63 percent of the people in the country supporting it. Still, it was not passing. The force of the opposition and the fact that legislative bodies kept turning the amendment down spurred even those who felt it was a waste of time to involve themselves in the campaign. As one member of a CD group explained: "I thought it would pass without me having to do anything. I was kind of peripherally involved, you know I'd go to a rally if it was convenient; but I kept noticing that the ERA wasn't passing."[9]

For those who decided at this point to get involved, there was a felt need to do something other than the "drudgery" involved in movement work. Civil disobedience means working outside the system and, as such, was seen as more meaningful involvement. Sonia Johnson attempted to pass a CD action at the 1981 NOW conference, but after much heated debate, members voted the measure down.[10] The majority of NOW members resisted both throwing away their previous efforts and the unstated assumption that their energies had been wrongly placed. Some NOW members reacted to this assumption (whether correct or not) by questioning the motives of CD groups. For instance, a longtime NOW activist wondered "who these actions are meaningful to. Here we are, doing grunt work for years and years, and they do one 'dramatic' action and tell us they're doing something meaningful."[11]

In a sense this assessment was true. The meaningful part of CD, as Sonia Johnson explains it, is not that you think this action is going to win a goal; it is to give women a feeling of empowerment: "You have to see CD as something besides changing the system—you do it to get women happy."[12]

CONSIDERATIONS OF FEMINIST PRACTICE: POLITICAL ACTIVISM AND DISCURSIVE POLITICS

As the preceding discussion shows, by 1980 the ERA had become a goal for feminists with widely varying inclinations. In looking at the last years of this campaign, two types of activism—one to shake the public up and the other to incorporate the public into their sphere—intermingled in the hopes of attaining the same goal.

Civil disobedience and other forms of direct action tactics are expressive forms of activism, which can be called discursive politics. Activism is meant to create dialogue, expand the realm of discussion, promote new ways of thinking, and, quite literally, change the way people see and experience the world. Political activism, on the other hand, is grounded in concrete and specific goal attainment.

Political activism and discursive politics exhibit distinctive orientations, yet these orientations are not exclusive, nor are participants exclusively involved in one type of group. Indeed, a significant characteristic of political and discursive groups is the interface that exists between overlapping membership. For instance, NOW has a diverse membership and, while the organization did not endorse CD during the ERA Campaign, when Sonia Johnson later ran for NOW president, 40 percent of the delegates voted for her.

The fact that individuals participate in more than one group does not negate the existence of a primary group orientation for different movement groups. Consequently, political activism and discursive politics, although nonexclusive in terms of what they are about and who participates in them, do contain distinct features that illustrate the purposes for which they serve. As categories, these two types of activism typically equate with their structural component. In other words, mass movement organizations are more likely to primarily engage in political activism, and small groups are more likely to engage in discursive (direct action) politics. NOW and A Group of Women/Grassroots Group of Second Class Citizens represent examples of contrasting forms of activism connected to structural form. As the following shows, these two social movement organizations contrast in terms of group structure, leadership philosophy, arena (legislative halls or the streets), tactics, long-term strategies, and motivation (ideological beliefs in social change process).

The most obvious difference is the organizational structure of groups that choose to primarily engage in either political activism or discursive politics. During the ERA Campaign, political activist groups had a national and/or state orientation, although some, such as NOW, also have a grassroots structure. Mass movement groups aim to have large numbers of participants to provide both practical effects and an image of representing the majority of women. Discursive activism is found in autonomous small groups that are often linked to other groups through multiple memberships and personal contacts. Seeing themselves as a core group, they do not necessarily feel they represent the majority of women even though they consider themselves advocates of all women. It is primarily (but not solely) structural components of social movement groups through which actions—that is, the *type* of actions—flow. Thus, it is not surprising to find that it is the mass movement organizations that do political activism and the small group sector that places an emphasis on discursive politics through direct action, keeping in mind that both types of groups can and do sometimes cross over into alternative types of activism.

Direct action groups using discursive politics operate by consensus and shared leadership with a philosophy of communalism. Consensus and rotating leadership eliminate hierarchical structures; they also require heavy time commitments and a degree of commonality in goal attainment. In the mass movement sector, size becomes a determining factor. Consensus rule is not possible when there are two thousand members voting on policy. Decision making in large groups is through majority rule with elected officers responsible for the implementation of goals.

The political and public arenas are where political activism takes place. Election work and education through marches, workshops, and public speaking are common activities. For discursive politics, group efforts are more centered in the personal and symbolic realm. Actions are expressive; they are meant to psychologically empower participants and draw media attention through unusual dramatic actions. Size interacts with arena to effect tactical implementation. Political activists use legislative means because they believe they have an opportunity, where numbers count, to have an effect on laws that are being passed. Discursive politics uses direct action tactics, such as zap actions and street theater, which lend themselves to size limitations. Their arena is the street, not legislative halls.

Ideological foundation (or motivation) is the underpinning for the differences between political activism and discursive politics. For instance, political activism is a method of gaining power within the system in order to change the system. The goal is the empowerment of women through structural change. Political activists believe that once changes are accomplished in laws, institutions, and the work structure, new opportunities and attitudes will benefit women throughout society. With these changes, women will begin to have a higher valuation of themselves and be more powerful in their personal relations. As Eleanor Smeal describes it:

> If you get full equality in pay equity, social security, insurance, etc., there's a profound change that affects the lower class; that is the people who make less money, mostly women. We want to improve women economically and lessen their dependency.[13]

Discursive politics is geared toward achieving power within the person. The goal is the empowerment of women through a changed self-image. Activism is meant to affect women on the personal and spiritual level to rid them of internalized oppression. It is after internal change has occurred, when women begin to feel strong about themselves, that their interactive relations improve and they can engage in the work of structural change. Sonia Johnson explains this position:

> Women have to begin to see themselves as a person who can change the world, really begin to have a vision of yourself and what you can do to create change. Once you have that changed self-concept, you begin to see opportunities where you can make changes which you didn't see before, when you didn't think you could do anything about it.[14]

Differences have been highlighted through an examination of contrasting approaches. Yet these differences do not negate the fact that both political activism and discursive politics share the goal of effecting personal *and* fundamental social change; where they differ is in the order and method of achieving these ends.

Even as the groups were sometimes at odds with each other, and in spite of occasional acrimonious relations, there were times, such as the spring of 1982 in Springfield, Illinois, when cooperation and support prevailed. For instance, after Sonia Johnson and six other women began a fast in the rotunda of the capital building, Smeal made provisions for the fasters to stay at a local hotel and for NOW members to take them back and forth.[15] It is important to remember that activists are often members of more than one social movement organization. Thus, it is not surprising to find that some of the activists engaged in the fast and CD (including Sonia Johnson) were also NOW members who attended NOW meetings and recruited NOW members to take part in direct action activities, or that NOW members took part in a CD act when they poured a massive dose of fertilizer on the Capitol grounds to enrich the grass so that the letters ERA would stand out in bright green. Unfortunately, they killed the grass instead.

DIVERGING PATHS OF MOVEMENT
SECTORS IN THE POST-ERA YEARS

The failure to achieve ratification of the Equal Rights Amendment left fragmentation over future direction. It was this state that led to the sharp reemergence of open confrontations over class, ethnicity, race, and sexuality. These confrontations, while often debilitating, nonetheless called for addressing issues that had been simmering under a cover of gender commonality.

With a unity issue gone, some activists dropped out of activism or entered into a spirituality search.[16] Sonia Johnson called a Gathering of Women searching "for feminist alternatives to the present direction of the women's movement."[17] She was still advocating CD, but she entered the political ring by running for president of the United States on a third-party ticket. At the same time NOW was supporting the Democratic ticket, which had a woman running for the first time as vice president, Johnson was running on the Citizen's Party ticket. Johnson's run was symbolic, to show that women could and should run for president, whereas Geraldine Ferraro's campaign was a serious one with hopes for victory. It would be a mistake to assume that these tactics pitted these two groups against each other. As an example, at a combined march and CD action in 1984 in Clayton, Missouri (St. Louis County), both NOW and A Group of Women banners were carried in the march. Perhaps the clearest indicator of combined support for both strategies were those women who wore campaign buttons from both campaigns, for example, a Geraldine Ferraro for Vice President button and a Sonia Johnson for President button.

After the election, in which neither woman won, Johnson began to speak of the despair she saw in the political system. She warned of the seductiveness to join it in order to make changes, when in reality it just "sucks women up." Over time, Johnson transformed the call for developing inner strength through confrontational tactics into a call for internal revolution by disengaging "psychically and emotionally from patriarchy and all its institutions" (Johnson 1989, i). For instance, she argued against marching and lobbying for the right to choose since such actions acknowledge that "men own us" (Johnson 1989, 23). In answer to the question "What shall we do?" Johnson answered, "How shall we be?" (Johnson 1989, 42).

By the mid-1980s, Johnson was no longer interested in challenging the system. Indeed, she eventually "dropped out" to live in a women's commune. Critics found her call for a separatist community and her focus on the overriding power of the patriarchy to be "limited by class and race bias because it denies the debasement of men who do not fit into the ideal of white middle class heterosexual masculinity" (*off our backs* 1988, 25). In addition, her solution shut out heterosexual women and created distance for women of color from their race/ethnic communities, both of which included men.

For political activists the question remained, "How can we go about creating change on the structural level?" NOW called for the reintroduction of the ERA because, as Eleanor Smeal argued, "the ERA doesn't take strength from the women's movement, it adds to it. Throughout the recent fight for ratification, the ERA was a major recruiter and consciousness-raiser" (Smeal 1987, 218). In answer to the question of how money would be raised to run a new campaign, she responded, "action begets money and money begets action. Do you think those marches are fund losers? They're fund raisers."[18] The ERA, however, was not able to revive flagging interest in feminist activism. When those efforts failed, NOW went further into political organizing. Symbolizing the change from earlier references to women's powerlessness through the "feminization of poverty," the call now was for women to take power by running for office.[19] Like the 59 cent button worn during the ERA Campaign (to highlight the gap in earnings between women and men), the new symbol became a 5 percent button representing the percent of legislators in Congress who were women.

NOW continued to stress engagement in politics, at both the local and national levels. Since the early 1980s, there has been an increase in women in political positions, although the sex ratio remains dismally low. By the end of the 1990s women held 58 out of 440 seats in the House of Representatives and only 9 out of 100 U.S. senators were women. To see this as progress, it must be remembered that before 1990 there were only two women serving in the Senate. Thus, there is forward movement, but it is terminally slow.

Since the ERA Campaign, there have been concerted efforts to address identity issues by increasing the participation of women of color and to further address issues of poverty, race, and sexual orientation in NOW, women's studies, and other women's groups. Identity politics, which became a primary division in the women's movement by the mid-1980s, refers to discourses and social activism focused on racial, religious, sexual, ethnic, gender, or national identity. Groups, such as NOW and A Group of Women, organized around identity (e.g., gender), are usually involved in power bids, particularly in making demands on the state, although some are more expressive than political in nature (Moghadam 1994). There are mixed opinions about the value of social movement organizing around lifestyle and personal identity characteristics. On the one hand, it is seen as something new (and, therefore, problematic); on the other hand, we could define identity politics broadly enough to include all social movements. It is safe to say that it is a complex and, in many ways, contradictory topic. Beyond that is contested territory.[20]

In reference to the contemporary women's movement, this discussion needs, first, to be grounded in the recognition that the question of identity politics in the women's movement did not arise when feminist groups organized on the basis of gender. Even though theorists who have not studied the women's movement think of it as typifying identity politics (i.e., that it is a unified movement of women), activists and students of feminism know that the politics of identity emerged out of challenges to the movement raised by those women who felt left out.

Identity politics is an issue because divisions among women have led to separate group formations and because there have been charges of racism and classism in the women's movement. In *Inessential Woman* (1988), Elizabeth Spelman points out that the "problem of difference" is not really one of looking at commonalities and differences among women; it is one of looking at the differences of women outside the norm of "woman." Feminist discourse about diversity, pluralism, multiculturalism, and identity politics is really a discourse about women who are the new "Other"—that is, *other than* white heterosexual middle-class women.[21]

The two most recognized identity divisions within the U.S. women's movement are those sectors established by lesbian feminists, particularly in what is sometimes called the women's culture, and the womanist organizing of women of color.[22] At their base, these divisions, as well as others, challenge the concept of "universal sisterhood" (Davis 1981; Dill 1983; hooks 1981; Moraga and Anzaldua 1983; Smith 1982).

Both of these gender-plus identities contest the primacy of comparing women with men. Historically, the women's movement has focused on gender equality, a position based on similarities between the sexes. This emphasis can be traced to the beginning of the organized woman's movement in the mid-1800s and can also be found in the ERA Campaign of more recent times.[23] However, alongside the similarity argument has run a difference argument. In this view, advocates call for changed social relations premised on women's particular needs and special values, a position found in one sector of the women's suffrage movement and in a new (much more radicalized) form in the women's culture of contemporary times.[24]

The framework, however, for both similarity and difference arguments has been the relation *between* women and men, an emphasis that has always failed to address differences *among* women. This, then, is the fault line from which identity politics arises. And it is identity politics, more than previous concepts, that has created a shift in focus in the women's movement.

Although identity in the women's movement constitutes a compelling issue (and need for resolution), as a reflection of the larger society, identity politics reveals not only the necessity of addressing the inequalities that exist among women but also the inequalities that exist among all people in the United States—indeed, the world.

CONCLUSION

The loss of a highly visible issue bequeathed a decade of entrenched resistance to feminists' goals and a reassertion of intense feminist group division. These divisions emerged in spite of the fact that a short time earlier the ERA Campaign, as new groups emerged to work for passage, had led to both concerted efforts to win a mutually desired goal and a generalized view that mobilization is dependent upon the engagement of many types of women working in multiple arenas.

This case study reveals cycles of intramovement division and intramovement cooperation, along with cycles of advance and decline—all in interaction with political/social change. The renewed threat to abortion rights in the 1990s led to the emergence of groups, once again working together using both legislative and confrontational direct action tactics (Scanlan 1989). Still, as the ERA Campaign reveals, a revitalized movement carries the danger of focusing too much energy on one goal, allowing other issues to recede into the background, and it is often background issues that address the needs of women from disadvantaged sectors of society. A high visibility issue can submerge divisions that need to be addressed and thereby thwart the engagement of women who feel the movement is not meant for them.

Rather than *a* mobilizing issue, the women's movement needs many mobilizing issues. As this study shows, inclusiveness is not just having a multicultural membership addressing multicultural issues; it is also organized actions for both personal and political engagement. An inclusive feminist movement is characterized by diversity in members, issues, leaders, organizational structure, tactical choice, and goals—all the areas that provide myriad opportunities to enhance feelings of self, change social conditions, and connect with others.

The need to work with "difference" to achieve goals is even more important today when activists are reaching across borders. A goal of the women's movement in the twenty-first century is to become worldwide, making women's lives, work, and values part of everyday consciousness. If women achieve autonomy for themselves, enter into decision-making positions, and show that working together for change—in spite of identity differences—is possible, they will have shown the possibility for a different kind of political/cultural system than exists today. If the women's movement succeeds, it has the opportunity to set an example of identity-with-unity that the rest of the world, individuals, and societies would do well to emulate.

NOTES

1. The text of the Equal Rights Amendment is: "Equality of rights under the law shall not be denied or abridged by the United States or by any state on account of sex."

2. See, for example, Arrington and Kyle (1978); Becker (1981); Berry (1986); Boles (1979, 1980); Buechler (1990); Carabillo, Meuli, and Csida (1993); Costain (1992); Cott (1987, 1990); Davis (1999); Deutchman and Prince-Embury (1982); Eisenstein (1982); Ferree and Hess (2000); Freeman (1986); Harrison (1980); Hoff-Wilson (1986); Langolis (1982); Mansbridge (1986); Marshall (1990); Mathews and De Hart (1990); McGlen and O'Connor (1988); Miller and Linker (1974); Mueller and Dimieri (1982); Nelson and Johnson (1991); Rosen (2000); Rupp and Taylor (1987); Ryan (1992, 1996); Slavin (1982); Wandersee (1988); White (1985).

3. For full details of data gathering, as well as an expanded analysis of the ERA Campaign, see *Feminism and the Women's Movement: Dynamics of Change in Social Movement Ideology and Activism* (Ryan 1992). Parts of this chapter were first published in that work.

4. See also Gamson (1975); Jenkins (1983); McCarthy and Zald (1977); Oberschall (1973); Tilly (1978); Zald (1992); Zurcher and Snow (1981).

5. For NSM theory, see Melucci (1985, 1988); Offe (1985); and Touraine (1981, 1988). For combinations of resource mobilization and NSM theory, see Ferree and Miller (1985); Klandermans (1984); and Morris and Mueller (1992).

6. STOP ERA is an acronym for Stop Taking Our Privileges and Extra Responsibility Amendment. The Heritage Foundation is a conservative think-tank. The profamily movement was spearheaded by Jerry Falwell's Moral Majority (now defunct). The Eagle Forum, formed in 1975 by Phyllis Schlafly, is an anti-ERA, antiabortion, and "profamily" organization. The eagle is used as the symbol because it stands for traditional American values and because the eagle is one of the few creatures that only has one mate for life. See Marshall (1984) and Fishman and Fuller (1981).

7. National Organization for Women (1982) and Mann (1982).

8. For a full account of CD actions Johnson was involved in, see chapter 2 of her book *Going Out of Our Minds: The Metaphysics of Liberation* (1987). For a detailed description of the fast she organized in the spring of 1982 in Springfield, Illinois, see chapter 4 of the same book. For much of her feminist philosophy, see *Wildfire: Igniting the She/Volution* (Johnson 1989).

9. Interview with an anonymous member of the CD group The Grassroots Group of Second Class Citizens (July 1983).

10. Interview with Sonia Johnson, August 1983, and field notes of 1981 NOW Conference, Washington, D.C.

11. Conversation with Norma Mendoza, Chapter President, Metro East (Illinois) NOW, March 1984.

12. Interview with Sonia Johnson.

13. Interviews with Eleanor Smeal, September and November 1983.

14. Interview with Sonia Johnson.

15. Previously they had been sleeping on the floor of a nearby church.

16. The women's spirituality movement surfaced in the mid-1970s with the reemergence of Wicca and the introduction of New Age awareness.

17. Mailing from Sonia Johnson, June 16, 1983; field notes of Women's Gathering, Washington, D.C., August 1983; interview with Sonia Johnson.

18. Eleanor Smeal, campaign speech and question/answer session, 1985 National NOW officer election, New Orleans, Louisiana.

19. Conversation with Eleanor Smeal after her talk "The Feminization of Power," Lafayette College, Easton, Pennsylvania, February 21, 1989.

20. See Ryan (2001a) for more in-depth analysis of identity politics on which this section is based.

21. Twist on de Beauvoir's concept of woman compared to man: "defined and differentiated with reference to man and not he with reference to her; she is the incidental, the inessential as opposed to the essential. He is the Subject, he is the Absolute— she is the Other" (from *The Second Sex*, 1952, xix).

22. Womanist, rather than feminist, is the term preferred by some African American women.

23. For sex similarity arguments of the early women's movement, see Buhle and Buhle (1978); Cott (1987); DuBois (1978, 1981); and Flexner (1975).

24. The social feminist position of the late nineteenth and early twentieth centuries can be found in Addams (1917); Lemons (1973); Gusfield (1970); and Papachristou (1976). For a lesbian feminist essentialist position, see Daly (1978); Echols (1989); Johnson (1989); and Johnston (1973).

5

The Politics of Decision Making in the National Organization for Women

Maryann Barakso

While participation in electoral politics always occupied a place in the collective action repertoire of the National Organization for Women (NOW), until fairly recently the group was best known for its use of tactics like legislative lobbying and grassroots mobilizing (Freeman 1975; Costain 1992). In 1992, however, the media-dubbed "Year of the Woman" in electoral politics garnered the enthusiasm of women's organizations (Handlin 1998, 44), and NOW proved no exception.

One of the principal questions this volume poses about feminist organizing is, "What factors lead feminists to choose certain actions over others?" (Banaszak, chapter 1). Why did the leaders of the NOW choose to invest more organizational resources in electoral politics? The most frequently cited explanations for social movement group behavior hinge upon the particular structure of political opportunities available to organizations. Broadly speaking, such opportunities can include the availability of resources, political allies, and local networks of mobilizable elites and/or activists (Tilly 1978; McAdam 1982; Tarrow 1983, 1994). More recently, scholars have focused on how factors including values, beliefs, group identity, and organizational form combine to influence organizational decision making (Banaszak 1996a; Minkoff 1999, 2002; Clemens 1996, 1997).

This chapter argues that the decision to effect changes in NOW's protest repertoire reflects not only the availability of political opportunities and resources but also the group's internal political system. This analysis of decision making in NOW follows Elisabeth Clemens's conceptualization of "organizational form," which "implies both a cognitive model that informs identity and those structures of relations that characterize social institutions" (1996, 207). NOW's particular political culture privileges certain values over others, and in turn this fact affects group leader's decisions as well as members' assessment of the legitimacy of those decisions. Further, NOW's formal structure provides its members with independent means of molding the group's agenda and tactical choices. Failing to take account of these components of NOW's political system underestimates the representation and participation of the group's grassroots members and chapters (whose importance is emphasized, for example, in Reger and Staggenborg, chapter 6) while overestimating the independence of NOW leaders.

THE STRUCTURE OF POLITICAL OPPORTUNITIES

Macropolitical changes in the American political environment since the 1970s made political campaigning a potentially more rewarding endeavor to a wider variety of interest groups than ever before. Post-Watergate modifications of campaign finance laws, together with the decline of political party influence (both in terms of the nominations process and within the electorate) and the rise of an increasingly candidate-centered election system, all provided incentives for interest groups to create political action committees (PACs) and otherwise focus their sights on participating in campaigns as a means of wielding political influence (see Berry 1984).

Feminist organizations joined other interest groups responding to these shifts. Buoyed by analyses of the 1980 presidential elections that revealed gender-linked political divisions among voters, the leaders of many women's organizations, including NOW, argued that this "gender gap" represented a new exploitable opportunity for feminists (*National NOW Times* 1980–1981; Mueller 1988). Media attention to several key concerns of feminists since President Ronald Reagan's election, including attacks on abortion providers and clinics and sexual harassment, also fueled feminist organizations' electoral activity (Kahn and Goldenberg 1991; Handlin 1998, 13, 15). New financial resources further encouraged these groups. Anita Hill's widely publicized testimony at Senate Judiciary Hearings on President George H. W. Bush's Supreme Court nominee Clarence Thomas in 1991 swelled the coffers of women's organizations, who reported that donations poured in as a result of the hearings (Carabillo, Meuli, and Csida 1993, 143). Finally, a scandal involving many congressional members' use of the House bank created a favorable climate for the recruitment, funding, and election of female candidates as viable alternatives to the discredited incumbents (Hershey 1993).

THE MISSING LINK: THE INTERNAL POLITICS OF GROUPS

NOW's leaders responded to shifts in the macropolitical environment by moving the group toward activities like the financial underwriting of political campaigns, the deployment of volunteer activists to campaigns supporting the election of feminist-friendly candidates, and the creation of candidate recruitment and training programs. However, NOW's political culture and structure also definitively shaped its participation in electoral campaigns. Activists' expectations about how the organizations they belong to should act are shaped by each group's unique political culture. Activists in membership-based voluntary associations often exhibit a great deal of interest and concern about how leaders' decisions affect "their" organization, particularly when the choices involve strategy or tactics (Riger 1984; Taylor and Whittier 1993; Arnold 1995; Barakso 2004).

Activists' influence on group policy, on the other hand, is shaped in large measure by the formal structure of the organization. As Elisabeth Clemens showed in her analysis of populist and progressive groups, such structures strongly affect tactical choices and even a group's political success (Banaszak 1996a; Clemens 1997). Groups whose bylaws call for regular elections of national leaders, for example, provide activists with greater leverage than groups whose bylaws stipulate that leaders are to be appointed by a board of directors.

Political Culture[1]

Although formally founded in 1966, the guiding principles that were to frame NOW's political culture were not fully established until 1971. Arthur L. Stinchcombe hypothesized that organizations become imprinted with a particular form during a founding period reflecting the available resources and constraints in the environment (Stinchcombe 1965). This form influences organizational behavior far into its future (Selznick 1992).

NOW's formal documents (Statement of Purpose, bylaws, and press releases) as well as documents capturing the group's less structured discussions (board meeting minutes, public statements at annual conferences, and interviews) reveal NOW leaders' and members' agreement on the goals and priorities of their group (Beyer 1981; Riger 1984). At all organizational levels, NOW activists consistently express the importance of five principles, repeatedly referring to them when describing the purpose of their collective endeavor. In brief, the principles that form the substrate of NOW's political culture include commitments to

- position itself at the vanguard of the women's rights movement;
- maintain the support and vitality of its grassroots base;
- pursue a multi-issue, multi-tactical strategy;
- remain politically independent; and
- focus on action-oriented (as opposed to educational or leadership-led lobbying) activities.

NOW's founders' experiences in politics informed the development of these principles. For example, the founders sought to counter the inability or unwillingness of existing women's organizations, governmentally sponsored committees, and political parties to enact substantive changes in women's political, social, and economic status. Hampered by their allegiance to institutionalized means of interacting with the state, the most prominent women's groups, (including the American Association of University Women, the Association of Business and Professional Women, and the League of Women Voters) had failed to produce a fresh, compelling vision for a society in which women shared equal status with their male counterparts. Established women's groups lacked the independence to confront political institutions, nor did they seem willing to expand their tactical repertoire or to harness the resources of a wider public in support of their goals. As advisory bodies, the federal and state commissions on the status of women were not empowered to take action on any issues. Finally, even when they managed to infiltrate the upper echelons of the political parties, women continued to face significant roadblocks in achieving support for women's rights measures within them (Freeman 2000).

The experience and interests of newer members, particularly those who became active in NOW between 1968 and 1971, also profoundly shaped NOW's political culture. Many of the activists who joined NOW during this period had cross-cutting memberships with the "radical" women's liberation groups and the new iterations of peace and civil rights movement groups. New members' experiences in other new social movement groups, many of which emphasized the involvement of the grassroots in organizational decision making, led them to expect more voice in NOW's management and policies. The new wave of NOW activists pushed the group to commit to a feminist philosophy that more clearly advocated for the empowerment of all women, regardless of sexuality, race, age, or class (Freeman 1975; Echols 1989; Evans 1979; Meyer and Whittier 1994; Ryan 1992; Sapiro 1989; Evans and Boyte 1986).

As a consequence, NOW's founders' vision soon stretched to incorporate the experiences and convictions of its new members. The group's repudiation in 1971 of NOW founder and ex-president Betty Friedan's position against adopting lesbian rights as a feminist issue marked this transition. From then on, internal debates over strategy choice and change in NOW consistently revealed members' and leaders' shared acknowledgment of the organization's guiding principles.

Political Structure: Leadership and Policymaking

NOW leaders, like those of any organization, make decisions within a particular internal political context. The organization's political structure is characterized by two primary elements: its electoral system and the annual meeting of its membership. Elections for the four national leadership offices (which are salaried positions) are competitive and are decided by members (via a delegate system). Candidates for national office must have been NOW members for a minimum number of years; once elected by the membership at a national convention, officers may serve a maximum of two consecutive terms.

NOW's national board consists of approximately thirty-four members elected to a maximum of two consecutive two-year terms by members attending one of nine regional meetings held yearly.[2] Bylaws require that a minimum number of board seats be filled by persons of color. The board meets three to five times a year; members are unsalaried, although their expenses are reimbursed.

Members have a hand in NOW's operation not only through the electoral process but also through their ability to influence policy at the national level. Annual meetings of members constitute "the supreme governing body" of NOW. These meetings provide the space for members to exchange ideas, to discuss grievances against the external political world as well as problems they have with NOW's leadership. Members have the opportunity to debate, and ultimately to formalize, changes in NOW's priorities or functioning. Except in the case of bylaws changes, resolutions can be formulated at the conference itself, which allows members from all over the country to organize themselves more easily. At these meetings, members, chapters, and regions are empowered to voice their opinion on NOW's direction and its policies, to develop and lobby for (or against) changes in NOW's political agenda or its tactical focus. Rank and file NOW members have the opportunity to draft resolutions to enact changes in NOW policy. Issue caucuses are held until the last day of the conference, which is reserved for a plenary session at which NOW delegates will vote on resolutions. Any NOW member who would like an issue addressed, or who advocates for some change in policy, may formulate a resolution and lobby for its adoption at one of these caucuses. If the resolution is approved by a majority of members present at one of the several caucuses held for this purpose, it is eligible to be brought before the entire body for a general vote.

If a member's favored policy resolution fails to move out of a caucus, or if the activist is doubtful of her chances of success in this venue, she may bypass the caucuses altogether by gathering a minimum number of signatures on a petition. Any member is further able to influence the policy process in NOW by speaking for or against resolutions at the final plenary session and by offering amendments to proposed resolutions. Conference delegates then vote on these resolutions, which, if approved by a majority of delegates, obligate national leaders to carry them out.

Finally, annual meetings provide national officers with the opportunity not only to share their visions with members but also to interact with and receive feedback from the grassroots. National leaders consult frequently with local, state, and regional leaders and are easily approached by rank and file members at these meetings.

Additional Factors Fostering Member Participation and Mobilization

Two aspects of NOW's financial structure are critical to understanding the dynamics of its internal decision-making processes. First, national NOW rebates a proportion of dues back to its 550 chapters, providing them with a modicum of financial independence. Second, NOW's income is heavily reliant on membership dues, particularly on renewals. Maintaining the loyalty of members is critical to the group's ongoing viability.

In addition, according to the organization's bylaws, local groups enjoy significant autonomy from the national level. At the same time, as Reger and Staggenborg note in chapter 6, the national level of NOW also provides its chapters, regions, and states with concrete advice on strategy and suggested plans of action, in addition to regular assistance in membership recruitment and chapter development.

ELECTORAL ACTIVISM AND NOW'S POLITICAL CULTURE

When the timing seemed auspicious, leaders of the National Organization for Women formed PACs, created workshops for members on electoral politics, and otherwise became more active in political campaigns. Yet NOW's guiding principles, principles further codified in the organization's formal structure, fundamentally shape *how* the group employs the tactic as well as the *extent* to which it is used.

Throughout NOW's history, both rank and file members and leaders have expressed concerns about the potential for electoral activism to erode their organization's political culture at the group's internal elections, board meetings, and annual conferences (Barakso 2004). Some NOW activists associated political campaigning with co-optation by political parties and/or individual candidates. Endorsements and other electoral activity, they feared, might cause NOW's leaders to temper their demands and draw the organization away from its vanguard position among women's groups. Participating in political campaigns would privilege NOW's national leadership at the expense of leaders and members at the local, state, and regional levels. Electoral activism could also encourage NOW leaders to focus less on mobilizing people in favor of mobilizing money for political candidates (for elaboration see Freeman 1973, 1992).

The destructive potential of electoral participation served to contain, but not eliminate, NOW's involvement in campaign politics. Although significant numbers of NOW leaders and members worked within political parties during the first sixteen years of its existence, national NOW launched few drives to involve its grassroots members in doing so. Perhaps the clearest evidence that NOW's early leaders did not expect their own organization to focus on electoral politics is the formation in 1971 of the National Women's Political Caucus (NWPC). Among the founders of the NWPC were several NOW members, who saw the caucus as the feminist movement's "political arm" and quite separate in purpose from organizations like NOW.

NOW members did, however, vote regularly to support NWPC activities at annual conferences: in 1971 one resolution approved of NWPC's proposals to "form women's caucuses within every party and every state . . . a caucus within every county in every party . . . a caucus within every congressional district in every party . . . to ensure that 50% of delegates to national conventions are women . . . [and to] teach women through school for political candidates" ("Revolution: Tomorrow Is NOW" 1972–1973). An internal survey of NOW members in 1974 also found that 16 percent claimed membership in NWPC ("Summary of Questionnaire for NOW" 1974). Nevertheless, in the mid-1970s, when a few NOW activists and leaders, including Politics Task Force Chair Charlene Suneson, ventured that NOW should create its own "political arm," the suggestion engendered accusations that proponents intended to disempower grassroots activists. Suneson responded that political necessity alone drove her suggestion:

> I have had a couple [sic] communications that indicate there is some misunderstanding about the political device. It has not been put forth because I or anyone else "likes" political action. My own involvement in NOW has been entirely legislative. Where legislative action can accomplish ratification of the ERA there is no reason to bring in political action. However, various state ERA coordinators have indicated they do not believe legislative action alone will ratify the ERA. (Suneson 1973)

After much internal debate at the 1977 national NOW conference in Detroit, by a narrow margin members approved the creation of a PAC (National Organization for Women 1977). Nevertheless, the organization continued to leave most of the political campaigning to groups like the NWPC and the Women's Political Campaign (WPC). In 1980, NOW's president, Eleanor Smeal, hoped to capitalize on the gender gap that appeared in that year's presidential race, but members continued to pressure NOW leaders to ensure that a broad range of kinds of tactics would continue to be employed (see Ferree and Hess 1985, 113–14.)

The ERA's failure presented Smeal with another opportunity to argue that NOW must turn its attention and resources to filling legislatures with feminist politicians. Smeal presented the electoral tactic as a critical tool to be employed at a propitious moment in time. NOW members and resources were at their peak, and in the process of campaigning for the ERA, leaders and members of the organization had accumulated valuable political experience, forged networks, and enjoyed a high degree of public recognition (Bennetts 1978; Mann 1979).

Smeal directly attributed the ERA's loss to the presence of a handful of "turncoat" and otherwise intransigent politicians in state legislatures who remained unmoved by massive numbers of people engaging in protests, marches, and lobbying (*National NOW Times* 1982). Moreover, the ERA's loss in the face of the apparently overwhelming support of the public allowed leaders to press the argument among their members and to the public that change at the electoral level was critical to women's progress. (Although, as Jane Mansbridge [1986] showed, public support for the ERA was not nearly as clear-cut as opinion polls seemed to suggest.)

As a result of its new emphasis, NOW increased the number of political workshops it held at its annual membership conferences. During President Goldsmith's tenure, NOW also endorsed a presidential slate for the first time, that of 1984 Democratic presidential candidate Walter Mondale and his running mate Geraldine Ferraro. In return for NOW's endorsement, Goldsmith understood that Mondale would afford the group an inside track in the campaign and that he would strongly consider nominating a woman as his running mate (Perlez 1984). While Smeal habitually presented the argument for electoral activism together with plans to invest and involve NOW's grassroots members, Goldsmith proved less successful in convincing activists of her own commitment to do so. Her enthusiastic lobbying for a female vice-presidential nominee threatened to sacrifice NOW's political independence. A Mondale staffer had called the campaign's affiliation with NOW "a good marriage," for example (Basler 1984). Goldsmith's apparently cozy relationship with the Democratic Party stoked ill-will among NOW's ranks (and contributed to her failed reelection bid).

The dismal performance of the Mondale-Ferraro ticket dampened the enthusiasm of NOW leaders and members for political campaigning for some time thereafter. One Washington lobbyist in regular contact with women's organizations identified the problem this way: "NOW is about being on the outside and shaking the foundations of the ruling class. . . . Judy misunderstood the role of the organization. She went to dinner at the Mondales' and got drummed out of the corps" (Gross 1992). At the same time, associating with NOW seemed as politically poisonous to politicians as involvement with politicians was to NOW (Toner 1986).

In the wake of the ensuing controversy within NOW, Smeal regained the office of president in 1985. Though still a strong proponent of electoral activism, Smeal reaffirmed the centrality of grassroots mobilization. Referring to Goldsmith's tactics of legislative lobbying and coalition building, Smeal said, "We tried that last year—but now it's time to go back into the streets"

(Klemesrud 1985). Ramping up her outsider rhetoric, using terms like "fascists" to describe those who would curtail women's reproductive rights, Smeal declared, "The worst thing we can do right now is try to become acceptable" (Gialey 1985).

Subsequent NOW leaders, including Molly Yard, Patricia Ireland, and Kim Gandy, emulated Smeal's tactical balancing act. In 1989, during Yard's tenure, NOW members voted to create a commission to study the possibility of forming a new political party (Herbers 1982). Bella Abzug and Eleanor Holmes Norton offered lukewarm support for the idea, but most of NOW's usual allies proved decidedly hostile to the suggestion. At a meeting of the National Women's Political Caucus, for example:

> Members . . . rejected a call by [NOW] . . . for a study of whether a third party should be formed to support women's rights. Though there was no formal vote on the issue, that sentiment was made clear in formal sessions and in conversations outside. "To divert yourself from the established power structure, which will go on and continue to make decisions anyway, to pull yourself out of it, it's absolutely stupid," said Maxine Berman, a Democratic state representative in Michigan. "Everybody here laughed at that thing," said Lana Pollack, a Democratic state senator in Michigan. (Dionne 1989)

The majority of political commentators, and perhaps more important, most other feminist leaders, including Harriet Woods (NWPC president), took Yard herself to task for potentially ruining years of feminists' hard work forging relationships with those inside the Republican and Democratic Parties. The press roundly derided NOW's "radical" stance and Yard's outlandish tactics (*New York Times* 1991). A coalition of progressive organizations formed the new party in the face of these objections. The "21st Century Party" wrote a platform invoking an uncompromisingly feminist, diverse, and progressive vision, but as the Democrats regained the White House in 1992, the project unraveled.

NOW's PAC did not endorse William Jefferson Clinton, but the organization, led since 1991 by Patricia Ireland, reasserted its presence in the political arena during that election cycle. The group provided funds and activists from its chapters and PACs to support the political campaigns of feminists like Carol Moseley Braun in her successful Illinois Senate race. Though activists occasionally complained (in fact, one woman used the fact as fodder to support her own campaign for NOW's presidency), dinners and auctions to benefit NOW's PAC became commonplace events at annual meetings. In the 1997–1998 election cycle, NOW ranked fourth in total contributions ($80,861) of thirteen "women's issues" PACs contributing to federal candidates. Among the sixteen women's issue PACs contributing in the 2001–2002 races, NOW ranked fifth ($69,894). NOW's overall spending on political campaigns increased over this period: In the 1998 election cycle, overall

NOW/PAC spent $161,114; four years later its campaign expenditures jumped to $304,737 (www.opensecrets.org).

Evidence of the way NOW aligns its PAC work with its guiding principles appears in the rules under which NOW PACs operate. While women's PACs all apply endorsement guidelines to potential beneficiaries of their funds, candidates hoping for support from NOW's PACs must pledge to support a far more substantial list of social and economic policies. Underscoring the fact that NOW's vanguard vision is carried through in its electoral activism, to win the organization's support, candidates must support affirmative action and commit to "nonpunitive" welfare policies and to "reproductive freedom without restriction." Candidates are required to declare their support for lesbian and gay rights as well as an equal rights amendment to the federal constitution that "guarantees women's equality, reproductive rights and non-discrimination based on sexual orientation" (www.nowpacs.org/facts.html).

NOW's involvement in electoral politics extends beyond the funding of political campaigns. At its 1992 annual conference, NOW members voted to support an "Elect Women for A Change" campaign crafted by Patricia Ireland, which "had projects running full force in Connecticut, Florida, Georgia and Tennessee, helping feminist candidates win Congressional, state and local primaries" (Carabillo, Meuli, and Csida 1993, 147). Intensive political action workshops intended to provide grassroots members with training in a variety of electoral strategies are also a continuing feature at NOW's annual meetings.

Ireland's emphasis on launching campaigns to develop NOW members' political skills and on funding NOW's PACs frustrated members who saw this as evidence of her lack of support for the group's guiding principles. Yet during her tenure, Ireland launched a host of special "summits" bringing young feminists, feminists of diverse ethnic and racial backgrounds, and lesbians together. Ireland spearheaded civil disobedience campaigns and helped organize grassroots campaigns to keep abortion clinics accessible. More recently, Ireland's successor, Kim Gandy, unveiled her newest initiative, a "Drive for Equality" whose centerpiece is a voter registration drive that, while still electorally focused, clearly centers on grassroots mobilization efforts.

CONCLUSION

David Meyer and Sidney Tarrow note, "Ironically, a movement organization concerned with effecting democratic reforms in the polity may be most effective by abandoning certain democratic and amateurish political practices" (1998a, 15). Even a brief sketch of NOW's internal politics, however, reveals that the organization's culture and structure conspire to maintain such practices—even when they appear counterproductive. For example, on its face, NOW's tactical repertoire is extraordinarily broad. Yet the deployment of that repertoire is constrained by the group's principles and practices. As a result, a political candidate who appears to be a potentially promising ally will nevertheless fail to garner NOW's support if she or he does not pass its stringent litmus test. Similarly, opportunities to join advantageous political coalitions will be ignored or dismissed if such coalitions clash with NOW's political values.

Shifting our gaze to groups' internal political systems also highlights the extent to which rank and file group members influence associational behavior, as several scholars have recently noted (see, e.g., Minkoff 2002; Foley and Edwards 1999). NOW members participated in forging the group's political culture and decision-making apparatus and furthermore work to maintain its integrity. Decision making in NOW can only be understood by placing these facts in the analytical foreground.

NOTES

1. Inglehart's definition of political culture applies to political organizations as well as to nation-states: "a system of attitudes, values and knowledge that is widely shared within a society and transmitted from generation to generation" (1990, 18).

2. The requirements for office in the bylaws state that "all national officers shall have been members of NOW for at least four years immediately prior to election and shall have served at least one year as a chapter or state officer or National Board member."

6

Grassroots Organizing in a Federated Structure: NOW Chapters in Four Local Fields

Jo Reger and Suzanne Staggenborg

Although national organizations are undeniably important to modern social movements (see Barakso chapter 5), grassroots mobilization of individuals and networks at the local community level is also vital to many movements. Local movements can energize community institutions, and some movements become political forces through grassroots action (see Button 1989; Naples 1998; Pardo 1998). The history of the U.S. women's movement testifies to the potential of concentrated grassroots mobilization. In the 1960s and early 1970s, feminists and other grassroots activists wrested control of the abortion movement away from medical professionals and demanded reproductive rights for women (see Buechler 1990; Lader 1973; Luker 1984; Staggenborg 1991). In the politically hostile 1980s, feminist social movement organizations survived attacks by the New Right through the development of grassroots agencies (Hyde 1995). In the 1980s and 1990s, feminist grassroots organizations mobilized thousands for mass demonstrations on abortion and women's rights (Ferree and Martin 1995). In short, much of the ongoing activity of the women's movement can be credited to grassroots mobilization. As Joyce Gelb (1995, 131) argues, "The continuation of grassroots activism, ongoing commitment to the progressive goal of transformation, and the existence of a large constituency that has maintained its independence from 'official circles' have contributed to sustaining the [women's] movement's vitality and strength."

In a federated social movement organization (SMO), such as the National Organization for Women (NOW), the national and local levels affect each other. The national organization can greatly influence the grassroots in both negative and positive ways (McCarthy and Wolfson 1996; Oliver and Furman 1989; Staggenborg 1991). On the one hand, national organizations create burdens for chapters, such as dues payments, and they may sap local energies by requiring more attention to organizational matters than to action campaigns (cf. Piven and Cloward 1977). On the other hand, national organizations can provide material support to chapters and the legitimacy associated with a nationally known organization. Local groups can provide democratic input into national organizations, and, in some instances, they may exert strong influences on the national organization. In some federated organizations, local members provide input, and national leaders create action campaigns, policies, and directives that are communicated to the chapters and shape their activities.

In NOW, chapters do provide such input, and some chapters make regular use of national NOW action plans such as the Equal Rights Amendment (ERA) and reproductive rights strategies. However, NOW chapters also construct organizational infrastructures and design means of mobilizing resources and action campaigns that may differ from national strategies (see Barakso chapter 5). In this chapter, we examine the ways in which NOW chapters are shaped by localized dynamics as well as by national structure. Our analysis focuses on the ways in which local chapters maintain themselves and carry out collective action, adjusting their structures in response to local needs as well as responding to national directives and taking advantage of national resources.

We identify two localized dynamics that shape the structural and cultural development of chapters. The first is the local organizational and political environment, which social movement theorists have conceptualized variously as the "social movement community" (Buechler 1990; Staggenborg 1998), "multi-organizational field" (Curtis and Zurcher 1973; Klandermans 1992), and local "political field" (Ray 1999). The concepts of social movement community and multiorganizational field call attention to the variety of community actors and organizations that interact locally, and the concept of a political field points to the "structured, unequal, and socially constructed environment within which organizations are embedded and to which organizations and activists constantly respond" (Ray 1999, 6). We argue that NOW chapters respond not only to the national organization and political environment, but also to the local movement community and political field containing other SMOs and community organizations, local political parties, and the state.

Leadership dynamics are a second localized influence. The styles and concerns of local leaders shape the organizational structures and action campaigns of NOW chapters. Leaders also play an important role in influencing levels of recruitment and collective identities of movement participants. As Disney and Gelb (2000) found in their study of women's movement organizations, individual leaders contribute greatly to the success of an organization. We argue that the structures and activities of NOW chapters are shaped in multiple ways by the style and content of the leadership and that leaders of grassroots organizations shape mobilization through their varying emphases on national directives and the requirements of local fields.

To explore the effects of national structure and directives and local fields and leadership, we use data that we have collected on four NOW chapters located in New York City, Chicago, Cleveland, and Bloomington, Indiana. While these four chapters are not a representative sample of all NOW chapters, their histories provide insight into the importance of NOW's grassroots organizations in the maintenance and development of U.S. feminism. Each of us had previously studied two NOW chapters (see Reger 2001, 2002a, 2002b; Staggenborg 1989, 1991, 1998), and we found that comparisons among the chapters allowed us to show how variations in local fields and leadership affect mobilization and collective action.[1] Organizational newsletters and interviews with chapter participants are the primary sources of data for all four chapters. These sources are supplemented by documents available in various archives, dating from 1966 to 1995, which contain information on national, regional, state, and chapter activities.

We begin by describing structural developments and action campaigns in the national NOW organization. We then describe how local political fields and leadership dynamics have affected grassroots maintenance of feminism. We conclude with some thoughts on the role of federated organizations in movement mobilization and grassroots continuity.

NATIONAL STRUCTURE AND STRATEGIES

Throughout its existence, NOW has modified and expanded its organizational structure and strategies in response to both the political environment and the demands of its members. National NOW's ability to influence its chapters has varied over time, and chapters have influenced the national organization at least as much as the national organization has shaped local structures and strategies (see Barakso chapter 5). Particularly in the early years, national NOW experienced many growing pains and was unable to contribute much to its chapters, though the chapters were essential to NOW's growth and development.

When NOW was founded in 1966, the organization consisted of several hundred members and had no real grassroots constituency. Realizing that the organization would be more effective and stable if it could mobilize participants on a local level, leaders began to organize chapters. Within a year of NOW's founding, fourteen chapters had been formed and, by 1973, 365 chapters had been established throughout the country (see Carden 1974; Freeman 1975; Hole and Levine 1971). As NOW began to grow in terms of individual members and chapters, its administrative and decision-making structure became inadequate, and the organization experienced several years of disorganization and conflict.

Initially, NOW was run by a national board of directors and officers elected at an annual membership conference, where a small membership made major decisions. By 1973, the organization had expanded enough to open three national offices with several paid staff each, including an administrative office in Chicago, a legislative office in Washington, and a public information office in New York City. But, as Freeman (1975, 83) reported, "this wide geographic distribution of functions made NOW very decentralized and often chaotic." NOW also had problems communicating with its chapters, which were growing and operating in a largely autonomous fashion. Regional directors had been elected in 1970 to coordinate chapter activities, but they "had no staff, no budget, no expense allowance, too much territory, and too much work" (Freeman 1975, 88). National level task forces suffered from similar shortages of resources. Consequently, there was not a lot of coordination of chapter activities with national strategies, and there was a decided lack of adequate communication between chapters and the national organization. This led to resentment of the national office by local activists because the national office was receiving a larger portion of the dues money than were the chapters.

There was also a growing problem with decision making at the national conferences, at which officers were elected and policy decisions were made by members. When the membership of NOW was small, it was feasible to have each individual attending the conference have one vote, but when several thousand individuals began attending membership conferences, it was clearly unworkable to make decisions in this manner. Moreover, many members were disenfranchised by their inability to travel to the membership conferences. The result of these difficulties was a period of internal conflict for NOW as the organization struggled to create a viable, and democratic, organizational structure (see Staggenborg 1991, 165–67 for details).

By the late 1970s, NOW had resolved many of its internal problems by establishing a single office in Washington, developing a delegate system of voting, paying salaries to its elected officers, and hiring additional professional staff as resources expanded. Chapters were essential to this structural development, as elected leaders of NOW typically work their way up from chapter to national office. Once a formalized structure was established, NOW was able to expand its resources and increase coordination among chapters through the use of direct mail and professional staff. In the late 1970s and early 1980s, NOW was able to coordinate a nationwide ERA campaign, which led to further growth and unity in the organization.

The development of NOW's structure resulted in a system where members join local chapters or remain "at-large" or unaffiliated. All chapters belong to a state organization that coordinates local activities. State organizations are grouped into nine regions that coordinate regional activity. From the regional level, members are selected to sit on the national board. The national level consists of a hired staff and four elected, salaried officers, including the president, executive vice president, action vice president, and secretary. The national board consists of members who represent regional areas, the national officers, and the president of the NOW Legal Defense and Education Fund, the nonprofit arm of the organization. The national board is the highest level of the organization and is in charge of day-to-day administration. The board is also responsible for developing nationwide actions and responding to the concerns of chapters, states, and regions.

Despite these set procedures for conducting business, however, national conferences are often controversial and volatile (see Rumph 2000). Delegates from different chapters prepare resolutions to be presented to the membership, and participants spend much of their time at conferences lobbying and arguing over issues. In some years, chapters have clashed with one another and with the national organization. Adding to the intensity of the conferences are the elections of national officers every four years. The elections are often contested, and lobbying can become intense and acrimonious.

Because of member input on organizational policy and the election of leaders, chapters are considered the "building blocks of NOW." Chapters can be developed wherever there is sufficient community interest, but to be chartered by the national organization they must have at least ten members, formulate bylaws, and elect officers. Since 1970, chapters have been free to create their own structures, policies, and procedures as long as they do not contradict the national bylaws. However, all levels of NOW including chapters are required to create an affirmative action plan to increase diversity (National Organization for Women 2001). This organizational flexibility within national guidelines permits chapters to pursue their own areas of interest and to adapt their structures to local changes while still allowing some national input.

Throughout its history NOW has adopted a wide variety of goals and initiated a multitude of action campaigns, with some of the most visible issues being the ERA, abortion and reproductive rights, and workplace and employment discrimination. NOW's founders were professional women concerned primarily with sex discrimination in employment (Freeman 1975). However, as the chapter system developed and younger women entered NOW, the organization's issue agenda expanded and the group became radicalized. At the organization's second national conference in 1967, NOW went beyond its focus on employment-related concerns and adopted then-controversial positions in favor of both the ERA and abortion law repeal in its "Bill of Rights for Women." Although some of the professional women who had founded NOW wanted to stick to employment issues, young women active in local chapters insisted on an abortion plank (see Lader 1973, 37). As a result, NOW was the first national organization to frame abortion as a "woman's right." Although initially divisive, the ERA and abortion rights eventually became "bottom line" issues around which all NOW members united.[2] In the late 1970s and early 1980s, NOW became increasingly focused on the campaign to pass the ERA. Never a single-issue organization, however, NOW's local activists continued to push the organization to take stands on numerous controversial issues, including gay and lesbian rights, violence against women, racism, and poverty. In addition to expanding issues, younger women also brought consciousness-raising or rap groups into the bureaucratically structured NOW, pushing the organization toward the more "person-centered" attitude of radical feminists (Freeman 1975, 92).

In short, the relationship between the national level and the chapters is one of mutual influence. The chapters, as conduits of members from diverse backgrounds, continue to shape NOW's ideology, strategies and tactics, and goals. At the same time, the national level organizational model is adopted by most chapters, and national NOW directs chapters in action campaigns focused on national issues. In the following sections, we examine how our four chapters have operated within both the federated NOW structure and their local fields.

LOCAL STRUCTURES AND STRATEGIES

NOW chapters vary significantly from each other and national NOW in their structures and strategies. They use national NOW guidelines and strategic initiatives differently, depending on the interests and approaches of local members and leaders and on the ability of the chapter to mobilize resources and organize activities in the local community. The decision-making structures of chapters are more or less formalized and centralized, with some allowing more input from individual members and others concentrating decision making in a core of leaders. Chapters also vary in their ability to attract cohesive "micro-cohorts" of activists (see Whittier 1995) who enjoy one another's company and share a common feminist approach.

Each of our four chapters struggled to develop internal decision-making procedures, mobilize resources, and initiate action campaigns. New York City NOW and Chicago NOW each succeeded in establishing a workable structure, using national NOW as a template, and both have enjoyed fairly continuous levels of mobilization. However, each chapter achieved stability differently, adjusting its structures and tactics to local conditions. Cleveland NOW enjoyed less stable mobilization than New York and Chicago, which can be attributed in part to failed structural adaptations to the problems of citywide mobilization. Bloomington NOW was the most erratic of the four chapters, as it struggled to survive amid the continual population turnover of a college town. In the following accounts of these chapters, we examine influences of the local fields and chapter leadership as well as chapter responses to national NOW.

New York City NOW

Soon after its formation in 1967, New York City (NYC NOW), one of the first NOW chapters,[3] developed a centralized and formal structure, modeled after national NOW's infrastructure. The original structure was also a response to the competitive NYC movement community in which a developed infrastructure (including multiple phone lines and a centrally located office) was one means for sustaining membership recruitment and fund-raising efforts. One activist recalled how this competition began in the early years of the movement:

> There are lots of different women's groups. . . . You have upper crust ladies' clubs with all the trappings of feminism. You have the National Women's Political Caucus. So even from day one . . . NOW in this town competed with a variety of other women's groups and so it was always differentiated. (Interview with NOW activist, March 3, 1996)

The modeling of NYC NOW's structure after national NOW was also largely influenced by one long-term and dynamic leader. Her experience in the early years of the movement with a decentralized women's liberation group led her to join NOW, where she advocated the development of structure. She said:

> If you don't have any structure, you spend more time. No one is designated to pinpoint [a] vision . . . and then there is so much in-fighting. There is even more in-fighting than when you have structure. (Interview with NOW activist, March 3, 1996)

As a result of her experience, chapter members have continued to stress the development of a formalized infrastructure with paid staff and a permanent office (features most NOW chapters are unable to develop).

As part of the chapter's infrastructure, members developed a formal leadership system and committee structure. The chapter's leadership system consisted of a clear chain of authority established through a hierarchy of officers. Chapter officers include the president, multiple vice presidents, a secretary, a treasurer, and a board of directors. The chapter has expanded its infrastructure in periods of heavy mobilization. For example, in 1985 the Women's Helpline, an information phone line, expanded, and in 1988 the chapter hired a full-time staff member to coordinate volunteers answering the phones. An important part of the chapter's infrastructure is the location of its office in Manhattan, the "heart" of the city. Even after three moves prompted by rising rents and financial difficulties, the chapter continued to maintain a Manhattan office, providing a location accessible to women throughout the city.

NYC NOW also has had a system of ongoing and active committees and subcommittees. While committees tend to focus on issues, subcommittees concentrate on sustaining the infrastructure. Regular chapter committees include family relations, consciousness-raising (C-R), lesbian rights, media reform, psychology, and reproductive rights. Subcommittee topics include working on communication and media, producing leaflets, tabling at different locations in the city, and coordinating volunteers. One of the oldest committees in the chapter is the C-R committee, which was institutionalized in 1972 in response to member demand and public interest. At this time in the women's movement, women's rights groups began to bring C-R into their organizations as a recruitment device and as a means to help women rethink their lives and understand the importance of feminist organizing (Carden 1974). The introduction of C-R into NYC NOW posed a dilemma in terms of chapter structure. Intrinsic to C-R is a need for women to experience the process in a decentralized and nonhierarchical setting, an organizational context not found in NYC NOW's main infrastructure. To deal with this structural dilemma, the chapter created an informally run, decentralized committee within a centralized and formalized infrastructure (Reger 2002a). This negotiation, accomplished by enacting boundaries between the C-R committee and the rest of the chapter, resulted in the committee becoming separated and somewhat alienated. The relationship between the C-R committee and the rest of the chapter is an uneasy one, with one C-R committee member characterizing it as an "us versus them" situation.

Situated in one of the national media centers of the country, the chapter quickly developed into a political force in the early years of the movement's second wave. The strength of the chapter led Jo Freeman to conclude that in the late 1960s "to many the New York [City] chapter was NOW" (1975, 81).[4] Because of its location and media connections, the chapter has been able to mobilize large numbers of activists. One of National NOW's first large events was the Strike for Women's Equality held in 1970, which brought an influx of members into the organization (Carden 1974; Freeman 1975). NYC NOW, along with other chapters, grew dramatically as a result, with some groups seeing an increase in membership of 50 to 70 percent (Carden 1974; Freeman 1975). By 1987, the chapter was estimated to have three thousand members (NOW York Woman 1987) and in 1993, after a flurry of pro-choice organizing resulting from the *Webster v. Reproductive Health Services* decision, membership rose to four thousand (NOW NYC News 1993). These peaks in mobilization brought in some new micro-cohorts of activists, particularly during the 1991 Anita Hill–Clarence Thomas hearings and the antiabortion campaign Operation Rescue in 1988 and 1992. However, the chapter's activist core is mostly made up of longtime members present through peaks and declines.

Since its inception, NYC NOW's action campaigns have been influenced by the local field as well as by national NOW. Throughout its history the chapter has focused on national issues such as the ERA, presidential political campaigns, and abortion rights. Events such as the fourteenth anniversary of *Roe v. Wade*, the Supreme Court decision legalizing abortion, drew large numbers of participants and well-known women's movement speakers, such as Gloria Steinem. When Operation Rescue targeted New York City abortion clinics in the spring and fall of 1988, NOW joined with other groups to form Project Defend to protect clinics from antiabortion forces. The chapter also maintained a presence nationally, sending 165 busloads of New York City activists to the NOW-sponsored 1989 March of Women's Equality, Women's Lives, a demonstration for passing the ERA and keeping abortion legal (NOW NYC News 1989).

Because of the amount of feminist protest in the city, the chapter sometimes benefited from other organization's actions. After one hundred feminists held a sit-in at *Ladies Home Journal* to protest the editorial content, the magazine published a special insert in August 1970 describing the women's movement and listing groups to contact (Freeman 1975). After the insert's publication, chapters saw an increase in members even though NOW was not listed as a contact group.

Because of the chapter's visibility and large membership, chapter members often compared themselves to national NOW in terms of power and control over the organization. This attitude led to the fear by other large chapters that New York would eventually take over all of NOW (Freeman 1975). These concerns also spread to NYC NOW's local field. In a particularly bitter debate in 1980, the chapter fought off attempts by another NOW member to start a chapter based in Manhattan. Again in 1986, the president of the Bronx NOW chapter voiced her concerns about New York City in a letter to the state NOW president:

> New York City NOW has so many people that belong, that it does not give the smaller chapters a chance, not unless it is ok with NYC. It is not written that NYC is right all the time. We all have ideas which also must be considered. (New York City NOW Document 1986)

While the dynamic local field helped the chapter position itself as comparable to national NOW, national level policies made the chapter susceptible to debates, controversies, and schisms. One of the first schisms affecting the chapter occurred in 1968, when more radically oriented feminists began to voice their discontent with the structure and hierarchy of national NOW (Carden 1974). At the time, the chapter held half of the national NOW membership and was the most active and best known of the chapters (Freeman 1975).[5] Desiring a less "elitist" structure, radical women, mostly from New York City, proposed a new form of organization that was less centralized and formal (Freeman 1975). Despite fears that their membership would drastically decrease if the measure did not pass, the chapter voted to keep the current structure. Proponents of the changes left in protest in October 1968, and Ti-Grace Atkinson, then president of New York NOW, resigned from the group and organized The Feminists, a radical women liberationist group (Freeman 1975; Friedan 1977). The second schism came in the form of two "purges" of lesbians from the national organization in 1969 and 1970. Betty Friedan, founder and then president, worried that lesbians constituted a "lavender menace" and were trying to take over NOW (Carden 1974; Freeman 1975; Friedan 1977). Many of the women who left NOW to form lesbian liberation groups were New York City members. Along with these schisms, the chapter experienced several internal disputes with the national and state level organizations over the years. Politically, the chapter clashed with other NOW organizations through its support of candidates for the national NOW presidency.[6]

In addition to these conflicts, the chapter has had financial difficulties, even with its large base of approximately two thousand members and strong activist core. In 1992, the chapter began a donor campaign to help the chapter pull out of its "constant money crisis." The call for donors reminded members that "NOW-NYC is the largest chapter of the most important women's organization in the world" (NOW NYC News 1992). Despite these efforts, the chapter relocated its offices in an effort to cut back on rising expenses in 1993 and 1995.

NYC NOW has continued to be active on both local and national issues. For example, in August 2000 members raised funds for domestic violence programs, protested police inattention to attacks on women in Central Park, and denounced sexist ads by the animal rights group People for the Ethical Treatment of Animals (PETA). Members continue to promote the chapter as one of the largest and most powerful within NOW, and leaders continue to promote the maintenance and development of a formalized infrastructure.

Chicago NOW

Whereas NYC NOW's structure was centralized and formalized from the start, Chicago NOW's structure became more so over time, allowing the Chicago chapter to achieve a similar stability. Chicago NOW was founded in 1969 as one of the first midwestern chapters of NOW, at a time of much movement activity in the city. The movement community included a very active socialist feminist umbrella group, the Chicago Women's Liberation Union (CWLU), also founded in 1969. While the CWLU attracted young feminists interested in radical social change, NOW appealed to somewhat older career women interested primarily in issues of employment discrimination. Yet the backgrounds of early NOW members were varied, with some members coming out of experience in the civil rights movement and others having experience in conventional organizations. Rather than there being one close micro-cohort, an informant recalled an early split between "direct action" people with civil rights experience and others who favored more "institutionalized" approaches. As a result, an informal power structure existed, consisting of "the people who met on Friday nights" alongside official leaders "who gave the nice speeches" (interview with early Chicago NOW activist, November 7, 1983). The formal structure consisted of monthly meetings run according to parliamentary procedure, working committees, and a board that originally consisted of officers, at-large members, and committee chairs. Committees were formed around issues, depending on the interests of members. NOW members protested sex-segregated want ads, integrated male-only lunch counters, filed complaints with the Equal Employment Opportunity Commission, and, owing to the efforts of a few members, supported legal abortion.

By 1972, the original "informal" leaders had become the elected leaders of Chicago NOW, and, as the 1960s protest cycle waned, early strategic differences also seemed to disappear. Influential chapter leaders decided that Chicago NOW could become a force in the local community by recruiting members, raising money, and paying attention to public relations. Leaders employed mobilizing strategies, such as an annual fund-raising walkathon and ad book, that allowed Chicago NOW to take advantage of its location in a large city with many potential supporters to greatly expand its membership. By the mid-1970s, when other Chicago feminist organizations such as the CWLU were declining, NOW was expanding; by 1984, the chapter claimed three thousand local members and supported a paid staff of five. As one informant put it, Chicago NOW considered itself a "local institution" (interview with NOW leader, May 22, 1984).[7]

To achieve this impressive growth and stability, chapter leaders steered Chicago NOW to concentrate resources on priority issues and to pay attention to public relations. The structure of the chapter was altered to achieve these ends. Similar to NYC NOW's subcommittees, more committees devoted to functional tasks such as fund-raising were formed. Leadership became more centralized as at-large members were removed from the board and, after 1973, issue committees were no longer allowed to form simply because some members were interested. Instead, the chapter began voting on several issue priorities per year in an effort to avoid diluting resources. Proposals for actions were submitted to the board for screening based on criteria such as whether or not the action would help to build the chapter's membership. To attract potential new members and to allow the chapter to address a range of issues beyond the official priorities, Chicago NOW began holding bimonthly meetings, with one meeting devoted to business and the other meeting open to the public, consisting of an educational program on an issue of public interest. In the 1980s, the chapter also held weekly work sessions at which members wrote letters to legislators, made phone calls to potential supporters, and worked on various projects together, providing an easy way for individual members to become involved in the chapter.

Some structural changes and strategic choices were influenced by the national organization. For example, beginning in 1978, the office of vice president was expanded into three vice-presidential offices (finance, chapter development, and action), mirroring a similar functional division of labor on the national level. Chicago NOW also worked closely with the national organization on the ERA Campaign in the late 1970s and early 1980s. But earlier in the 1970s, when national NOW was in turmoil, Chicago NOW went its own way, orienting itself to the Chicago community. At the same time, the chapter recognized the advantages of being part of a nationally known organization and wanted to contribute to NOW's national success. Indeed, the chapter saw itself as an organizational model for national NOW, and contributed a number of leaders and strategies to the national organization. Although Chicago NOW was also involved in some of the national level conflict in the 1970s,[8] the chapter continued to mobilize local feminists for an impressive program of activities. This involved raising funds from the local community and creating campaigns aimed at local targets, such as the city of Chicago, which the chapter sued successfully for sex discrimination in the 1970s. Influenced by local leaders and opportunities, Chicago NOW developed a model of local feminist organizing that helped sustain feminism at the grassroots level.

Cleveland NOW

The Cleveland chapter, founded in 1970, was heavily influenced by the local field and chapter leadership. Whereas the Chicago and New York City chapters were similar in structure to national NOW, Cleveland NOW did not develop an organizational infrastructure capable of sustaining the group through periods of "abeyance" (Taylor 1989a). The chapter worked on several national campaigns but, as a result of fluctuations and tensions inherent in the local field, eventually developed an organizational strategy that focused on community mobilization.

The emergence of the Cleveland chapter came as a result of the growing media attention to the women's movement in the late 1960s. Initially, Cleveland NOW focused on issues promoted by national NOW. Chapter members protested the sex-segregated want ads at a local newspaper and a "gentlemen-only" policy at a local restaurant and gathering place. Over the next several years, the chapter became involved in a variety of nationally focused issues. In 1973, lobbying for the ERA became the top priority of the chapter, and Cleveland NOW joined with other organizations to form the Cuyahoga Coalition for Ratification of the ERA. In the same year, members participated in legislative hearings on the state of abortion clinics. Even in the early years, however, chapter actions focused on the community, particularly local politics. In 1971, for example, a chapter member ran for mayor and the chapter participated in the first Cleveland Women's Political Caucus.

As the chapter continued to grow, it began meeting bimonthly.[9] By 1974, Cleveland was the ninth largest NOW chapter in the country, and Ohio had seventeen chapters with a total of 1,291 members (correspondence between Lana Moretsky and the National NOW records coordinator, November 13, 1975). With the growth of the chapter came increased complaints about the lack of locally focused actions and the need for more communication among chapter members. After much debate, members voted to allow the formation of a multiple chapter system. Arguments against the proposal stated that the system would further divide chapters into east-versus-west-side mentality, promote chapter competition, and inhibit any kind of diversity in the chapters (Greater Cleveland NOW newsletter 1974). Despite these reservations, six suburban chapters had formed by 1976, and a coordinating council of presidents and board members was created to coordinate actions and facilitate chapter communications (Greater Cleveland Coordinating Council 1976). The chapters met national NOW's requirements of having at least ten members, officers, and bylaws. However, each developed a structure of committees and task forces determined by member interest and community issues. For example, some suburban chapters focused on issues such as day care, finding a babysitter, and school lunch programs, while others adopted issues more in line with national campaigns and events.

After the failure of the national ERA Campaign in 1982, the women's movement began to demobilize, and suburban chapters lost membership and eventually dissolved or merged. One activist concluded that the suburban system had not been effective in building the organization and was in fact "a disaster." She added that the system fragmented activists and "people found it demoralizing and drifted away" (interview with NOW activist, December 5, 1996).

By the beginning of the 1980s, the suburban chapters had begun to merge with the large chapters, leaving only the Cleveland and Cleveland East chapters. The membership of the two chapters came, for the most part, from different socioeconomic bases and did not constitute a united micro-cohort.

Members of the Cleveland East chapter were predominantly affluent middle-class suburban women, many of them homemakers. The Cleveland (West) chapter also had some members from middle-class neighborhoods but was made up primarily of working-class women. As predicted in the debates over the suburban system, the chapters did compete with each other for credit in organizing events, publicity, and members, and that history of competition moved one Cleveland president to write in a newsletter article:

> I extend my hand in friendship and co-operation to the members of Cleveland East. I'm hoping . . . that we can forget the past and join together; after all, we're all work[ing] for the same goals. (Feminist View, May 1981)

This competition was partially based in the members' different socio-economic backgrounds. However, the class-based competition was less visible during periods of high mobilization.

From 1989 to 1993, Cleveland's feminist community underwent a period of heavy mobilization during which the remaining two chapters merged. The merger eased the class divisions between the two chapters somewhat as they became involved in a series of local and national marches for abortion rights and began to work in coalition with each other and community organizations. With the city's abortion clinics targeted by Operation Rescue, Cleveland NOW members adopted a strategy that focused on community events. In their attempts to keep clinics open, Cleveland feminists joined in coalitions and responded in "crisis mode" (interview with Cleveland NOW activist, October 29, 1995). By August of 1990, the chapter was the largest in the state and reported an increase of one hundred new members joining primarily to work on reproductive rights. While the chapter participated in national campaigns, actions influenced by the local field were the ones that mobilized the chapter. For example, members became involved in a sexual harassment case brought by a local teacher and succeeded in getting the school board to settle her case. Members also held weekly demonstrations outside the office of an Ohio legislator and engaged in tactics such as street theater and spontaneous zap actions on a variety of issues. As a result of this mobilization, the chapter was able to move into its first office, located in a west-side women's center. One member began to hold C-R sessions for the chapter, and members formed a feminist reading group that continued to meet for a few years.

The more focused on local events the chapter became, the more members began to criticize and distance themselves from national NOW. In particular, members equated national NOW's emphasis on hierarchy and fund-raising with a lack of effective activism (interview with NOW activist, July 19, 1996). These ideas were promoted by a dynamic leader in the 1990s. Reflecting on the chapter's action under her direction, she noted:

The thing was—we had autonomy. We did pick and choose what we want[ed]. Yeah, we are going to follow this rule if we want to, if [National did not like it] too bad. Because that was what being feminist was all about. . . . We never did anything unethical or anything and we did our little record keeping and all that but I mean there were times when we were told what we could and could not do. . . . I think at one point we were even told that we were a little too activist sometimes. That made the folks [at the state level] uncomfortable. (interview with Cleveland activist, October 29, 1995)

Under this leader's guidance, Cleveland members began to equate a formalized organizational structure with patriarchy and the status quo. As a result, the chapter was quick to respond to community issues but had a difficult time maintaining an organizational structure. In addition, class divisions continued to plague the chapter. The chapter rotated meetings from one side of the city to the other, finally settling on a more central downtown location. Members from the eastern suburbs found the location too distant, however, and were not comfortable with the safety of the meeting location. Many members also were concerned with the location of the office, which was situated in one of Cleveland's poorer west-side neighborhoods.

By 1994, Cleveland NOW was struggling to stay alive. When the chapter's active and dynamic leader decided to step down, no one would assume leadership for the chapter. To reduce the president's duties, the chapter devised a steering committee structure that would rotate leadership every two months. The steering committee met a few times and finally ceased scheduling meetings. By 1995, the chapter had completely stopped meeting and planning activities.

For Cleveland NOW, the local field and chapter leadership contributed to a tumultuous history with multiple organizational adaptations, social class divisions among the membership, and fragmentation due to a lack of cohesive micro-cohorts. The chapter was able to mobilize around periods of crisis, but the focus on community over national issues distanced the chapter from national NOW and prevented it from taking advantage of national strategies that may have prevented the chapter's decline.

Bloomington NOW

In the small college town of Bloomington, Indiana, the opportunities were far different for feminist organizers than in the large cities. Founded in 1972, Bloomington NOW went through many ups and downs of mobilization, sometimes relying on local initiatives and at other times barely surviving with the help of national strategies. The chapter initially drew on a local constituency of women involved in the Democratic Party and in organizations such as the League of Women Voters. As in Chicago NOW, however, some members also had backgrounds in the protest movements of the 1960s, and there were initially a variety of ideas about what strategies NOW should pursue. As a local reporter described:

> One of the new groups to make the most impact last year [in 1972] was the local chapter of the National Organization for Women (NOW), which underwent a long period of growing pains to recently emerge as a viable and expanding organization. As an observer at one of the first organizational meetings this reporter could only wonder at the potential success of NOW. There were approximately 30 women present, with approximately 30 different ideas on which direction NOW should set itself. Through the following months several task forces were set up, which alternately petered out and developed with fluctuating membership. A small core of women, however, kept the group going through the summer, and it emerged in the fall with a charter, purpose and slate of officers dedicated to the feminist movement. (Larson 1972)

The main reason that NOW was able to prosper in the early 1970s was that passage of the ERA became a unifying goal for activists. Although national NOW's support for the ERA was certainly an impetus for chapter involvement on the issue, the national organization was not capable of providing much assistance to state campaigns in the early 1970s. It was the local political field, rather than the national organization, that provided support for Bloomington NOW's ERA campaign. The chapter was able to link up with the state NOW organization and other groups throughout the state, and this joint work helped to organize activists. For example, Bloomington NOW participated in a state meeting of groups working to support the ERA in Indianapolis in 1972 consisting of workshops and panels (*Courier-Tribune* 1972). The ERA Campaign provided the focus for a flurry of activity for the chapter, including letter writing, pamphleteering, petitioning, educational forums, and rallies. When the ERA was defeated in the state legislature in March 1973, the chapter lost momentum as the first round of intense campaigning for the amendment in Indiana came to an end. In the mid-1970s, however, Bloomington NOW again became involved in the state ERA Campaign as a result of the leadership of local activists involved in Democratic Party politics. Owing to the efforts of a statewide coalition that worked to elect Democrats pledged to support the ERA to the state legislature, the ERA passed in Indiana in 1977.

Bloomington NOW was never large or stable enough to develop a formalized organizational structure, such as that of New York City or Chicago NOW. The chapter worked best when it attracted unified micro-cohorts who found a sense of community in NOW and became engaged in issue campaigns. In the early 1970s, like-minded liberal Democrats worked through NOW in the ERA Campaign and also enjoyed the experience of meeting in small groups to share their excitement about the new feminist movement. In the mid-1970s, after a few years of reduced activity, another micro-cohort that included a number of Indiana University students enlivened the chapter with C-R groups and renewed activity in the state ERA Campaign. In the late 1970s and early 1980s, yet another micro-cohort, which included many lesbian feminists from the local community, was attracted to Bloomington NOW through the leadership of a dynamic president, the use once again of C-R groups to create internal community in the chapter, and participation in the national ERA Campaign. After the ERA Campaign ended in defeat in 1982, however, many members left Bloomington NOW, and the chapter found itself without a cohesive micro-cohort.[10] Although the chapter managed to stage some successful events from the mid-1980s to the 1990s, it never succeeded in attracting a solid micro-cohort and lacked a unifying issue campaign after the demise of the ERA.

Both the successes and difficulties involved in maintaining ongoing activity in Bloomington NOW had to do with the nature of the local field. On the one hand, Bloomington provided a community of potential activists, including "faculty wives" and other women active in organizations such as Planned Parenthood and the Democratic Party, lesbian feminists, and students. When issue campaigns were mounted, these constituents could be readily mobilized. On the other hand, there is always a great deal of turnover in a small college town, as students continually come and go, and professionals frequently move away in search of greater opportunities in larger cities. This feature of the local community made it very difficult for the NOW chapter to retain leaders and members for more than a few years.

In this context, connections to national NOW were important. During the struggle to pass the ERA in Indiana, the chapter's strategies came from interactions with other organizations in the local political field. After 1977, however, the chapter relied more heavily on nationally generated strategies and thrived or declined depending on local leadership and the appeal of issue campaigns. In the late 1970s and early 1980s, the chapter participated in the nationwide campaign orchestrated by national NOW, uniting around what was then the burning issue of passage of the ERA before the (extended) deadline was due to expire in 1982. After 1982, the chapter relied on a small core of activists and connections to national NOW to sustain itself. The national organization regularly provided its chapters with blueprints for strategies that sometimes resulted in successful events sponsored by Bloomington NOW, such as a 1984 news conference and rally to call attention to the consequences of Reagan economic policies for women and a 1986 "back alley vigil" in support of abortion rights. In addition to these ideas for action, the chapter received NOW literature to distribute, thereby lessening the burdens of local organizing. Moreover, chapter leaders attended state and national NOW conferences and reported on these to other members; this contact with larger feminist communities provided the local chapter with periodic infusions of energy. As long as Bloomington NOW had capable leaders willing to generate events, the chapter could maintain itself. After numerous leadership problems and failures to attract a cohesive membership, however, the chapter finally dissolved in the mid-1990s.

CONCLUSION

Our histories of four NOW chapters in different local fields demonstrate the various ways in which national level organization and local dynamics interact to maintain feminist mobilization and action campaigns. Local leadership and the nature of the local field affect chapter mobilization at least as much as national direction, and in some instances chapters contribute to national direction. It is no accident that our two largest chapters, New York and Chicago, are located in very large cities. Leaders in both chapters recognized that a more formalized and centralized organization would allow them to capitalize on the support available in their cities, and both chapters managed to distinguish themselves from other organizations in their local fields. Both chapters contributed leaders and strategies to national NOW early in its history, and both took advantage of national organizational forms and strategies. Both chapters achieved a balance between national directives and attention to local dynamics. Because of their size and organizational structure, cohesive micro-cohorts were probably less important to organizational maintenance than in smaller chapters.

Cleveland NOW and Bloomington NOW were less successful in making use of national resources while responding to local conditions. Cleveland NOW was faced with the difficulties of mobilizing in a class-divided and geographically dispersed city that lacked a vital downtown core, such as Manhattan, in which activists from both sides of the city could come together. The organization had difficulty attracting unified citywide micro-cohorts as a result. Cleveland NOW leaders saw the chapter as a community-based organization rather than a part of NOW's federated structure. Although the chapter did participate in some national campaigns, leaders generally rejected national direction and, as a result, failed to take advantage of many resources and strategy plans provided by national NOW.

Bloomington NOW also faced a difficult local field, characterized by a great deal of population turnover. During periods of peak mobilization, the chapter was able to take advantage of local constituencies, and the group attracted cohesive micro-cohorts at several different times. When energetic leaders took charge of the chapter, they were able to keep the chapter going by using national strategies, even in the absence of a united micro-cohort. However, the chapter was never large or stable enough to create the type of formalized structure that sustains the New York and Chicago chapters, and, in the absence of leadership, the chapter failed to maintain itself.

Despite the varying successes of our chapters, their stories indicate a positive role for federated organizations in maintaining the feminist movement. Whereas national organizations may drain scarce resources from poor people's movements, as Piven and Cloward (1977) argue, in a relatively resource-rich movement such as the American women's movement, a formalized, federated organization such as NOW helps to keep the movement mobilized. Local chapters and national level organization have been mutually beneficial in NOW. In the early 1970s, when the national organization was weak and divided, grassroots organizing kept NOW alive. In some local fields, such as New York or Chicago, chapters are capable of sustaining feminism without a great deal of national help, but they also benefit from national undertakings such as the ERA Campaign, particularly those with strong local connections. In times when local organizing is difficult, national resources and strategies can maintain a local chapter such as Bloomington NOW. However, local leaders are needed to take advantage of these opportunities. Formalized national organizations like NOW have played an important role in maintaining the U.S. women's movement, but opportunities present in local fields, together with local leadership, are also critical.

NOTES

1. In a study of Memphis NOW, Stephanie Gilmore (2001) also shows how the local culture and politics affect chapter actions.
2. However, some members claim that there is too much emphasis on abortion by organization leaders (see Barakso 2004).
3. The chapter, proud of its history, continues to promote itself as "NYC, the founding chapter of NOW" on all its stationery and in its newsletter mastheads.
4. Even after interest in feminism began to fade, the chapter continued to successfully use the media. The *New York Times, Wall Street Journal*, NBC, CBS, and *Good Morning America* covered the chapter's ten-year anniversary banquet in 1977 (NOW York Woman 1977).
5. It is difficult to get accurate membership figures for the New York City chapter in the early years. Part of the problem is that the chapter was referred to as the New York County, New York, and New York City chapters in state NOW records until 1977. The most accurate estimate of the chapter's size in the late 1960s is approximately 600 members in 1967. The next membership figure recorded is 606 members in 1977, which made the chapter the largest in New York State. (Series 2, Box 3, New York State NOW Records 1977–1978, Lists—Chapters, Delegates, Etc. 1976–1978, "List of State Chapters," February 16, 1977. From the Eugene P. Link Papers, Archives of Public Affairs and Policy, University of Albany, State University of New York.)
6. The 1974 national conference in Houston, Texas, saw a hotly contested power struggle between a New York candidate, Karen DeCrow, and a Chicago candidate, Mary Jean Collins-Robson. When the New York candidate won the presidency, she found herself in a power struggle with the other officers (Freeman 1975). In 1985, the

New York City chapter became embroiled in another controversy when members supported incumbent NOW president Judy Goldsmith over former president Eleanor Smeal. When Smeal won, relations with the national level were strained. Once again, in 1987, the chapter came up against other NOW leaders when it supported a New York City member's unsuccessful bid for the presidency against the powerful Smeal (NOW NYC News 1987).

7. Although the chapter was unable to afford paid staff in the 1990s, it did maintain some level of activity into the twenty-first century and reportedly had a very active year in 2000 (see "Our Year in Review," www.chicagonow.org, May 25, 2001).

8. For example, at the stormy national NOW conference in 1974, the Chicago chapter campaigned hard for four of its members running for national office and was accused of acting like a "machine" (Act NOW 1974).

9. Feminist organizing, in general, flourished in Cleveland in the early years of the movement. Carden (1974) notes that in 1969 only one Cleveland women's liberation group existed; a year later, the number had climbed to between ten and twelve groups.

10. Around the same time that the ERA deadline expired in 1982, there was an internal conflict in the chapter over the C-R groups. The chapter member who had done most of the organizing of the groups was a therapist who recognized that some of the women in the groups were in need of therapy rather than consciousness-raising. Consequently, she sent participants in the C-R groups a letter about a private therapy group that she was offering and that they might want to join (for a fee). Others in the chapter, including its president, were outraged by this solicitation of C-R group members. The result of the conflict was an end to the C-R groups in NOW. In addition to this problem, the chapter's dynamic president was forced to resign as a result of a terminal illness.

Part II

WOMEN'S MOVEMENTS IN COMPARATIVE PERSPECTIVE

7

Political Mobilization: African American Gendered Repertoires

Belinda Robnett

This chapter is particularly concerned with African American political cohesion and solidarity since the decline of the civil rights movement. I argue that the adherence to familiar African American gendered repertoires of political organization has contributed to a weakening of mobilization in the post-1960s era. A central concern of mine is, "Why, given the civil rights backlash in the 1990s, has there not been a Black social movement comparable in scope and scale to that of the 1950s–1960s civil rights movement?" While social movement scholars focus attention on movements that succeed or fail, short shrift has been paid to why it is that social movements don't begin. While admittedly this is a difficult, if not impossible, question to answer, it should not preclude us from attempting to gain insight into this problem. With few exceptions (see, e.g., Banaszak 1996a), we do not know why it is that groups do not take advantage of opportunities to protest. Most theories of political opportunity structures are based on post-hoc analyses of social movements. Consequently, there is a gap in the scholarly research that ignores "missed opportunities."

Numerous social movement scholars have traced the development of specific social movements, and many agree that while movements cannot succeed without resources, political opportunities are central to the development of such movements (e.g., McAdam 1982; Tilly 1978; Oberschall 1973; Oberschall and Kim 1996; Tarrow 1994; della Porta 1995; and the recent work of Johnston and Snow [1998] on Estonian Nationalist Opposition between 1945 and 1990).

Most recently, scholars such as Gamson and Meyer (1996) have begun to unpack the meaning of political opportunities by examining its treatment in various studies, and, in part, they conclude that what is most important to a social movement is how political opportunities are recognized and framed. Gamson and Meyer's macro-micro analysis points to the importance of subjective judgments of political opportunities. Moreover, both Elisabeth Clemens (1996) and Kim Voss (1996), in examining organizational models, connect these to political opportunities and structures. Clemens argues that if a movement wishes to successfully take advantage of a political opportunity, it must create an organizational form that will "fit" with the specific type of opportunity. Moreover, these forms must be developed out of culturally acceptable or familiar repertoires of organization. Banaszak's (1996a) analysis of the Swiss suffrage movement highlights the ways in which familiar values and beliefs can undermine collective identity, stifle tactical innovation, and, therefore, hinder the ability of groups to take advantage of political opportunities.

Similarly, this chapter questions the suitability of African American gendered repertoires of political mobilization, arguing that in the face of political opportunities to challenge civil rights backlash, gender divisiveness is a contributing factor in the failure of African Americans to mobilize. Most assuredly, others have attributed this failure to increased class stratification among African Americans, but this chapter argues that, although class provides a partial explanation, it does not explain all of the divisiveness.

POLITICAL OPPORTUNITIES

Commencing in the late 1970s, the federal government and courts have demonstrated a decreased commitment to programs aimed at remedying racial inequality in the United States. The Reagan administration ushered in an era of counterreforms bent on the destruction of civil rights legislation, which conservatives, and increasingly most of mainstream America, deemed either useless or too socialistic in nature. Several Supreme Court decisions contributed to the erosion of legal remedies. In 1978 the *Regents of the University of California v. Bakke* ruling held that racial quotas are unconstitutional. The court struck down set-aside plans for minority contractors[1] in 1980, after hearing arguments in *Fullilove v. Klutznick*. In the *Memphis Fire Department v. Stotts* decision in 1984, the justices ruled that seniority systems take precedence over affirmative action plans.[2] Similarly, in the *Wygant v. Jackson Board of Education* ruling in 1986, the court "emphasized that lawful affirmative action programs cannot require that incumbent white workers be discharged to make way for minority workers."[3] In 1995 the court, in *Adarand Constructors v. Pena*, issued a "'strict scrutiny' standard for proving race-based discrimination,'" which the ACLU deems "a ruling which critically undermines affirmative action."[4] The University of Texas School of Law's affirmative action program was ruled unconstitutional in 1996 in *Hopwood v. University of Texas School of Law*. According to the American Civil Liberties

Union (ACLU), Latino admissions dropped 64 percent and African American admissions dropped 88 percent in one year.[5] Equally damaging to minority college enrollment was the passage in 1997 of Proposition 209, which bars race-based admissions policies in the University of California system. A similar measure, I-200, passed in Washington State in 1998. Based on Governor Jeb Bush's Executive Order 99-281, in 1999 the state of Florida ended "affirmative action in state contracting and higher education."[6]

In sum, by the 1990s, programs such as affirmative action and laws to protect against racial discrimination were severely weakened. While it is true that the U.S. Supreme Court upheld affirmative action for universities in 2003 in *Gratz vs. Bollinger* and *Grutter v. Bollinger*, the mechanisms to ensure minority enrollment have been weakened. This ideological shift is due, at least in part, to the global economy characterized by a reduction in resources, including jobs, and the decline in real wages. With increased competition, many African Americans find themselves squeezed out of the game. Yet with all of these sweeping changes and the increased hostility toward egalitarian remedies, African Americans have not united to form a large-scale countermovement. This is neither to deny the resistance of local or issue-specific organizations nor to ignore Jesse Jackson's ongoing campaign, Louis Farrakhan's and the National Association for the Advancement of Colored People (NAACP)'s former president, Benjamin Chavis's, Million-Man March, the Million Woman March, or the Million Youth March. Rather, this chapter argues that the bifurcation of these marches by gender has contributed to our failure to successfully wage a movement comparable in scale to that of the civil rights movement.

Many social movement theorists would argue that this phenomenon is due to a lack of political opportunities and the absence of a charismatic leader and/or resources. Their view is that faced with a conservative court and Congress, a movement could not possibly succeed. Yet the election of former president William Clinton should have signaled a more favorable political shift in spite of his rather conservative stances. In point of fact, Clinton supported affirmative action programs, albeit with qualifications, even though he was responsible for sweeping welfare reform. Even given his mixed signals, one can certainly make the case that African Americans had no reason to be less optimistic than their counterparts of the 1940s and 1950s. In 1992, a record number of blacks won political office. The Congressional Black Caucus increased from twenty-six to forty members and become an even more powerful voting bloc. That same year, Carol Moseley Braun became the fourth African American to serve in the U.S. Senate. The first two served in the 1800s. Moreover, African Americans possess more financial resources and political power than they did at the start of the civil rights movement. While charismatic leaders don't develop overnight, the lack of such "a" leader in itself deserves attention.

Philosopher Cornel West, while not specifically addressing these issues, and sociologist William Julius Wilson would argue that increased class stratification within the African American community has created economic, social-psychological, and cultural barriers between the Black middle class and those below. Such an analysis, I argue, neglects many aspects of the declining cohesion of African Americans. While class is obviously a factor, pre-1960s solidarity has also been splintered by an increase in identity politics. The African American community now faces ideological clashes, which unlike those of the past are seemingly irreconcilable. Most assuredly, there has been the rise of conservatism among our small but significant Black elite, but gender relations have also affected our unity.

THE ROOT OF GENDER DIVISIVENESS

In the late 1960s, the apparent divisions between Black men and Black women can be marked with the acknowledgement by some members of the Student Nonviolent Coordinating Committee (SNCC), a civil rights movement organization, that sexism was a problem in the movement. With this understanding, founder Frances Beal and several other women in New York City initiated the Black Women's Liberation Committee of SNCC in 1968. Initially, this small group focused its efforts on Black women's multiple oppressions. These women felt that the Black movement did not address the specific needs of Black women. Over time, their analysis stretched beyond their specific needs as Black women to include a critique of Black male chauvinism as manifested in Black nationalism. In 1970, the organization grew beyond SNCC members to include all women, and they named their group the Black Women's Alliance. Later, they merged with other women of color into the Third World Women's Alliance. In the 1970 book *The Black Woman*, Gwen Patton, a co-organizer of these organizations, commented on sexism within the Black Power movement as contributing to the division of "potential revolutionaries"(1970, 146–47).

Equally critical of the new posture of Black male leaders were the contributors to *Black Women in White America*. Margaret Wright, a member of a Los Angeles women's liberation group, criticized Black men's perceptions of Black women as emasculators and oppressors (Wright 1970). Another feminist, Lorretta Ross, in *Theorizing Black Feminisms*, writes that Black feminists of the time were challenging Black nationalists' claims that birth control was "genocide" (Ross 1993).

Sexism within the Black Panther Party is also well documented in *A Taste of Power* by Elaine Brown, *Angela Davis: An Autobiography* by Angela Davis, and *Assata* by Assata Shakur. Brown writes that Black women in leadership were viewed as "counterrevolutionary, man-hating, lesbian, feminist white bitches" (1992, 357). Black women leaders were viewed as traitors to the race who undermined Black masculinity.

Many Black women activists felt that unless gender issues were articulated and redefined, divisions along gender lines would fracture the movement. Toni Cade Bambara (1970) was aware of the need for men and women to understand and confront sexism in the movement. In "Is the Black Male Castrated?" (1970) Jean Bond and Paticia Perry argue that the movement needed to create its own definitions of masculinity and femininity. Similarly, Shakur (1987) concluded that sexism erodes political solidarity between men and women.

Gender divisions have continued to fracture the movement, with the grassroots mobilized by women and national political representation dominated by Black male leaders and ministers. Previous Black mobilization rested upon an organizational repertoire in which Black women worked as bridge leaders (much as they did in the Black church), connecting the masses to the organizations led by nationally recognized male leaders. This was true of both the civil rights movement and the Black Power movement. The break in gender relations has created a disconnection between the grassroots and national-level leaders. Instead, women's leadership remains localized while Black national leaders attempt to mobilize from the top down. The essential mobilizing work of women bridge leaders remains largely unconnected to that of Black national leaders. (See Robnett 1996, 1997 for a discussion of the role of Black women as bridge leaders.)

THE STUDY

This study is part of a larger project that employs both macro-level and micro-level analyses. At the micro-level, I research the ideological differences among African Americans, arguing that identity politics and the politics of identity have splintered the "community." I argue for a more complex analysis of the position of African Americans, analyzing internal differences and increased internal stratification in the post-1960s realignment of the racial/ ethnic hierarchy in the United States. Sixty-five interviews have been conducted thus far. I plan to interview a total of one hundred individuals of Black African descent. They include the following subcategories: for nonimmigrant U.S. African Americans, and for both males and females, I interview individuals from the under class, working class, middle class, upper class, intellegentsia (i.e., Henry Louis Gates Jr., Cornel West, etc.), local activists and national level activists, gay/lesbian activists, and biracial and multiracial individuals. For individuals who are first- or second-generation immigrants of Black African descent, mainly from Africa or the Caribbean, I have interviewed with the same subcategories outlined for the nonimmigrant group. I analyze differences based on class, gender, sexual orientation, immigrant versus nonimmigrant status, activist versus nonactivist, and local versus national activist. I also analyze generational differences. With regard to class, I use self-identification, and I ask them about their education, job title, and residence. So, while class is a slippery concept, I am relatively certain of the interviewees' class assignments. Moreover, these interviews are representative of the four regions of the United States. The interviews consist of forty open-ended questions. Each interview takes approximately three hours. All interviewees are assured of anonymity. Also, included in my analysis is a cultural analysis of Black resistance and change that includes studying music, the media, and other cultural shifts that may now serve as alternatives to or additions to Black organizational and institutional forms such as the Black church and civil rights movement organizations.

Internal stratification, ideological rifts, and cultural shifts cannot be analyzed without an analysis of macro-level social-structural factors. My macro-level analyses include a social-historical analysis of ideologies that emerged during previous Black social movements, including the Black Power movement, the civil rights movement, and the Black women's liberation movement, and their continuity into the 1990s. These ideological antecedents may, in part, explain current political divides. In addition, I analyze the post-1960s political activities of local and national Black organizations. I also examine the political and legal opportunity structures of the 1970s through the 1990s.

THE FINDINGS

The issue of the applicability of African American gendered repertoires of political organization emerged during my interviews. Gender issues were raised across class and generational lines. The data indicate that class alone is not perceived as *the* central cause for divisions among African Americans. Nor do my findings suggest that class differences explain all of the variation in interviewee responses. None of the respondents indicated that this alone was the central problem regarding Black solidarity. While all agreed that Black cohesiveness has been severely weakened since the 1960s, fifty-five of the sixty-five interviewees pointed to a breakdown of family and gender relations as key to the weakening of African American collective identity. Class was only significant with regard to their analysis of post-1960s integration patterns that many argued depleted the community of professional resources.

All but one interviewee believes that the Black middle class is a part of the community and that most are not "sell-outs." For example, a forty-six-year-old working-class male from South Central Los Angeles stated:

I can't understand speaking in terms of upper-class African Americans or Blacks or whatever I mean, you're Black, if you're African American you're African American. You [sic] definitely been oppressed for a long time and you'll continue to be oppressed until some type of changes, whatever in the laws, you know, these are some of the differences I see on the national front and personal front too, you know. You're Black first of all, you're African-American and regardless of whatever height you ascend to you'll never be considered the good half, the ruling body in America, okay?

This response was typical, with all of the interviewees agreeing that the Black middle class is very much a part of the African American community. However, all pointed to the post-1960s breakdown of the Black community, particularly the Black family and gender relationships. What was especially surprising about the responses was the level of conservatism among the interviewees given that forty-six of the sixty-five grew up and/or remained in predominantly Black communities. Only eight of the twenty-nine working-class interviewees, and eleven of the thirty-six middle-class interviewees, grew up in integrated communities. Of the sixty-five interviewees only eight, the eight who did not name the breakdown of the Black family and gender relations as the most pressing problem in the Black community, connected the ills of the Black family and gender relationships to unemployment and racism. These eight were three working-class women, one working-class man, two middle-class women, and two middle-class men. The other fifty-seven based many of the ills of the community on a breakdown of morals and values corresponding to a breakdown in family cohesion and gender relations. For example, when asked, "Do you believe that the cohesiveness of the Black community has changed over the last thirty years? If so, how and why?" the forty-six-year-old working-class man from South Central Los Angeles replied:

Yes, that's a very good, very interesting question, the cohesiveness of the Black community. Of course it has. There's more interplay and more struggle going on in our community amongst ourselves. Gang rivalries, you know, people wanting safe and secure streets and got young idiots, that's what they are, thinking that this is family. Family is where you come from. Family is mother and father first of all. And I think they'd better get back to what really the family is because that's just not family that gang. Over the last thirty, oh it's changed dramatically. I mean shoot. Something that I haven't seen in the last twenty years, teenagers or youngsters getting any discipline. No discipline in the home, that's what's uprooting and changing the way Black families and Black communities are. No discipline. Why do I think it happened? Well a number of reasons. You start having more children having children since the mid to late-'60s. I mean you lost your moral identity and you have no values or anything.

One fifty-three-year-old middle-class man from a segregated Midwestern city connected government policies to the destruction of the Black community, but in doing so, he discussed the development of moral breakdown as a by-product of the loss of strong families:

> The policy was set up not to support people remaining in the family unit. I think that they exchanged one form of slavery for another when they took that spoon called welfare. I think that it's just as addicting as any heroin or crack or any of that stuff. I think that it really destroys the fabric of the community and the spirit of the people that has that perseverance and that ability to be resourceful.

The eight who disagreed with the "breakdown of morals and values thesis" centered their analyses of the ills of the Black community on the history of slavery, the legacy of assaults on Black families' structure, and economic inequality. For example, a forty-eight-year-old self-described Pan-Africanist, lumpen proletariat, urban peasant from South Central Los Angeles stated:

> I think compared to some kind of non-existent ideal that I don't know who came up with all that ole "stable Black family." That was never known. Look, you couldn't get married when you were a slave, somebody gave you up. You get people talking about the breakup of the Black family, I mean from what? There wasn't no Father Knows Best. You never had no long period of time where all the Black men, 90 percent of them got married and all that, stayed married. Besides institutions like marriage are organized around economic structures. Marriage in America period, there's a big divorce rate period. I mean marriages are breaking up because of the way the society's organized, because of employment. It's because of the way things are organized economically and politically.

It is difficult to discern why few of the interviewees connected economic and structural antecedents to the current state of the Black family. Of course, this could be a result of the small subsample, or perhaps it can be explained by careful analysis of the post-1960s conservative political and media campaigns around issues of family values and morality, with the Black female portrayed as the quintessential "welfare queen" and Black males as violent criminals, as in former president George Bush's use of Willie Horton in campaign speeches.[7]

Several of my interviewees offered more detailed analyses of their conservative stances. Some discussed the loss of self-esteem and self-respect within the Black community and, surprisingly, connected this to the post-1960s shift in the expectations of Black women.

The forty-six-year-old man from South Central Los Angeles believes that the Black Power movement was positive but may have hurt the identities of Black women. He elaborates his feelings:

> The slogan say it loud, "I'm Black and I'm proud." You know, that was a positive message but it did not come across to some as well as it did others. And I really see where it could have hurt Black women's identities because they

should have been the proudest. They're the mothers. You know? It shouldn't have hurt their identities at all. I mean, I know they went through a monumental struggle on their own. Women in general, not just Black women, but women in general. But it shouldn't hurt their identities at all, because, it should make them proudest.

And the fifty-three-year-old working-class man from a segregated Midwestern town elaborated on this theme:

I know that the out of wedlock birthrate is higher than it's ever been or was. So that can be said to be a direct result of the [Black Power movement]. I think that there were certain pressures that were put on African women at the time to conform to certain ideals of what, maybe Black males thought they ought to be. What comes to mind is when I look at the experience of the American Muslim movement here, Farrakhan and all that, that women were placed in a very rigid perspective: that they should be supportive and submissive and all that and I'm not so sure that what we didn't get out of that demand placed on Black women was the backlash that was that "I'm gonna be free Black and Proud." You know that movie *Waiting to Exhale*, I think that movie sort of epitomizes that. And I think that was to the detriment of Black women and I think that they are still reeling from that and that is part of all of this rap thing where they're denigrating Black women and all that. I think that now what we're seeing is the fallout from that very structured way of being that was imposed upon them by the Black Power movement.

He believed that this fallout, in conjunction with the development of welfare programs, has actively disrupted the family unit and led to the disintegration of the Black family. This as well as racial integration, he argued, contributes to the lack of solidarity of the Black community. He continued:

The whole social fabric falling apart actually goes back to integration and then I think it was exacerbated by the Black Power Movement and the demands that were placed on women at that time to be loyal and you know "You have to be with your Black man no matter what!" And staying with him and all that. And then the Black man saw that there was no future in Black Power because there's no base for that and if they begin to fall off and look for other things, I think that Black women were left with nothing.

While some of my interviewees connected the Black nationalists' definition of Black women's place to some of our current ills, others suggested that it was feminism and Black women's failures to meet men's needs that contributed to the problems. The forty-eight-year-old working-class, self-defined Pan-Africanist, lumpen proletariat, urban peasant from South Central Los Angeles believed that Black Power

helped the hell out of Black women, helped the hell out of Black wounds. Black women who be talking about feminism need to check their recent history out.

You don't know how bad Black women had it before the movement. Boy they had it bad. You think they got it bad now, you hear these people talking about calling Black women hos and bitches. . . . Black women back then would have hoped that they had it as good. You know the man in charge was supposed to keep the Black man and the white woman apart. This was the threat to him. He wasn't thinking about no Black woman. Black woman was trash. Black woman, that's your maid. You can do what you want to her, that's your maid. . . . If you got white folks at the top and Black people at the bottom, Black women was at the bottom of the bottom, and Black women in bathing suits and all that, papa talking about "she's the finest thing in the world." She wouldn't have been do-ing that. [Back then] cat say, "I don't want nothing black but a Cadillac." The feminist movement wasn't nothing but a whole lot of bullshit. . . . Some of them Black women feminists better check out what the Black movement did for Black women period in terms of them giving them enough confidence and enough recognition among everybody to take any kind of other step.

A fifty-year-old working-class woman from South Central Los Angeles who did not view male chauvinism as a central problem in the community re-marked:

I think that Black women do not speak highly enough of Black men. [They] are not giving Black men enough consideration. It's as if we, we think that we can out-think them or out-smart them or we're smarter than they are. I don't see it as a problem with the Black man, I see it as something missing with us. I think that Black women push to the point of being angry and mad. I went through it when I was working. If I hadn't believed in the Bible I think that I probably would have been, quote/unquote a bitch. Because I think a lot of us act like bitches and it's because of sometimes external forces. It's not necessarily "I wanna be angry [but] something's driving me, aggravating me, pushing me" to the point where you act a certain way and it's something that guys may not be attracted to.

She further suggested that Black women ought to understand what Black men are going through and that "Black women can help Black men under-stand what's going on if we just sit back and not bitch."

Half of my respondents, however, felt that Black men no longer respected Black women. For example, a twenty-one-year-old middle-class man from a northern California inner city elaborated these feelings:

Sometimes I don't think the Black male respects the Black female. You know, you've got the hos, the bitches, stuff like that and it's like, man. It's like it's one phrase you learn when you're young, you know. Would you say that about your mom? You know? I think it starts right there, that mind-state. Ho, bitch, or whatever. Then you get in that mind-state and then you're with your Black woman and you have that mind-state. You know it's not going to work out. It's really not.

The fifty-three-year-old interviewee from the Midwest who earlier characterized Black nationalists' demands on women to be submissive as having
contributed negatively to Black women's identities further attributed much
of the downfall of the Black community to the sexism of the Black Power
movement. He suggested that

> before [Black Women] were the pillars of the community, they were the one
> who basically upheld all that. But when all of that went away and the status as-
> sociated with being a teacher in the Black community, involved in the Black
> church and all of that—when all that went away, you know the status among
> Black women, their self-esteem was affected. And it seems, watching during
> that time, I feel they were more victims in a lot of that. Maybe greater victims in
> a different way, let me put it that way, they were victims in a different way than
> the Black men.

Much like all groups in America, the gender divide has increased since the
1960s, yet the impact on African Americans has had detrimental effects on
political forms of organization and mobilization. The legacy of Black gendered repertoires has increasingly bifurcated political solidarity.

GENDERED COLLECTIVE ACTION IN THE POST-1960S ERA

Interestingly, the Million Man and Million Woman Marches are the most large-
scale organized collectivities of African Americans since the 1970s, yet these
marches are largely gendered. Each drew an estimated attendance of close
to one million participants. The tone and organization of the marches were
distinct, with men and women organizing much as they did during the civil
rights era, but this time separately. This bifurcation in organization includes
high-profile men organizing nationally and local women organizing at the
grassroots. Such gendered organizing mirrors the activities of men and
women during the civil rights movement, as I have argued elsewhere (Robnett 1996, 1997).

The Million Man March, which was held in Washington, D.C., on October
16, 1995, caused an enormous amount of controversy among African Americans, not only because it was initiated by Louis Farrakhan, the controversial,
anti-Semitic leader of the Nation of Islam, but also because women were
asked not to attend. Instead, they were to remain at home, pray, and teach
their children family values.

The rally drew few women, although the famous poet Maya Angelou, the
mother of the civil rights movement, Rosa Parks, and longtime civil rights activist Dorothy Height were among the honored guest speakers. The platform
participants were largely composed of national level Black male leaders, including co-organizer and former executive director for the NAACP Benjamin

Chavis, elected chairman of the Congressional Black Caucus Representative Donald Payne, Reverend Jesse Jackson, Reverend Al Sharpton, philosopher Cornell West, and Martin Luther King III. In addition to the aforementioned representatives and ministers, a total of thirty-one ministers and reverends constituted the leadership as well as former mayor Marion Barry, former congressman Gus Savage, and Congressman Kweisi Mfume. Several longtime civil rights movement activists, such as Reverend Wyatt T. Walker, Reverend James Lowery, and Reverend James Bevel, all of whom worked with Dr. Martin Luther King Jr. and the Southern Christian Leadership Conference, were also present.[8] In addition, many celebrities, including rapper M. C. Hammer, singer Stevie Wonder, and comedian Dick Gregory, addressed the crowd.

Conversely, the October 25, 1997, Million Woman March, held in Philadelphia, with attendance rivaling that of the Million Man March, included few big names. Winnie Madikizela-Mandela, the former wife of South African President Nelson Mandela, Congresswoman Maxine Waters, Congressman John Conyers, Philadelphia Mayor Edward Rendell, singer Sister Soulja, and Julia Wright, daughter of the deceased famous author Richard Wright, comprised the few high-profile speakers. Though invited, Coretta Scott King, widow of Martin Luther King Jr., and Rosa Parks declined to attend. Co-founders of the march Asia Coney, a housing activist, and Phile Chionesu, a local businesswoman, shook up the status quo by ignoring conventional methods of march organization. They did not work through the traditional high-profile civil rights groups, the NAACP, Southern Christian Leadership Conference, the Nation of Islam, or labor unions. This was, in fact, the first large-scale African American mobilization not organized through male-dominated, national organizations. Instead, they organized at the grassroots by printing flyers, posting the march on the Internet, and relying on community leaders to get the word out.[9] That such efforts could result in such mass attendance is a testament to the need to consolidate mobilization efforts.

The theme of the Million Man March undoubtedly resonated with many African Americans. The message was one of atonement and a return to family values, personal responsibility, and high moral standards of behavior. While this theme was also present at the Million Woman March, twelve platform issues included a focus on the eradication of drug trafficking, the development of Black independent schools, an increase in health facilities, professional development for Black women, intervention in human rights violations against those of African descent, an increase in housing, greater care for the elderly, and enrichment sites for youth.[10] Congresswoman Waters stated that Black women had no need to atone but instead should use their power to counter negative public policy and other societal ills.[11]

In contrast, the Million Man March program "made no mention of the destructive role played by poverty, unemployment and discrimination. Nor did it make a single demand on the government against racism, police brutality or massive Republican cutbacks."[12] That the platforms diverged in such a way is important because it highlights the detrimental effects of the gender divide on Black mobilization. The Million Woman March clearly reflected the day-to-day experiences of many African Americans and situated the crisis within the context of political mobilization rather than personal atonement.

Many Black scholars and writers, including Michael Dyson, June Jordan, and Julianne Malveaux, were disturbed by the exclusion of women from the Million Man March. Black journalist Julianne Malveaux expressed dismay over the support offered by many Black feminists and activists (Malveaux 1995). Malveaux explained that the message that women should stay at home fails to capture the historical reality of African American women's participation in leadership. She acutely pointed out, "The African-American community can't build much momentum from the imperfect vehicle of an exclusionary march" (Malveaux 1995).

Black writer and scholar Michael Dyson, who attended the march in spite of the objections of his Black women friends, noted that the march should have more adequately highlighted community problems, including "drugs, homicide, gang violence [that] dramatically affect the health and character of their communities" (Dyson 1995). The lack of connection to the grassroots was affirmed by many of my interviewees. For example, one nineteen-year-old working-class woman from a southern California suburb noted:

> The Million Man March was an historical event. You know, it was good to see a whole bunch of Black men getting together. But I mean, how many people, I mean most of the people that were involved were those that already had something going for them, you know? They didn't take the drug dealers and the gang-bangers. At the march, I mean maybe it inspired them but what did it actually do for the, you know. It was good to see Black men rallying together but what still was happening? Nothing really.

When asked what she thought the message was for women, she responded:

> It was inspiring to see Black men together but as for women, I mean I really didn't see a message. How many women did you actually see at the Million Man March? I mean I think it should have been incorporated for everyone because the Black men aren't the only ones in the struggle. There were some Black women in the past who led. It's been Black women pushing Black men to get something done.

Many of the interviewees felt similarly, indicating that it would be much better to have a two million Black person march to show solidarity. It is clear that gender divisions among African Americans began to emerge in the late 1960s and continue to play a significant role in identity politics today.

Whether or not African Americans identify a lack of sufficient attention to sexism in the community or focus on the ways in which Black feminists are misguided, the politics of gender shakes the foundation upon which political solidarity is forged.

CONCLUSION

In the face of political opportunities to protest, African Americans in the post-1960s era have found it difficult to mobilize. This chapter argues that familiar and culturally acceptable gendered repertoires of political organization have impeded African American mobilization. It is precisely the attempt by Black leaders, both male and female, to use 1960s forms of organization that has led to the lack of political cohesion between Black men and Black women, as demonstrated by the Million Man March and the Million Woman March. Clearly the organizational repertoire of religious Black men as the formal and visible leaders of the movement, as supported by women serving as grassroots leadership, is still in place. But this familiar and acceptable model has failed to achieve the type of mass mobilization needed to address current problems, and it is dangerously divisive. This chapter examined the leaders and keynote speakers of the Million Man March and the Million Woman March, and it is clear that the former consisted primarily of national leadership and the latter of grassroots local leaders.

As I have argued elsewhere, women in the civil rights movement provided a form of leadership that bridged the masses to the movement. Much of women's leadership is now further marginalized. Few of my interviewees had even heard of the Million Woman Marches. Media coverage was weak, and the goal of that movement was unclear to my interviewees. Moreover, and perhaps even more troubling, while political mobilization is occurring at the grassroots level, national level leadership appears to be almost exclusively guided by a moral mandate, as evidenced by the call for atonement at the Million Man March. In addition to conservative political and media campaigns focused on morality and family forms that never existed, a similar focus by national level Black religious leaders may explain the conservative responses of my interviewees.

Unfortunately, grassroots level activism appears to be quite separate from national level leadership. Rather than extending the organizational repertoire to include women's leadership in national level organizing, women largely mobilize the grassroots. Unlike the women of both the civil rights movement and the Black Power movement, they are now splintered from the top echelon of leadership. Thus far unable to develop new and more effective models, African American leaders are rendered ineffectual by an adherence to familiar cultural and political repertoires of organization.

NOTES

1. Joseph Cordero, "Major U.S. Court Cases," *Institutional Diversity & Equal Opportunity, CSUSM,* September 4, 1997, at www.csusm.edu/affirm_action/court.htm (accessed December 10, 2003).

2. Cordero. "Major U.S. Court Cases."

3. The Civil Rights Coalition for the 21st Century, *Affirmative Action Court Decision of the Supreme Court,* 2002, at www.civilrights.org (accessed December 10, 2003).

4. *ACLU Position Paper: Affirmative Action,* n.d., at www.aclu.org (accessed December 10, 2003).

5. *ACLU Position Paper: Affirmative Action.*

6. *ACLU Position Paper: Affirmative Action.*

7. When Willie Horton, a convicted murderer, was released on a weekend prison pass, he entered a home in an affluent community, shot a man, and raped his girlfriend. Bush used this case to confirm his commitment to a "safe America," that is, a white America safe from Black male criminals.

8. CNN at www.CNN.com/US/9510/megamarch/whowasthere.html.

9. Cynthia Tornquist, The Associated Press, and Reuters, "Million Woman March Seen as Step Toward Unity," October 25, 1997, atwww.cnn2.com/US/9710/25/million.woman.march/index.html (accessed December 16, 2003); and "Women Gather for Show of Unity," October 24, 1997, at www.cnn.com/US/9710/24/million.women .march/index.html (accessed December 16, 2003).

10. *Million Woman March Platform Issues,* October 25, 1997, at members.aol .com/lilbitz/platform.htm (accessed December 12, 2003).

11. *"The Million Woman March—10.25.97,"* *The Philadelphia Inquirer,* November 5, 1997, at www.mwmsisters.com/themarch.html (accessed December 12, 2003).

12. Sharon Smith, "On the Road Again," *Socialist Review* 191 (1995), at pubs .socialistreviewindex.org.uk/sr/sr191/smith.htm (accessed December 10, 2003).

8

Gendered Opportunities: The Formation of Women's Movements in the United States and Chile

Lisa Baldez and Celeste Montoya Kirk

In many countries, women's movements have developed in three phases: a first wave movement centered on the demand for suffrage, a period of relative quiescence, then a second wave women's movement focused on women's equality. According to conventional historiography, first wave feminism in the United States began with the Seneca Falls Convention in 1848 and ended with the Nineteenth Amendment in 1920. The first wave was followed by a period characterized by conflict and division among women's groups, primarily regarding the Equal Rights Amendment (ERA) (Costain 1992; Harrison 1988). Women did not altogether retreat from public life during this period, which lasted from 1920 to the 1960s, but relative quiescence among women's organizations prompted Leila Rupp and Verta Taylor (1987) to refer to it as "the doldrums." The second wave feminist movement began in the 1960s. While it still exists today, it has been supplanted by myriad feminisms (plural) that focus on particular constituencies among women, such as women of color, disabled women, and transgendered people—feminism's "third wave" (see Whittier chapter 3).

A similar pattern characterizes women's mobilization in many other countries. In Chile, for example, the first wave movement began when women organized around the right to vote in the late 1800s and ended just after women won full voting rights in 1949. Next came a period characterized by a dearth of mobilization by women. After women won the right to vote, the women's movement became "atomized" and "submerged" within political parties. Women participated more frequently in "women's divisions" created to address their concerns within political parties than in independent women's organizations. Chilean scholar Julieta Kirkwood coined the phrase "the feminist silence" for this period (Kirkwood 1986). The second wave women's movement began in the 1970s, as women mobilized in opposition to the military government of General Augusto Pinochet. In Chile, as in other Latin American countries, women mobilized primarily against human rights abuses, poverty, and sexism. Since the return to democratic rule in 1989, many new forms of feminist activism have emerged in Chile, ranging from women's studies programs, to feminist radio stations, to reproductive health networks, to informal collectives among poor women.

The historical context in which women's movements emerged in these two countries differed dramatically. In the United States, feminism emerged during a period of economic expansion in a stable democratic system. In Chile, feminism emerged during an acute economic crisis in the midst of a brutal military dictatorship. Yet women's movements in both countries (and many others as well) shared certain patterns in common. They experienced an initial period of activism centered on the right to vote, followed by a period of low activity and lack of common agenda, and then a resurgence of autonomous mobilization around a common set of concerns. A similar cycle of mobilization among women's movements in different countries signals the possibility that women mobilize in response to common causal factors. This pattern raises the following question: What are the conditions that trigger the mobilization of women as women, on the basis of their gender identity?

THEORETICAL APPROACH

Existing literature identifies three theoretical approaches to explaining social movement origins: resource mobilization, political opportunities, and ideational factors (see Banaszak chapter 1). According to the resource mobilization perspective, movements emerge as a function of individual decisions about the costs and benefits of collective action—or as the result of material resources brought to bear on organizing (McCarthy and Zald 1973; Olson 1965; Zald and McCarthy 1987). The political opportunities approach maintains that movements rise and fall in response to changes in the external environment, particularly within the political arena (Gelb 1989; Kitschelt 1986; McAdam 1982; Tarrow 1994; Tilly 1978). Analyses of ideational factors highlight the role that ideas, beliefs, culture, and discourse play in shaping collective action; they focus on the way in which activists perceive their status and convey their concerns to the public (Banaszak 1996a; Gamson and Meyer 1996; Snow 1992; Snow and Benford 1988). We concur with what McAdam, McCarthy, and Zald (1996, 2) have identified as the "emerging consensus among movement scholars regarding the importance of these three factors" for explaining mobilization and contentious action. Our analysis here focuses on the relationship among them. We seek to explain how these three factors—resources, opportunities, and framing—relate to one another, in causal terms.

Our argument presumes that an organizational network already exists, and maintains that new political opportunities shape the way in which activists frame their arguments. Like Jo Freeman's analysis of the origins of the women's liberation movement in the United States (chapter 2), we consider a preexisting communications network to be a necessary condition for the formation of a movement. In both Chile and the United States, women participated in many different kinds of organizations well before a "women's movement" could be said to exist. In Chile, arguably the most highly mobilized period in the country's history occurred just prior to the coup in 1973; women participated extensively in political parties (across the political spectrum), student groups, and neighborhood organizations. In the United States, women participated in the Democratic and Republican Parties, civil rights groups, and labor unions. Many women's groups existed, but they pursued a diverse array of objectives. In both cases, the way in which women envisioned their agenda changed dramatically following a change in political context. Women participated in civil society for many decades but pursued divergent goals determined in large part by their alliances with different, nongender-specific, groups. A change in political opportunities *expanded* the number of organizations that existed and attracted new activists—but an organizational infrastructure was well in place before political opportunities changed.

We build upon the arguments that Freeman and others have made to articulate the specific nature of the conditions that catalyze existing organizations into a unified movement. In both cases, there are two relevant changes in political opportunities that prompt women in various organizations to overcome their differences and forge a common agenda. First, a change in the general political context heightens the salience of gender differences, and second, a failure of women's male colleagues to take action to resolve a pressing problem moves women to take action themselves. The first change leads to the evolution of a new rhetorical framework by which to understand women's situation and articulate a new set of demands. In each case, the development of a new way to frame women's issues facilitated coalition building among groups with previously distinct, even conflicting, agendas. In Chile, political repression and economic recession at the hands of the military affected women and men in different ways, forcing men out of the public arena and pushing women into it. The politicization of women's traditional concerns, centered on home and family, provided the impetus for reframing that became a powerful tool against the dictatorship. In the United States, the Presidential Commission on the Status of Women (PCSW) created by President Kennedy provided a venue that facilitated dialogue among groups with conflicting visions of women's goals. It allowed women to frame their concerns in terms of equality, but in a way that was free from the dissension caused by the way equality was understood in the ERA.

The second relevant change in political opportunities is the "precipitant" (Freeman's term, see p. 28, this volume) that prompts women to take action. In both cases, the failure of women's male colleagues to act on women's concerns prompted women to take matters into their own hands. In Chile, the failure of the male-dominated political parties to agree on a unified strategy to defeat the military regime compelled women to unite both to provide an example of what needed to be done and to articulate a set of specific demands. In the United States, the failure of the Equal Employment Opportunities Commission (EEOC) to enforce Title VII of the Civil Rights Act (banning sex discrimination in employment) motivated women to form the National Organization for Women (NOW) to demand government accountability to women.

In the sections that follow, we provide an extensive analysis of the emergence of the women's movement in Chile, followed by a more concise analysis of the U.S. case as the basis for comparison. We treat the U.S. case more briefly on the assumption that readers will be more familiar with it than the Chilean case.

CHILE

September 11 is a day of somber remembrance for many Chileans—but not because of the events of 2001. September 11 is the anniversary of the 1973 coup in Chile, the day that a military junta seized power from President Salvador Allende. Allende had been elected three years earlier on the promise to pursue a "peaceful road to socialism" within the framework of Chile's long-standing democratic institutions. His government nationalized private industry in order to redistribute profits to the poor—but his policies unleashed economic chaos and sparked trenchant political opposition. The opposition further destabilized the government by blocking legislation and organizing massive strikes and demonstrations, supported and generously funded by the U.S. government. When military planes bombed the presidential palace the morning of September 11, it put an end to a spiral of political violence—and to Allende's life.

The coup had catastrophic effects on Allende's supporters, but many other Chileans welcomed it. Allende's opponents envisioned the coup as a temporary means of ending the chaos that, for many reasons, had taken hold of Chile during the Allende administration. But it soon became clear that the military junta, led by General Augusto Pinochet, meant to stay in power in order to rebuild the fundamental structure of Chilean society by means of severe repression. The military did not simply restore order and step down; instead, it governed Chile for the next sixteen years, until 1989. The Pinochet government carried out its plans primarily by means of political repression and economic restructuring. The military arrested tens of thousands of people, many of whom were tortured or killed or "disappeared" without any record of their whereabouts. The junta closed congress, banned political parties, and severely restricted civil liberties. The new regime implemented stringent neoliberal economic reforms, fired more than a hundred thousand people from their jobs for political reasons, and replaced university faculty with military personnel. Chileans faced high unemployment and increases in the cost of living. A climate of intense fear pervaded the country.

These measures had gendered effects. The military aimed its fiercest repression at the male-dominated arenas of political life: political parties and labor unions. Most of the people who were detained, tortured, or killed or who disappeared were men. Of the 2,279 disappeared persons identified in the government's official report on human rights violations, 94.5 percent were men (República de Chile 1991). The military subjected men and women alike to severe, sexually violent torture and rape (Bunster 1993), but men constituted a far greater percentage of the regime's victims than women. Soldiers inflicted humiliating and violent punishments upon the bodies of their victims; they assaulted detainees with verbal and physical abuse and applied electric prods to their sexual organs.

The gendered nature of repression created a political vacuum that women slowly began to fill. The change in regime provided a political opportunity for women to organize autonomously from men. As Sonia Alvarez (1990) found in her analysis of the Brazilian women's movement, banning the parties created a space in which new forms of mobilization could emerge by restricting the possibilities for men to move within that space. In retrospect, it is possible to argue that the policies pursued by the military government prompted a surprising unintended consequence: the mobilization of women.

In Chile, as in other Latin American countries living under military rule, women mobilized along three main trajectories: human rights, poverty, and feminism (Chuchryk 1994; Frohmann and Valdés 1995). The female relatives of people who had disappeared formed networks to collect information on their loved ones, to press for writs of *habeas corpus,* and to publicize cases of human rights violations, as well as to provide support for one another. Poor and working-class women, primarily in the shantytowns that ringed the city of Santiago, organized to provide food and shelter for their communities in the face of economic crisis. University-educated women, many of whom had been active in leftist politics prior to the coup, organized to challenge patriarchal norms and practices that became particularly acute in the context of dictatorship. Women also reacted against the perversely sexualized nature of torture; female political prisoners who were released from detention began to discuss what had happened to them, and this opened the space for discussion of, and action against, domestic violence.

While women made up the majority of activists in human rights groups, economic survival networks, and feminist study circles, they did not immediately perceive themselves to be part of a broader women's movement. Awareness of a common agenda began to emerge as the result of contact with the growing international feminist movement. This contact was another consequence of the military regime. Women learned the new language of feminism from living in exile and from participating in international organizations that sought to depose the regime. These experiences introduced new ideas into Chilean culture and allowed women to understand their situation in a new way. They also helped women to establish distance between themselves and the culture the military instilled in Chilean society. Awareness of feminism helped women conquer the climate of fear and articulate a new, positive vision of democratic politics and society.

Many women began to learn about feminism while in exile. Hundreds of thousands of Chileans went into exile during the sixteen years of the military government. They fled to avoid being arrested or left to find better opportunities abroad. For many women, living in exile required them to bear the full responsibility for household chores and child rearing for the first time in their lives (Kay 1987). In Chile, many middle-class families had taken their reliance on domestic servants for granted; in exile, in the compromised economic circumstances that many encountered, having a maid became a luxury that few could afford. The experience forced women to confront firsthand the oppression of women in the domestic sphere. Feminist movements then brewing in the West, especially in countries with active feminist movements, such as Sweden, Canada, Austria, West Germany, and the United States, gave Chilean women a language with which to interpret their experiences. Women who returned to Chile after spending time in exile brought back ideas about feminism with them.

Ideas about feminism were not entirely new to Chile; media sources from the period indicate awareness of women's liberation movements in other countries. Prior to the 1980s, however, Chileans tended to view feminism either as radical man-hating that violated traditional gender norms or bourgeois false consciousness that betrayed the prospects for socialist revolution. Living in exile provided some Chilean women with a different context in which to interpret feminist ideas. Feminism gave these women a language to make sense of their experiences and showed them the value of identifying with women as women in a way that transcended national boundaries and national identity. Chilean women did not accept foreign ideas about feminism uncritically, but rather forged uniquely Chilean interpretations through a process of discussion and reflection.

Chilean sociologist Julieta Kirkwood played a critical role in the process of "translating" feminist ideas through her writings and many workshops that she conducted in Chile. Under dictatorship, Kirkwood maintained, women found themselves "face-to-face with a well-known phenomenon: authoritarian culture is their daily experience" (Kirkwood 1986, 186). Female activists began to frame their demands for an end to military rule in feminist terms, linking the struggle against *machismo* to the struggle for democracy. They drew an analogy between military authoritarianism and dominant patterns of behavior within Chilean families and Chilean society. This analogy became the basis for the slogan "democracy in the nation and in the home."

Participation in international organizations, and in domestic organizations funded from abroad, provided a relatively safe space in which women could gather. The United Nations Conference on Women in Mexico City in 1975 set this process in motion. Within this community, female academics began to conduct research on the status of women. Academic research on the status of women, such as studies published by the Center for Women's Studies (CEM), documented systematic patterns of discrimination against women and made it easier to refute the then-predominant sense in Chilean culture that women did not face inequality. Studies such as *World of Women: Change and Continuity*, published by CEM, raised awareness of women's subordination and helped to build support for the movement (Centro de Estudios de la Mujer 1988). Participation in regional and international conferences strengthened the incipient movement and provided a space for the further articulation of autochthonous understandings of feminism (Alvarez et al. 2002; Sternbach et al. 1992). These factors contributed to a growing awareness that the problems women faced in Chile were shared by women in other countries and other contexts elsewhere in the world.

During the first ten years of the dictatorship, women's mobilization remained relatively isolated and small scale, primarily due to fear of repression. Many groups, particularly human rights organizations, did not mobilize on the basis of gender identity despite the predominance of women as leaders and members; they did not identify themselves as women's organizations, but rather as human rights groups. Among those who did mobilize as women, cross-cutting interests prevented the formation of a united front. Conflicts proved particularly acute between organizations of poor women shantytown dwellers and middle-class feminist groups. Economic differences made many "middle-class" solutions to women's problems untenable for poor women. Partisanship constituted another fault line among women: Groups led by former party members tended to advocate taking an active stance against the military government, while other groups refrained from becoming part of broader political conflicts. Only in retrospect did it become possible or plausible to identify these diverse and often conflicting groups as part of a broader movement.

In 1983, after ten years of military rule under General Augusto Pinochet, women began to weave together these disparate strands of organizing. Their efforts eventually converged in the form of a mass movement. In May 1983, Chileans opposed to the regime organized a mass demonstration in Santiago. This was the first public protest the opposition had organized since the coup. Economic recession had hit hard the previous year, weakening the regime's claim to have produced an economic miracle. The mood had shifted and people everywhere began to believe that Pinochet would soon fall. Thousands took to the streets. "¡Va a caer!" ("He's going to fall!") became the rallying cry. Organizations representing labor, students, human rights groups, feminists, the poor, and white-collar professionals took to the streets to denounce the regime. The success of this initial demonstration triggered a series of general protests that took place every month for the next three years, until 1986 (Oxhorn 1995).

The emergence of the protests took everyone by surprise. The political parties that were opposed to Pinochet—those on the center and the left—had been underground for the past ten years. They moved quickly to assume leadership of the new mobilization. Defying the regime's ban on party activity, opposition politicians formed two separate alliances. Both alliances sought to control the protests and to promote popular mobilization as a strategy to unseat the military, but they remained deeply divided on other points of strategy. As Chilean scholar Manuel Antonio Garretón (1995, 222) writes, "hidden behind [their common concerns] were different perceptions of the nature of the transition, which became evident in the difficulty of establishing a common platform. The partial attempts at unification . . . either never overcame their marginal importance or simply fell apart quickly." The divisions that emerged between these two coalitions seriously threatened the opposition's chances to unseat Pinochet.

The first coalition was known as the Democratic Alliance (Alianza Democrática, AD). It was made up of centrist political parties (primarily the Christian Democrats) and the more moderate leftist parties. Foremost on the AD's agenda were acceptance of democratic institutions, rejection of violent tactics, and support for capitalism. This center–left coalition represented a significant shift in relations within the opposition forces. Prior to the 1973 coup, the Christian Democratic leadership vehemently opposed Allende and supported the military takeover; their ability to form an alliance with the Left had not come about easily. Moreover, while support for capitalism and democracy may seem obvious for a coalition negotiating a transition to democracy, embrace of these ideologies represented a significant break for many members of the Socialist Party, which had advocated violent revolution in the 1960s. The AD initiated negotiations about the terms of transition with the Pinochet government, a move that generated great hope for the possibility of a peaceful return to civilian rule. It soon became clear, however, that Pinochet had no intention of devolving control back to civilians. The AD had been premature in its efforts to engage in a dialogue with the government, and the process stalled dangerously (Silva 1996).

A second coalition emerged in response to the AD's miscalculation. Several radical Left parties formed the Popular Democratic Movement (Movimiento Democrático Popular, MDP). The MDP coalition advocated armed confrontation with the regime, in keeping with the agenda of the Communist Party that led the coalition. The MDP opposed any effort to negotiate with Pinochet and did not support democracy or capitalism. At least some of its members viewed the AD as "a futile, U.S.-concocted pact to return Chile to bourgeois democracy" (quoted in Constable and Valenzuela 1991, 276). The MDP sought to pick up where Allende had been forced to leave off.

The deep conflicts that brewed between these two coalitions galvanized women in the opposition. The two coalitions, dominated by men who had been party leaders for several decades, engaged in endless and futile discussions about what to do, discussions that frequently broke down due to long-standing partisan disputes. Meanwhile the military continued to engage in ferocious repression against the protests that were taking place in the streets. One particularly horrific event stood out. In November 1983, police arrested several people after a protest in the southern city of Concepción. Some of those detained were the children of a fifty-year-old man named Sebastián Acevedo. Acevedo searched for his children at police stations, but the police said they had no information about them. They had disappeared. Thousands of people before Acevedo had encountered the same desperate frustration. In despair, Acevedo staged a protest at the entrance of the cathedral, in the city's main plaza. He shouted about his children, begging the secret police not to torture them. He then covered himself in gasoline and threatened to set himself on fire. When police challenged him, he struck a match and instantly went up in flames. A widely disseminated photograph of this tragic event further enraged the opposition.

A few weeks later, a group called Women for Life (Mujeres por la Vida, MPLV) formed and sought to unify women across party lines. Sebastián Acevedo's death compelled them to take action. As one member of the group recalled:

> This event struck us all as something extremely painful that could not go on. It was at this point that we women said, "Women support life, against the culture of death that is the dictatorship." (quoted in Baldez 2002, 155)

The sixteen women who formed the group were party leaders who represented the full spectrum of political parties within the opposition, the AD and the MDP. They served as referents of various positions but did not represent their parties in an official capacity. Women for Life framed its actions in terms of women's status as political outsiders. It sought to establish unity among the opposition political parties and claimed that women possessed a superior ability to transcend partisan divisions. Women for Life saw the task of inspiring unity within the opposition as one that women were uniquely qualified to carry out. In the opposition paper *La Época*, on January 4, 1988, for example, MPLV leader Fanny Pollarolo claimed that the group's task was "to inspire the spirit necessary to unify the opposition, to overcome the ineffectiveness of the men" (quoted in Baldez 2002, 156).

On December 29, 1983, MPLV held a massive rally in the Caupolicán Theater in downtown Santiago. This gendered appeal drew ten thousand women representing a diverse array of issues and interests. The event brought together women from all the factions within the opposition, the AD as well as the MDP, and activists from human rights groups, subsistence organizations, and feminist collectives. The rally catalyzed the formation of a broad-based, multisector women's movement. As María Elena Valenzuela notes, "Women for Life became the reference point for political organizations on women's issues as well as the most important arena for convening and discussing the social mobilization of women" (Valenzuela 1995, 172). Women had formed separate organizations prior to this point, and many of them had even participated in the general protests, but not in a coordinated way under a single banner. Thus, in the Chilean case, men's inability to take decisive action against the dictatorship prompted women to reframe their participation in terms of women's status as political outsiders, "above" partisan conflicts.

In the 1980s, Chilean feminists maintained they were practicing a new way of "doing politics" that sought to erase the gendered boundaries between the private and the public. Women demanded a place inside the political arena, albeit a transformed version of politics. The appeal to women's status as political outsiders fostered participation among women who had never been active in politics before. Their reliance on practices and rhetoric that effectively placed them outside politics proved to be an important source of leverage. Yet the discourse of the movements also contributed to women's eventual marginalization. Although the women's movement coalesced under the leadership of MPLV in 1983, by no means did the movement remain united in the years to come. Intense conflicts emerged over goals and strategies, tending to parallel the divisions that existed between the AD and the MDP.

Ultimately, when a newly elected democratic government came to power after the 1989 elections, the women's movement persuaded it to adopt some of its demands—an outcome Franceschet (2004) attributes to the ability of the women's movement to meet the new government's need to mobilize mass support. The opposition political parties faced enormous uncertainty at the time of the democratic transition; they had spent ten years underground and had no way to gauge their support. They had little access to reliable public opinion surveys and no recent electoral results. Meanwhile, women's organizations proved consistently capable of mobilizing tens of thousands of women; the parties sought to capitalize, or perhaps co-opt, this resource for their own purposes. This mutual need benefited women to a certain degree. The government moved quickly after the transition to create a government agency for women, the National Women's Service (SERNAM) (Matear 1996; Valenzuela 1998). Change on other policies affecting women has come more slowly (Haas 2000). It took fourteen years for the Chilean Congress to pass a law allowing divorce, for example.

At the same time, feminism has expanded and taken on a multiplicity of new forms. Political scientist Marcela Rios observes a "growing plurality and heterogeneity" in terms of discourses, institutions, and organizations (Ríos Tobar 2003). Feminism has become more professionalized and led by nongovernmental organizations dedicated more to research and social service delivery, but it has also become more "massified." It has moved beyond the major cities and into smaller towns and rural areas. *Casas de la mujer*, community centers for women, are common at the local level and are often funded by municipal governments. Feminist ideas, although still seen as radical, have become more prevalent in the media and in mainstream discourse. Perhaps one of the most dramatic indicators of the degree to which Chileans' views of women have changed is the fact that a woman may be running for president in 2006. Many consider Michelle Bachelet, the current minister of defense, to be one of the more viable presidential candidates of the governing coalition in the upcoming election.

THE UNITED STATES

After women won the right to vote in the United States, latent differences among women's groups emerged and the suffrage movement declined. Although women's mobilization fragmented, it did not come to a complete standstill. A lack of consensus about what constituted women's political interests hampered unity among women's groups between 1920 and the early 1960s (Cott 1987). Significant differences among the many women's groups that existed in the United States prevented them from forwarding a common agenda. Some—especially those associated with the Democratic Party—supported protective legislation for women, while others—associated with the Republican Party—advocated the extension of complete legal equality to women. These groups competed with one another to control the political agenda with regard to women's issues. As Anne Costain (1992, 30) maintains, "Many of the resources [women's groups] expended to influence government went to neutralize the political influence of other women's groups."

The political context for women changed when President Kennedy created the Presidential Commission on the Status of Women (PCSW). Advocates for women had lobbied for the creation of a commission to examine how to advance women's issues numerous times since World War II. Esther Peterson, the woman whom Kennedy had appointed as head of the Women's Bureau, spearheaded a coalition of women in liberal and labor organizations aimed at exerting pressure on Kennedy. Kennedy bowed to such demands partly in response to Peterson's efforts and partly in an effort to derail the campaign for an equal rights amendment (Harrison 1988). In 1961, passage of such an amendment seemed possible, even imminent, with "eighty-two House resolutions on the ERA in the hopper" (Harrison 1988, 119). Labor leaders—key constituents of the Democratic Party—opposed an equal rights amendment on the grounds that it would eliminate protective legislation. Kennedy hoped the PCSW would deflect attention away from the amendment. He appointed Eleanor Roosevelt to chair the commission and staffed it with high-profile people "from 'the power structure'" (Duerst-Lahti 1989, 256). The executive order that created the PCSW pledged to focus on issues of sex discrimination, primarily in the workplace (Harrison 1988).

The creation of this commission radically changed the profile of women's issues in the political arena. In the period since the extension of suffrage to this point, the government had devoted little attention to women's concerns. Congress created the Women's Bureau in 1920 in response to mobilization on behalf of suffragists, but conflicts among women's organizations stymied the agency's ability to move forward (McBride-Stetson 1995, 256). In creating the PCSW, Kennedy prioritized the issue of gender inequality in the public eye. As Cynthia Harrison (1988, 163) writes, "the president's commission, by openly acknowledging the validity of the quest for equal treatment, nudged public opinion along." Appointing a high-profile leader like Eleanor Roosevelt to chair the commission further underscored its importance. As Betty Friedan noted in *The Feminine Mystique*:

> The very existence of the President's Commission on the Status of Women, under Eleanor Roosevelt's leadership, creates a climate where it is possible to recognize and to do something about discrimination against women, in terms not only of pay but of the subtle barriers to opportunity. (quoted in Harrison 1988, 160)

Kennedy created the commission to address women's concerns and to advance the status of women. Unlike the Chilean case, heightened salience of gender issues in the political arena in the United States came about as the result of the president's explicit efforts to achieve that goal. In Chile, on the other hand, gender became politically salient as an unintended consequence of military policy; General Pinochet in no way intended to put the issue of women's equality on his agenda.

How did the PCSW forge unity among a constituency that had been sharply divided for more than four decades? Under Peterson's guidance, the commission left the ERA off its agenda; it avoided discussing the most contentious issue in order to allow room for other issues to surface. This strategy resulted in a series of measures that effectively achieved what advocates of the ERA sought—full legal and even constitutional equality for women— without the blanket language entailed by the ERA. Commission member Pauli Murray promoted a plan to interpret the equal protection clauses of the Constitution (the Fifth and Fourteenth Amendments) in a way that would include women. Another prominent example is the project that would become the Equal Pay Act of 1963 (Harrison 1988; Costain 1992).

The commission garnered widespread publicity through its association with the executive branch and through the many hearings it organized, but its most visible product was its final report, titled *American Women*. The report offered not only compelling evidence of sex discrimination but specific recommendations for dealing with it. The report, which appeared six months after the publication of *The Feminine Mystique*, was disseminated widely throughout the United States—to the fifty state-level commissions on the status of women—and abroad:

> By October 1964 the government had distributed eighty-three thousand copies of *American Women* (which had also been translated into three languages: Japanese, Swedish and Italian), and in 1965 Charles Scribner's sons published a commercial version edited by Margaret Mead. (Harrison 1988, 173)

Extensive documentation of women's inequality from the White House proved difficult to ignore.

The PCSW forged a new consensus among women—but it did so not by introducing a new frame for activism but rather by facilitating cooperation and dialogue among groups that had interpreted existing frames in incompatible ways. The commission provided a venue in which a new agenda could be articulated; as a result of its work, activists redefined an existing frame, the frame of *equality*, in a more inclusive way.

Freeman maintains that the Presidential Commission on the Status of Women proved a key factor in "convincing previously uninterested women that something should be done" (page 31, this volume). Comparison with the Chilean case suggests a slightly different interpretation. The PCSW not only brought new women into the movement—it created a shared understanding of the problem that women faced as women. While the PCSW expanded an existing network of women's groups, it also created a sense of "similar concerns" among existing organizations and activists who had been pursuing a wide array of conflicting interests and objectives up to that point (Costain 1992).

The PCSW also motivated Congress to address women's issues more aggressively, largely by raising the public's expectations that the government would take concrete actions to reduce women's inequality. The result that has borne the most fruit over time is Title VII of the Civil Rights Act, which bans discrimination on the basis of sex (and race, color, religion, and national origin) in the workplace.[1] Title VII was exactly the kind of action for which *American Women* had called—although initially it did not have this intended effect.

Title VII, in its original form as drafted by the Kennedy administration, was one of the strongest provisions of the Civil Rights Act. By the time it went through the Senate Judiciary Committee, however, it had become little more than a statement prohibiting employment discrimination. Although the inclusion of "sex" in the language of the Civil Rights Act was an extraordinary achievement, the victory would remain a shallow one until Title VII was implemented. The use of Title VII as a vehicle for the liberation of women had two major obstacles. The legislation itself was weak, and so was the institution designed to enforce it, the EEOC. It did not provide powerful mechanisms for preventing discrimination. The original bill called for its main regulatory agency, the EEOC, to act as a "cease and desist" agency, similar to the National Labor Relations Board. Instead, it was reduced to hearing legal complaints, and filing *amicus curae* briefs if the cases went to court. Title VII essentially required individuals or organizations to take the initiative to bring cases forward.

Initially the EEOC did not treat the sex provision seriously. Herman Edelsberg, the first EEOC commissioner, publicly renounced the sex provision of Title VII as being nothing more than a "fluke . . . conceived out of wedlock" (Freeman, chapter 2, this volume). He and other members of the commission publicly derided it, in crude terms that echoed the sexist jokes that male members of Congress made when they passed Title VII in the first place. The jokes had more serious implications: In 1965, when women began flooding the agency with grievances, the EEOC shocked activists by ruling in favor of sex-segregated help-wanted ads. The agency strenuously pursued cases of racial discrimination but did not treat sex discrimination anywhere near as seriously.

A small core of "feminist insiders," including Esther Peterson, Congresswoman Martha Griffiths, and several EEOC members, chastised the agency for its failure to enforce the law. They reminded the EEOC of its duty to uphold all the distinct components of the law. This group saw the need for an outside pressure group, similar to the NAACP. The opportunity came at the third annual meeting of the state commissions on the status of women, when a group of women met in Betty Friedan's hotel room to form NOW.

With the creation of NOW, the process of working for the implementation of Title VII began in earnest. One of NOW's first actions was to start lobbying the administration for the reappointment of the sympathetic Richard Graham to head the EEOC. In 1967, NOW took issue with the EEOC ruling on want ads, organizing pickets against it. In 1968, the EEOC overruled its previous ruling and barred sex-segregated want ads.

However, even with a more sympathetic leadership, the EEOC remained weak and unable to bring cases to court. So women's organizations took on this responsibility themselves. When the EEOC issued guidelines regarding pregnancy discrimination, for example, feminist organizations took the EEOC to the courts for enforcement. When the Supreme Court ruled unfavorably in *General Electric v. Gilbert,* women mobilized to form a coalition, the "Campaign to End Discrimination Against Pregnant Workers" (Costain 1992). In 1976, Congress proposed the Pregnancy Discrimination Act, a bill amending Title VII. Through the lobbying efforts of the coalition, including testimony in subcommittee hearings, the legislation was passed in 1978, overturning the Supreme Court ruling. NOW also started pressing the government to ban sex discrimination. In 1967, NOW began lobbying President Johnson to incorporate sex equality into his agenda, giving it the same treatment that he had given race. In 1965 Johnson had signed an Executive Order banning racial discrimination in businesses and institutions that received funds from the government. NOW demanded that Johnson issue a new Executive Order that banned sex discrimination in government contracting as well.

In sum, the failure of male political actors to address women's concerns ignited women's mobilization. Specifically, the fact that the EEOC did not enforce the sex equality provisions of Title VII of the Civil Rights Act prompted women to engage in collective action. Once women organized separately and autonomously, outside the formal political system, the EEOC began to respond.

Elsewhere, Baldez (2002) argues that framing activities in terms of *women's exclusion* triggers the coalescence of different women's organizations into a movement. Comparison of the U.S. case with the Chilean case suggests a somewhat different conclusion. President Kennedy created the Commission on the Status of Women and incorporated women's issues into politics in a new way well before women mobilized collectively to demand inclusion. Kennedy was not inclusive in terms of promoting women's participation; he did not appoint many individual women to government posts (Harrison 1988). But women did become aware of their shared interests as women as a result of the analysis of gender discrimination that the CSW conducted. Once documented, and publicized by a well-organized network of government insiders, gender inequality proved difficult to ignore (Duerst-Lahti 1989).

This analysis highlights a critical distinction between putting women's issues on the political agenda and taking concrete measures to address those
issues. In the United States, President Kennedy put women's equality on the
political agenda by creating the Presidential Commission on the Status of
Women; it is safe to say that achieving equality for women was not his primary goal in so doing. Similarly, legislators changed the terrain on which battles about the status of women would be contested when they added sex
equality to Title VII—but only a handful of them voted for that bill with that
intention in mind. Both of these actions raised the profile of women's issues
in the public arena and created expectations that the government would do
something to improve the status of women. When the government instead
did nothing, women took matters into their own hands and formed their
own group, NOW.

CONCLUSION

In this chapter we argue that changes in the external political environment
highlight the salience of gender identity and allow existing women's groups
to forge a new language to articulate a set of demands that women share in
common. Our argument demonstrates that movements coalesce when
changes in political opportunities affect cultural framing. To illustrate this argument, we compare the emergence of second wave feminism in Chile and
in the United States in the late twentieth century. Our cases differ in numerous ways in terms of economic status and political context; in a sense, they
constitute "most different cases." Even in two such radically different cases,
however, women's mobilization unfolds along similar paths. These similarities provide an opportunity for exploring commonalities in examples of
women's activism.

In Chile, the second wave women's movement emerged in the 1970s in response to the gendered dynamics of the 1973 military coup. Women mobilized in the midst of a fiercely repressive military dictatorship in the context
of demands for the restoration of democracy. The repression unleashed by
the military heightened the political salience of gender identity and created
a climate in which organizing as women provided a way to mitigate political
repression and survive the crisis. While most women did not initially perceive their activism in gendered terms, the inability of men in the opposition
movement to take decisive measures against the dictatorship catapulted
women to action.

In the United States, two events catalyzed the formation of the second
wave women's movement. The first was the creation of the Commission on
the Status of Women, an initiative that generated substantial evidence of
women's inequality and brokered a compromise among groups that had

been unable to cooperate for nearly forty years. The evidence of discrimination provided in *American Women*, the commission's report, proved so compelling that it broke the ERA/anti-ERA deadlock among women's organizations and prompted them to refocus their efforts around a shared agenda. The addition of sex discrimination to Title VII of the 1964 Civil Rights Act constituted the second critical political opportunity. Title VII raised women's expectations that the government would take concrete steps to address sex inequality. When this proved not to be the case, women mobilized in response. The government's failure to take action to enforce laws against sex discrimination facilitated cooperation among a diverse array of already existing women's organizations whose conflicting interests had kept them apart before then.

The EEOC's failure to implement Title VII catalyzed women's mobilization. As Freeman notes, "the repeated contradictions between these ideas and the actions of their male colleagues created a compulsion for action which only required an opportunity to erupt" (see chapter 2 in this volume). This statement applies equally well to the women's movement in Chile, where heightened expectations and the profound hope of taking action clashed with the reality of inaction on behalf of the male-dominated political parties. Frustration with men's failure to take decisive action against the military regime served to unite women around a common agenda.

NOTE

1. For the full text of Title VII, go to www.eeoc.gov/policy/vii.html.

9

Women Organizing Women in the Russian Federation

Carol Nechemias

In 1990, in the midst of *perestroika*, an American colleague asked me about the future of feminism in the new, democratic Russia. Without hesitation, I told her that feminism had no future whatsoever in my country—that women's problems had been solved long ago, in Lenin's time. . . . I told her that, if anything, Soviet women suffered from an excess of the rights Western feminists were fighting for, and that they would be happy to share their excess of independence with others.

—Nadezhda Azhgikhina (1995a)

As in U.S. history, Russian women's activism has been intermittent, with lengthy periods of little or no public organized effort on behalf of women's rights. While Russian women and men participated in a rich and variegated women's movement from the 1860s to 1917 (Stites 1978), and in a Communist Party–state directed campaign to transform women's lives from 1917 to 1930 (Lapidus 1978), nearly sixty years passed before the reemergence of a nascent women's movement in the late 1980s.[1] Since the fall of Communism in 1991 a new set of women's movements has emerged in Central-Eastern Europe and in the countries of the former Soviet Union, adding significantly to the diversity of women's movements across the globe. This chapter explores one of these cases—the contemporary Russian women's movement—with attention directed toward how it parallels and differs from its U.S. counterpart.

According to Russian feminist activist Olga Lipovskaya (1994), the relationship between the two movements may prove more akin to stepsisters or cousins than to sisterhood. The U.S. and Russian situations differ sharply from one another with respect to time frames and historical-cultural contexts. Although the contemporary U.S. and Russian women's movements appear part

151

of the same wave of women's movements that marked the final decades of the twentieth century, the two movements arguably belong to different phases of women's activism. The global environment changed dramatically from the time the U.S. women's movement emerged in the 1970s to the birth of the Russian movement in the 1990s. The burgeoning growth of Russian women's organizations took place in a context in which feminist movements thrived in many countries, transnational feminist networks carried ideas and resources across national borders to local movements, and gender issues routinely appeared on the United Nations' (UN) agenda (see Sperling et al. 2001; Henderson 2003). Western and international assistance played a significant role in shaping the Russian women's movement, especially its more feminist groups, generating accusations that "feminism in any form is alien to Russian soil and . . . nothing more than an artificial Western graft" (Azhgikhina 2000, 2). Exploring the intersection between the global and the local provides insight into the women's movements in the United States and Russia.

THE RUSSIAN WOMEN'S MOVEMENT
AND SOCIAL MOVEMENT THEORY

As chapter 1 indicates, there are three major concepts central to social movement theory—political opportunity structure, resource mobilization, and ideational factors such as culture and framing. These concepts provide a conceptual framework for explaining the rise of women's movements and structure our analysis of the Russian women's movement. To provide a context for this endeavor, it is important to present an overview of the social, economic, political, and international changes that shaped the emergence of the contemporary Russian women's movement, and to draw explicit comparisons with the U.S. experience. This approach highlights the extent to which Russia as a post-Communist country possesses unique components and traditions that may profoundly shape the direction of women's activism.

The Social Context

In contrast to the U.S. situation, the dominant stereotype of women's place in Soviet society involved the worker-mother rather than the happy homemaker, an image subjected to a devastating critique by Betty Friedan in *The Feminine Mystique*. The worker-mother image, however, fit reality: Soviet women had high labor force participation rates, with roughly 90 percent of women of working age gainfully employed. In the Soviet Union, the full-time housewife had disappeared—a good citizen, male or female, worked full time, with women taking off brief periods for childbirth. Although there were gender patterns in areas of employment, with women dominating certain fields like nursing, retail trade, and teaching, women had made substantial inroads into traditional male fields like construction work as early as the 1930s. Indeed, the decade of the 1930s formed watershed years as the Soviet state launched an all-out campaign to draw women out of their homes with slogans like "Women to the factories."

Aside from labor force participation, Soviet policies had opened educational opportunities to women as early as the 1920s. By the end of the Communist era, women's educational credentials exceeded those of their male peers. With a few exceptions like military academies and foreign service institutes, Russian women enjoyed access to a wide array of professional educational programs. As a result, women constituted 33 percent of the country's engineers, 38 percent of agronomists and veterinarians, 40 percent of academics, 70 percent of physicians, and 65 percent of economists (Nechemias 2003, 547). Thus Russian women gained workplace and educational opportunities earlier than their U.S. counterparts did.

Official propaganda counted the emancipation of women among Communism's achievements. Stalin had actually declared that process fundamentally completed in 1929! While the initial conception of women's emancipation stressed work as the key to women's independence and self-fulfillment, Stalin's introduction of plans for rapid industrialization in 1929 drew women into the workforce as an essential aspect of the state's central goal of building a powerful socialist state. Women's liberation thus meant that women were perceived as a productive (and reproductive) force rather than as individuals.

Although Soviet women achieved substantial access to the labor force and to the educational arena earlier than their U.S. counterparts, there are nonetheless striking parallels with the U.S. experience in that these accomplishments do not readily translate into equal pay or into leading positions in the economy. Soviet women earned roughly 70 percent as much as men, a gap that rested upon several factors, including women's lower skill levels, low relative pay for "women's work," and outright sex discrimination. And as in the United States, gender pyramids were evident even in female-dominated occupations: women formed 70 percent of the medical corps but only 6 percent of surgeons; in education women made up 83 percent of teachers but only 39 percent of head teachers (Nechemias 2003, 551). Only 5.6 percent of managers were female. A glass ceiling was clearly in place.

Soviet mother-workers shared another commonality with American working women: the burden of housework and child rearing. Soviet-style emancipation did not extend to a critique of traditional divisions of labor within the home. Women's lives were especially hard—they suffered from the triple burden of working, housework, and standing in long lines at stores. The failure to address inequities within the home was reinforced by the routine use of biological rather than societal explanations for distinctive gender patterns like women's underrepresentation in the Academy of Sciences, among factory managers, and among high-level party and state officials. It was considered "natural" that "real" women would place more emphasis on family responsibilities and thereby forgo high-powered or overly demanding careers. Motherhood was touted as women's central identity and destiny, and gender ideology stressed that while women were equal with men they nonetheless fell, along with children and invalids, into the category of those in special need of state protection (see Attwood 1990).

In stark contrast to the American experience, Soviet social policy aimed at helping women combine work life with family obligations. The welfare state included a day care system, children's summer camps, free health care, and a host of maternal benefits and protections that fell under the rubric "protection of motherhood." While there was an acknowledgment of the difficulties that plagued women's daily lives, there was no priority assigned to tackling those issues. Communist Party leaders insisted that women's plight would automatically ease as larger issues were resolved—as the economy grew and the country prospered. It was assumed that an improved service sector and the wider availability of modern consumer appliances like washing machines, vacuum cleaners, and so on, would facilitate women's task of combining work and family responsibilities.

What did command attention about women's behavior involved demographic issues, especially with respect to growing concerns about whether women could fulfill both their productive and reproductive roles in society and a growing recognition that there could be a tension between the two. During the 1970s a preference for smaller families emerged, with Russians opting for only one or two children (Peers 1985). The demographic situation worsened during the post-Communist transition, with Russia losing population as deaths exceeded births. The centrality of this issue as a political question separates the United States from the Soviet Union and its primary successor state, Russia. Unlike in the United States, there was more of a tradition of relying on the extensive growth of the labor force to achieve economic growth and a historical association between population growth and national power and the health of society as a whole.

Like abortion rights in the United States, demographic matters spill over and become entangled with other policy areas. During *perestroika*, for example, discussions of women's health centered on boosting birth rates by reducing maternal and infant mortality rates, and those goals in turn spurred calls for removing women from occupations that involve heavy physical labor, since such work was deemed injurious to women's reproductive health (Nechemias 1991). It should be noted that in 1989, 56 percent of Soviet women were engaged in jobs that involved laborious physical labor, compared to 11 percent of U.S. women (Nechemias 2003, 550). Here we have two ships passing in the night: the demand that women leave "unwomanly" jobs like working in coal mines, while U.S. women demand the right to work in coal mines.[2]

Demographic discussions also spilled over into the area of reproductive rights. Discussions about the high abortion rate—the average woman has had multiple abortions—often point to how reliance on abortions as the primary means of birth control contributes to a low birth rate by leaving women subject to chronic infections and high infertility rates. Yet proposals to address this problem by increasing Russian women's access to modern contraception or by introducing sex education in the schools encountered increased political opposition from nationalists, Communists, and others who believed such measures would exacerbate the demographic crisis, that is, reduce population growth even further.

The Economic Context

Economic reform during *perestroika* and the accelerated, full-scale, pro-market policies introduced in the 1990s led to economic implosion and collapsing safety nets, leaving populations largely impoverished following decades of relative security if not prosperity. Women especially bore the brunt of job loss, losing seven million positions, compared to one to two million for men. Even with a decline in labor force participation, women's employment remained high compared to the United States, standing at 75 percent in 1996 compared to 80 percent of men, a relatively small gender gap (Zhenshchiny 1997, 50). Official attitudes were not always sympathetic. As one of President Yeltsin's ministers of labor put it: "Why should we employ women when men are unemployed? It's better that men work and women take care of children" (Gennady Melikian, cited in Bridger et al. 1996, 51).

As marketization of the economy proceeded, women's employment remained disproportionately in the sectors of the economy funded by the state, like health care and education, while men seized better-paying opportunities in the private sector. A further complication for women involved the soaring price of day care and summer camps and the declining value of cash benefits like children's allowances and pensions. A substantial number of women sought to supplement family income by engaging in small-scale trading and the use of private plots for subsistence farming. Middle-aged women with higher and specialized secondary education—engineers, economists, technicians, and research staff—figured heavily among the unemployed and out of desperation turned to trade, catering, and operating small kiosks (see Bridger et al. 1996; Khotkina 2000).

The deteriorating economic conditions generated a number of negative trends. The share of single-parent families (overwhelmingly headed by women) stood at a stable 13 percent from 1970 to 1989, but soared to 25 percent by 1995; nonmarital births increased from 14 to 33 percent from

1989 to 2000 (Nechemias 2003, 557–58). Women's health deteriorated, evident in the growing prevalence of pregnancy and birth complications. Protective legislation—state-mandated benefits for working women—made young women less desirable as employees (UNICEF 1999, 26), and the sexualization of women's images that accompanied democratization and marketization led to greater problems of sexual harassment. It also caused many young women to dream of careers as prostitutes, to seek foreign husbands, or answer ads that promised work abroad but instead led to the underworld of sexual trafficking.

The Political Context

Compared with the United States, where the 1960s generated antiestablishment questioning, political activism, and widespread expectations of radical change, the Soviet Union underwent far-reaching, revolutionary change starting with Gorbachev's policies of *glasnost'* (greater openness) and *perestroika* (restructuring) in the mid- to late 1980s. The transformation in the Russian political structure was of far greater significance than in the American case. Within a few years the USSR had collapsed and a newly independent Russian state simultaneously faced the massive challenges of constructing a new nation, a new political system, and a new economic order. The contrasts are sharp: "between planning and markets, dictatorship and democracy, one party and many, transmission belts and civil society, a big state and one in retreat and often disarray" (Bunce 2002, 1).

The political consequences for women were significant. These included the questioning of old shibboleths about the emancipation of women; the emergence of a more pluralist debate over women's place in society; the freedom to organize independent women's organizations free from state control; and greatly expanded interaction with women's movements in countries like Great Britain, Holland, Canada, and the United States. The lively discourse over women's place included diverse positions, but the predominant view emphasized backlash against the Soviet concept of women's emancipation. Gorbachev (1987, 117) himself set the tone with his view that emancipation had gone too far and his hope that ongoing debates about women and family would lead to proposals making "it possible for women to return to their purely womanly mission." The end of censorship did not bring feminism to the fore but rather advanced neofamilial ideologies calling on women to be more home-centered or family-centered as part of the process of nation building, of distancing from the Communist past (Zhurzhenko 2004).[3]

The initial competitive elections reflected this "send the women home" theme. During the Soviet era, women were well represented in legislative bodies due to the practice of descriptive representation, whereby substantial proportions of women, peasants, and factory workers were included in institutions like the USSR Supreme Soviet. These legislatures were not centers of power but rather provided a façade of democracy, window dressing for the Soviet regime. In reality, few women had access to high-level decision making as they rarely held key political and economic posts within the party and state hierarchies, and those that did served largely in areas considered appropriate for women like pensions, education, health care, and culture.

Gorbachev's reforms, however, promised to transform once largely symbolic legislatures into real, working parliaments. The partial lifting of quotas for the 1989 election of the USSR Congress of People's Deputies (CPD) saw women's representation plummet from 33 percent in the last USSR Supreme Soviet to 15.7 percent in the CPD. The complete dropping of quotas a year later for the Russian republic election saw women's representation plunge from 35.3 percent to 5.4 percent. Women suffered highly visible setbacks in the political arena, and a clear message about women's true status—one of exclusion from power—was highlighted.

The International Context

With the fall of Communism, the international arena strongly endorsed the development of feminist organizations in Russia. The United States and other Western countries sought to promote democracy in post-communist countries by bolstering civil society, and several donor organizations singled out gender concerns as a thematic funding focus (Henderson 2003, 120). Heightened UN activity on behalf of women also contributed to the rise of activism. The strength of the international women's movement forms a crucial backdrop in influencing new directions in aid programs and in forging direct contacts between women's nongovernmental organizations (NGOs) in the West and in Russia.

Summary

From electoral results to trends in the economy and social benefits, since 1989 Russian women have endured stunning reversals at odds with the experiences of American women in the 1960s. In contrast to American women's struggle to extend the American dream of equal opportunity, many in Russian society rejected women's emancipation as part of a discredited communist ideology. Poverty and a broken social contract loomed as key issues, and demographic concerns occupied a far more salient place in Russian society. While U.S. women sought to improve their status by widening access to professions and careers, Russian women found their careers disrupted, encountered employment discrimination, and faced reductions in benefits that threatened to erode their security.

This context provides us with the necessary background for exploring the trajectory of the Russian women's movement through a focus on the three interrelated factors considered central to the development of women's movements: resource mobilization, political opportunities, and culture and framing.

THE RISE OF WOMEN'S MOVEMENTS: RESOURCE MOBILIZATION, POLITICAL OPPORTUNITY STRUCTURE, AND CULTURE/FRAMING

The number of women's organizations burgeoned during *perestroika* and especially during the post-Communist transition. By the mid-1990s a resource book on women's organizations listed over six hundred groups (Abubikirova et al. 1998). The emergence of a host of women's organizations working to improve the status of women rapidly led to a situation in which Russian women activists and foreign observers alike routinely employed the label "women's movement" to describe ongoing activities. For our purposes these organizations can be divided into three major categories: 1) the Women's Union of Russia (WUR) and *zhensovety* (women's councils); 2) the independent women's movement that involves feminist groups like the Moscow Center for Gender Studies (MCGS) and the Information Center of the Independent Women's Forum (ICIWF); and 3) a myriad of grassroots organizations working mainly on issues like unemployment, handicapped children, and poverty.

A focus on these lines of women's activism reveals rifts within the women's movement that stem from differences in origins, sources of support, and understandings of women's problems. As chapter 1 notes, the three major concepts in social movement theory are interdependent, and this creates difficulties in sorting out phenomena into neat, self-contained categories. Choices have been made to include subject matter where it seems most relevant. International aid to Russian women's organizations, for example, is placed within the discussion of resource mobilization, yet that assistance could readily count as part of the political opportunity structure. These types of interactive effects will be evident in much of the following discussion.

Resource Mobilization

The Women's Union of Russia (WUR)

What, then, were the skills, networks, and resources that spawned women's activism? What was the spark that galvanized women into action? The WUR demonstrates the central importance of preexisting networks; this is an organization with strong ties to the Soviet past. The popular view is that Communism destroyed civil society, but this did not mean the country was bereft of mass organizations. There were two Soviet-era, state-sponsored organizations for women: the *zhensovety* (women's councils), a nationwide network; and the Soviet Women's Committee (SWC), which as late as 1985 was the lone women's organization at the national level. The SWC had been a tame organization that represented an elite "track" for women party politicians (Nechemias 1991; Caiazza 2001). In 1987, however, Gorbachev called on the women's councils to take a more active role in society and placed them under the leadership of the SWC. By the late 1980s SWC was engaging in more outspoken criticisms of Soviet society and along with the women's councils played a leading role in filling seats allocated to women in the CPD.

With the collapse of communism the SWC faced massive cuts in its state-provided budget, unpopularity due to its close ties to the Communist Party leadership, and the loss of its role of filling legislative and executive positions in government. Seeking a new niche in Russian society, the SWC registered as the Women's Union of Russia (WUR), a nonstate, independent organization. Although many women's councils disappeared in the wake of the dissolution of the Soviet Union, the WUR entered the post-Communist transition with a head start, with substantial advantages and resources compared to the independent women's organizations that developed in the late 1980s outside the structure of state sponsorship. The WUR could count among its resources leadership, organizational skills, hundreds of local affiliates, insider ties to (often former) Communist Party and state connections, office space and equipment, and international ties with women's organizations in 120 countries plus consultative status with the UN. In an impoverished Russia the WUR stood ready to exploit long-standing relationships and secure scarce state assistance in the form of in-kind benefits and public monies to support programs in areas like women's employment, the family, and child welfare.

These very advantages represented disadvantages in the eyes of some beholders. Independent women's organizations feared WUR's Soviet-style, hierarchical structure; they suspected that WUR aspired to unite all women's groups under a single umbrella and to claim a role as the lone voice of Russian women. Feminist groups shared with their Western counterparts an aversion to hierarchy and orders from above. The WUR's leadership itself evoked distrust. The head of WUR, Alevtina Fedulova, had been one of the few successful female political figures of the final decades of the Communist era, holding positions like head of the Young Pioneers (the state-sponsored organizations for ten- to fourteen-year-old children), head of the Soviet Peace Committee, and finally head of the SWC. She qualified as an *apparatchik*, a professional Communist Party politician, and as such, many found it difficult to look past her close association with top party leaders in the past (see Khudiakova 1993).

What drove the WUR leadership to transform the SWC and advance action on behalf of women? Putting aside self-interest, salvaging careers in a setting where neither the state nor political parties showed an interest in women leaders and women's issues, Fedulova points to other factors. For WUR and many women, activism flowed from the "colossal education" that resulted from the onslaught of "send-the-women-home" rhetoric and from the 1990 Russian republic legislative election, the quota-free context that saw women's share of seats shrink to 5.4 percent. There was a sense of crisis, or as Fedulova put it, a need to challenge the wisdom of constructing illusions that women's greatest happiness involved confinement to domestic concerns (Khudiakova 1993). For a longtime party *apparatchik*, Fedulova had learned new lessons, including the idea that women are individuals and should decide their own fate rather than be objects and have decisions made for them. New frames thus came into play, as will be discussed later in this chapter.

Feminist Organizations

Contemporary feminist activities originated in the late 1980s in the burst of activism associated with the growth of "informal" groups independent of state control. Yet state action did inadvertently set off a chain of unintended events. In a process reminiscent of President Kennedy's Commission on the Status of Women, Gorbachev's reform-minded government wished to explore new directions with respect to public policy and women's issues. As a consequence, the Academy of Social Sciences (under the Central Committee of the Communist Party of the Soviet Union) sponsored seminars that brought women together, including a handful of previously isolated feminist academics. These women shared Western frames on women's issues: As academics, several of them had specialized on topics like women's movements in countries like France, Britain, and the United States. Privately, they had applied those feminist critiques to Soviet society. As these women became acquainted, they discovered commonalities, established friendships, and began to transform their personal interaction into independent organizational activity by forming the League for Emancipation from Societal Stereotypes (LOTOS), one of the first feminist informal (nonstate) organizations (Sperling 1999, 103–5).

The Soviet government nudged events forward in 1989 by asking Natalia Rimashevskaia, director of the USSR Academy of Science's Institute of Socio-Economic Population Problems (ISEPP), to formulate a position paper, "The State Program to Improve the Status of Women, the Family, and the Protection of Motherhood and Childhood."[4] LOTOS members participated in the writing of this paper, which was published in 1989 and rejected traditional approaches to women's issues that emphasized essential, biologically determined differences between men and women, with the latter innately destined for the nurturing of children and domestic duties. The LOTOS scholars advanced egalitarian and gender-neutral approaches that stressed equal opportunity and called on men to shoulder more responsibility within the home. They drew attention to socialization—to the idea that "society is destiny"—and broke with the policy tradition of addressing women through the prism of the protection of motherhood.

The nascent feminist movement possessed a key resource in Rimashevskaia, who had a personal friendship with Gorbachev dating back to their days as fellow students at Moscow State University. She secured a resolution from the Presidium of the USSR Academy of Sciences to create within ISEPP a scholarly center—the Moscow Center for Gender Studies (MCGS). The MCGS represented the first unit in the Soviet Union dominated by feminists and committed to promoting gender research and reducing gender discrimination (see Nechemias 2001). Feminists thus secured a niche within the USSR Academy of Sciences. This provided key resources with respect to office space, meeting rooms, phones, typewriters, a certain social standing, and salaried positions, although inflation and the inability of the state to support the extensive network of research institutes soon rendered the remuneration purely symbolic. Despite beginning with only five staff positions, the MCGS accumulated resources, particularly with respect to grants from Western foundations, and has significantly contributed to the institutionalization of a feminist women's movement (Nechemias 2001, 294–97).

The actual birth of an independent women's movement occurred in March 1991, with the First Independent Women's Forum in Dubna, a small town near Moscow (Cockburn 1991). The meeting called together women's organizations that were forming from below, outside of state control, with the idea that activists would get to know one another and exchange information about the work of their groups. Over two hundred women representing forty-two organizations across the USSR responded to advertisements and participated in the conference, along with twenty-six foreign guests from Western Europe, the United States, Canada, and India. The program included plenary sessions and discussions on an array of topics, with the goal of developing an understanding about the central issues facing the women's movement. Of the nineteen members of the committee that organized the conference, seven either worked at MCGS or were shortly to join it. Several came from the host organization, the Institute for Nuclear Research in Dubna, where a group of lively and energetic women had transformed their women's council into an independent, active women's organization. An early feminist organization, SAFO (Free Association of Feminist Organizations, but in reality a small group of feminists), also played a major role and raised some of the early money from Russian entrepreneurs.

With a second forum at Dubna a year later, which drew twice as many participants and more Western women, it became clear not only that the movement would persist but that greater coordination and cooperation would develop as well. And it is in this area that problems similar to those encountered by the U.S. women's movement occurred. Dubna leaders like Anastasiia Posadskaia of the MCGS placed a high value on the independence of the women's movement and on tolerance and pluralism. She believed the forum should offer a public arena where any woman or woman's organization could speak. After decades of manipulation from above, these attitudes are understandable, but they also undermine the solidarity and cohesiveness necessary for wielding sustained influence (Marsh 1996, 291).

There has been a drift toward greater structure over time. Indeed, the second Dubna conference took the first steps toward coordination when it created a new organization, the Moscow-based Independent Women's Forum (IWF, later the Information Center of the Independent Women's Forum or ICIWF), to provide independent, feminist-oriented women's groups in Russia with information services, educational seminars, and support for a wide variety of projects. Although ICIWF embraces an antihierarchical ideology, it has reached out to feminist activists in the regions and sustained a network that has strengthened horizontal linkages between women's groups across Russia and facilitated joint activities like lobbying efforts.

What galvanized the forum leaders to seek the creation of an independent feminist women's movement? It was not the campaign to "send women home" but rather the power of feminist ideas. Unlike WUR leaders, the women who formed the core of the early feminist organizations were intellectuals who had specialized in the study—and critique—of Western feminist movements. In reality they found themselves inspired by their exposure to Western feminist literature and drawn to applying feminist analytical frameworks to their own society. These are women passionately committed to the revival of feminism as the key to women's emancipation.

Yet Rosalind Marsh observed (1996, 292) that even at the Dubna forums there was a tremendous gulf between the sophisticated theorists and the bulk of the participants, for whom the issue was "What is feminism?" There were tensions between the more feminist organizers and other groups that preferred to speak about women and avoid the label "feminist." Those distinctions persist, with the core of the movement strikingly more feminist in its orientation than many independent women's organizations, especially those outside the metropolitan areas of Moscow and St. Petersburg.

In contrast to U.S. feminists, Russian feminists represent a small wing of the women's movement. Feminists are not as marginalized as they might appear, however, due to the efforts of highly committed and energetic women coupled with an infusion of international assistance and close interaction with the global women's movement. The pipeline of funding from the West to women's organizations became substantial in the mid-1990s, with feminist groups receiving the lion's share. In a setting of economic scarcity, domestic indifference, and institutional fluidity, the infusion of money was crucial in boosting activity. According to Sperling et al. (2001, 1174), the Ford Foundation granted $250,000 to ICIWF between 1994 and 1996, $200,000 to the United States-Newly Independent States (U.S.-NIS) Women's Consortium, and $75,000 to MCGS.[5] The Eurasia Foundation channeled $900,000 in United States Agency for International Development (USAID) monies to Russian women and women's organizations from 1993 to 1996. In 1999 USAID began a three-year, $600,000 program of small grants, administered by the International Research & Exchange Board (IREX), to support the development of rape and domestic crisis centers in Russia. European governments and Canada also contribute funding, while women's NGOs in many countries engage in collaborative work with Russian counterparts, sponsor travel, give lectures, and conduct training seminars.

The feminist women's movement is "almost completely dependent on foreign aid" (Henderson 2003, 47). This reality is unimaginable in the U.S. context, where women's organizations garner money from domestic sources like membership dues and contributions, the provision of services, grants, and state funding. More important, there are concerns that this stream of foreign funding has resulted in some unintended, negative consequences. Key charges include that funding is concentrated on groups in Moscow, that support goes toward a narrow agenda favored by funders' priorities, that grant competitions pit women's groups against one another and therefore encourage fragmentation rather than cooperation, and that the acceptance of foreign assistance brands groups as nonindigenous or more attached to the West than to Russia (Sperling 1999, 220–56).

The Moscow focus has eased over time, as some Moscow organizations serve as redonating organizations that direct funds to NGOs in the provinces. Donors may regard a Moscow focus as justified. As John Squier (2003), program officer for Russia and Ukraine, the National Endowment for Democracy, puts it: "If you want to have an effect on a political system as centralized as Russia's you have to work with organizations in Moscow, because Moscow is where all the people who make the important decisions are." Clearly, however, the goal of building civil society extends across the vast Russian expanse. In July 2002, USAID announced a shift in focus to smaller loans and grants to grassroots programs in the provinces rather than at the national level (Gutterman 2002). The Moscow-based organization Consortium of Women's Nongovernmental Associations (formerly US-NIS Women's Consortium) received large USAID grants and held grant competitions, rechanneling monies to women's organizations in places like Bashkortostan and Naberezhnye Chelny. In addition, a number of foundations (Ford, MacArthur, Eurasia, Soros) encouraged the "indigenization" of the grants decision-making process by involving Russians, or at a minimum Russian-speaking foreigners, in leading organizational positions.

A particularly thorny issue involves whether foreign assistance shifts organizational activity away from the purposes and priorities that would bubble up "naturally" from grassroots organizing. International assistance favors an agenda that emphasizes women's rights, technology networks to connect women's groups, domestic violence, gender expertise on public policy, gender/women's studies curriculums, and, most recently, trafficking. Donors favor women's organizations working to change women's status, organizations that focus solely on women. They could readily interact with feminist leaders in Moscow and St. Petersburg who had foreign language expertise, an affinity for the West, and the cultural skills to work with Western organizations. Speaking the language of gender studies, civil society, and advocacy (see Richter 2002), many grant competitions privileged academic feminist groups in Moscow and St. Petersburg.

In some cases, Russian women's organizations work around donor preferences by adjusting Western projects and thereby rooting them in Russian conditions. Thus Julie Hemment (2004) found that provincial women's crisis centers, though established with the mission of addressing sexual and domestic violence, were in fact providing counseling and legal advice on a wide array of "crises" ranging from housing to unemployment to poverty to military service. Here, an issue—domestic and sexual violence—that many Russian women did not consider most pressing was "translated" in a way that made sense to them but that also endangered their status with Western sponsors.

The feminist movement has shown little propensity to strive toward mass membership and, in the eyes of many, remains overly fragmented, with jealousy and competition overriding opportunities for cooperation (Sperling 1999). Writing in the major Russian newspaper *Nezavisimaia gazeta*, Galina Mikhaleva (2002, 2) noted that despite the number of women's organizations, there is not one feminist organization ready to call for a mass action that could result in women filling a city square. This is a movement lacking demonstrations and the public visibility so characteristic of the U.S. and Western European women's movements in their formative years. Worse, it is a movement that seems peculiarly indifferent to developing a mass membership. Some analysts hold that an orientation toward Western donors, coupled with economic distress, generates a situation in which women activists are wary of sharing scarce resources and exhibit little interest in cooperation with other women's groups or building a larger membership. There is no tradition of outreach, and building organizational strength through a mass base and membership fees represents a formidable task in a society in which poverty is widespread and there is little interest in participating in public organizations.

Western assistance thus runs the danger of reinforcing and institutionalizing a feminist movement that lacks a mission that connects with Russian women at large. The bulk of independent women's organizations focus on other groups, like the disabled or children, or fight for economic survival rather than struggling to broaden women's rights in the larger society (Kay 2004). The charge that feminists ignore the urgent needs of women and concentrate on larger or more important issues echoes charges that the U.S. women's movement promotes the goals of privileged white women while downplaying programs crucial to poor women.

Yet the feminist movement shows signs of seeking its own roots, a development that will deflate the perception that it is a foreign import. In 1998 key feminist organizations sponsored a conference in Moscow entitled "The Women's Movement in the Context of Russian History," held to commemorate the ninetieth anniversary of the First All-Russian Women's Congress in St. Petersburg in 1908. The feminist leaders of the independent Russian women's movement now seek to recover and publicize Russian feminist traditions, a history that had been lost during the Communist era. They traced their lineage and inspiration from Anna Filosofova, one of the organizers of the 1908 Congress and a pioneer feminist activist who established higher education courses for women and shelters for abused women and children.

Grassroots Organizations

Feminist organizations are vastly outnumbered by grassroots women's organizations, which form out of a determination to provide tangible, practical support for women facing extreme hardships, not to advance abstract goals regarding women's rights. Examples include groups of mothers of many children, groups formed to organize summer camps for children, and so on. These organizations face extraordinary challenges with respect to resources; buying paper and envelopes, maintaining paid staff, and access to office equipment pose major barriers. They rarely receive Western assistance, making Western aid agencies appear indifferent, callous toward the suffering people endure on a daily basis.[6] Key resources involve volunteer labor and nonmonetary forms of support like office supplies donated by businesses. Dedicated leaders typically exhibit a strong sense of social responsibility and often make personal sacrifices in terms of using personal phones and personal funds to carry on the group's work. Burnout is frequent. The motive behind activism involves survival: The contraction of the economy and the collapse of the welfare state left the most vulnerable in situations where joining together provided moral support if not tangible help. These organizations cannot replace the safety net of the past—it is a Band-Aid covering a large wound.

A unique grassroots organization that does not address traditional welfare issues is the Committee of Soldiers' Mothers of Russia (see Caiazza 2001).

This highly visible organization utilizes the ideology of motherhood to defend the rights of draftees and servicemen, combat human rights abuses in the military, end the war in Chechnya, and fight for alternative service. It has forged links with organizations in Western Europe, but its place in the women's movement is unclear. It rejects the label "feminist" and does not have strong ties to other women's organizations.

Summary

In contrast to the U.S. women's movement, the Communist legacy and the global women's movement played key roles in resource mobilization in the Russian women's movement. Communist-era structures provided a foundation of resources in terms of networks, leadership skills, personal contacts, and office space for WUR, while the feminist branch of the women's movement was able to short-circuit what would have been a much slower process of development by taking advantage of resources (money, information, and training) from Western governments, foundations, and NGOs. It is unlikely that this model of feminist women's movement mobilization—substituting international support for domestic popularity—can work indefinitely. Despite differences, there are also striking parallels with the U.S. experience, including tensions over organizational issues involving independence, horizontal relationships, and building consensus from below versus hierarchical, top-down structures. Moreover, there are similarities in how discourses centering on women's homemaker roles spurred activism, with Russian women battling against the introduction of a version of the "feminine mystique" that was totally at odds with the realities of their lives. They fought to retain positions they held in society, while in the United States women sought to dismantle a gender ideology that formed a barrier to the expansion of women's opportunities.

The Political Opportunity Structure

For both the U.S and Russian women's movements, the political ferment and reformist impulses that held sway during crucial formative periods gave way to a more conservative climate, in which widespread disillusionment and alienation replaced civic engagement. Yet American women were able to secure a firm position within the political setting. The U.S. women's movement is a political player, a significant force in areas ranging from electoral fund-raising to lobbying to aligning with the Democratic Party. The Russian women's movement has yet to establish a sure footing in the political arena; initial successes were followed by setbacks, and women's political clout weakened during the course of the 1990s.

The Russian women's movement faces an uphill battle in that seventy years of Communist rule left the population short on social capital—the trust, social cooperation, and leadership skills that facilitate working in networks or coalitions. It is extraordinarily difficult to build organizational strength. Participation in voluntary associations in post-Soviet Russia is strikingly low by American standards. Ninety percent of the Russian population does not belong to a voluntary association, though counting passive forms of participation like attending church services several times a year or labor union membership drops that figure to 60 percent. By contrast, 70 percent of Americans report belonging to voluntary associations, and half of these participants consider themselves active members (Remington 2002, 84–85). A poll conducted in June 2001 found that Russians had no interest in participating in voluntary organizations and that only 5 percent of them are active in public organizations ("Russians Not . . . " 2001). It seems that Russians are appreciating the freedom not to have to participate.

Despite this dreary picture of civil society, Russian women's organizations stood ready to devise political strategies designed to advance women's status. The key year was 1993, when the first parliamentary elections in the newly independent Russian Federation were scheduled. Here WUR and IWF took strikingly different paths. WUR chose to form, along with two smaller women's organizations, the women's electoral bloc Zhenshchiny Rossii, or Women of Russia (WOR), to contest the 1993 election.

This decision was made after WUR leaders reviewed the positions of thirty political parties and found a universal absence of the "woman question." Fedulova served as coleader of WOR along with Ekaterina Lakhova, a prominent woman political figure who, though not associated with any of the three organizations that coalesced to found WOR, provided an energetic and younger face to the electoral bloc. Lakhova was part of an entourage of Yeltsin supporters from the president's home base of Sverdlovsk. She had reformist credentials and had served in the Russian Republic CPD in 1990, chaired its Committee for Women, Protection of Family, Motherhood, and Childhood, and headed the President's Commission for Women, Family, and Demography.

Though invited by Lakhova, feminist organizations did not join WOR. They disapproved of a women's electoral bloc, predicted that WOR would fail, and accused the women's bloc of taking the gender out of gender politics by downplaying women's rights in favor of campaign rhetoric that stressed social protection for men, women, the elderly, and the young. Embracing a Western model, the IWF leadership preferred engaging in long-term efforts to develop women's factions and quotas within party organizations along the lines of some Western social democratic parties (Posadskaya 1994, 9). Sensitive to the Communist past of orders from above, the IWF did not endorse any political party, believing that it was up to each woman to decide for herself. Yet a number of leading feminists actively campaigned for and were included on the ballot of Grigorii Yavlinski's Yabloko Party, a party strongly committed to Western-style democracy and a market economy. None of the women were elected. More importantly, feminists failed to gain a toehold as part of a significant political force in the Russian political scene, as Yabloko proved a falling star over the course of the 1990s and was virtually wiped out as an electoral force in the December 2003 State Duma (parliamentary) elections.

In contrast, WOR was one of the biggest surprises of the 1993 election, finishing fourth among the twenty-one parties and blocs contesting the party list balloting, securing 8.10 percent of the vote and twenty-three seats in the Duma, doubling women's representation to 13.5 percent. Over one-third of the women deputies came from WOR. The electoral system was a factor, as virtually all WOR deputies were elected from the party list ballot. Unlike the U.S. electoral tradition of single-mandate districts (SMD), the State Duma fostered the formation of small parties that can compete for the 225 seats elected from proportional representation lists, with a 5 percent threshold to win list seats (an additional 225 deputies are elected from SMDs). Yet even in countries with proportional representation systems, women's political parties rarely meet with electoral success. The political environment in 1993 provided favorable conditions for a women's political party, but those conditions had evaporated by the next parliamentary election in 1995 (see Nechemias 2000).

Like so many Russian political parties or electoral blocs, WOR proved ephemeral. For two years WOR pursued a centrist position, siding with the Communist Party and the agrarians on land reform issues, supporting President Yeltsin on no-confidence votes, and avoiding a clear-cut stance on the war in Chechnya (Slater 1995; Ishiyama and Kuntz 2000; Nechemias 2000). The faction worked hard on a new family code and the Children of Russia program, a multifaceted set of social programs that included support for the provision of modern contraception. But WOR failed to surmount the 5 percent barrier in 1995 and pulled barely 2 percent of the party list vote in 1999.

The WOR experiment ultimately demonstrated more about the weaknesses within the Russian women's movement than its growing political strength. The 1995 electoral defeat led to a fissure within WOR, with Lakhova breaking away and forming a new organization, the Movement of Women of Russia (MWR). The relationship between the two leaders was poor, and Fedulova felt betrayed as Lakhova sought to transfer WOR support to her new organization. Both organizations strove to present themselves as the key public manifestation of the women's movement. While the two groups share many goals, WOR is seen as more conservative and less committed to democratic reform. Personal acrimony as well as policy differences obliterated the potential for close cooperation.

The absence of solidarity among women's groups and women at large contributed to the erosion of women's political credibility. By drawing 14–15 percent of the women's vote in 1993, WOR had increased the visibility of women in Russian politics and sent the message that women might represent a distinct bloc within the electorate. Politicians responded by courting the women's vote, especially in 1995, but that effort faded as a gender gap in voting behavior failed to materialize across several electoral cycles (Nechemias 2000; Belin 2000).

Women's representation in the State Duma fell from 13.5 percent in 1993 to 10.2 percent in 1995 and 7.5 percent in 1999, then rebounded slightly to 9.8 percent in 2003.[7] The 2003 figure is below the high mark achieved in 1993, a pattern inconsistent with the American experience, in which the growth of the women's movement helped bring about incremental improvements in women's representation in the U.S. Congress. Worse, women deputies across the four Dumas that have met since 1993 report a steadily diminishing level of cooperation among women deputies across party lines and far fewer women deputies who perceive problems specific to women (Cook and Nechemias 2004). WOR had rallied a critical mass of deputies around a women's agenda, a position taken up by Communist and left-oriented parties in the 1995 Duma, though women's issues were submerged within a broader collectivist and nationalist agenda that pressed for the restoration of Soviet-era social policies.

Overall, women's political fortunes continued to erode. Programmatic parties—democratic parties like Russia's Choice and Yabloko and other parties like the Communist Party on the left—were losing out to more nationalist parties and especially to "parties of power," organized to support the current Kremlin incumbent. And women continued to bet on the wrong horse. In the 1999 State Duma election, both WOR and the MWR entered into a close alliance with the Fatherland–All Russia bloc, a good bet at the time since the bloc's leaders included the two men most favored as possible successors to Yeltsin as president. The bloc had pledged to tackle women's unemployment, violence against women, and maternal and infant mortality, and to reserve 30 percent of the party list and single-member district slots for women (*Zhenshchiny* 1999). The 30 percent became 10 percent, leading to WOR's decision to withdraw support and contest the election on its own. The final weeks of the parliamentary campaign witnessed the meteoric rise of Vladimir Putin and the Unity electoral bloc, ending the aspirations of the Fatherland–All Russia bloc. Women's electoral strength splintered across several political blocs, with no clear gender gap that women's movement leaders could leverage as bargaining power.

Summary

The political world both domestically and internationally has become more hostile or simply indifferent. At home the representation of women's issues has weakened within the State Duma, and female representatives are reluctant to raise issues like family planning and modern contraception because they are branded antipatriotic. Women do dominate the "feminized" world of NGOs and civil society, but that niche is rather isolated from the Russian political realm, where the development of political parties with grassroots linkages remains largely a work in progress. Yet the picture is not altogether negative. There have been instances of cooperation, such as that between feminist groups and WOR deputies in 1995 to explore the need for the gender analysis of policy proposals. Gender expertise as well as lobbying experience has accumulated during the past decade. In 1997 Lakhova reached out to feminist organizations with the Charter of Women's Solidarity, an effort to increase cooperation among women's organizations with respect to lobbying; more than three hundred groups signed the charter (WUR did not), but mechanisms for coordinating lobbying remain underdeveloped. And there are victories like the State Duma's passage in 1997 of the Conception on Securing Equal Rights and Equal Opportunities, a measure that outlines legal strategies for achieving gender equality. That "victory," however, unless followed by substantive measures, reflects a lengthy tradition of declarative statements about women's equality. There has been no lack of provisions like the ERA in Soviet and Russian legal frameworks.

Internationally, a new project—the war against terror and the democratization of the Middle East—threatens to displace the mission of "growing" civil society and consolidating democratization in post-Communist countries. At the same time, however, the Russian economy has started to grow, and domestic sources of support may become more available in the future.

The Cultural Framing of Women's Issues

There are significant divides within the women's movement with respect to how women's issues are framed. One Russian woman activist described the women's movement in her country as reminiscent of a communal kitchen, an image that called to mind life in crowded communal apartments, with families sharing kitchens and baths with other, unrelated family units.[8] In this imagined communal kitchen, women in one corner come together in a style evocative of traditional, rural gatherings, while in another corner there is a procession of bellicose amazons (Papkova 2000, 2). As a metaphor, the communal kitchen captures the liveliness as well as the fragmentation of the Russian women's movement.

This analysis of cultural framing explores that diversity by identifying the dominant strands of gender ideology found in the major streams of activity within the women's movement. This approach overlooks the complexity embedded in different wings of the women's movement but highlights fundamental differences in conceptual approaches to women's issues.

Women's Union of Russia

WUR's understanding of women's position in society shares strong elements of continuity with the Communist past. The central emphasis is on a broad-based program of social protection that will create the conditions that permit working women to fulfill their central mission: motherhood. The protection of motherhood and the equating of women's issues with family and children's issues persist as major prisms for viewing women's lives. As in the Soviet era, improving women's lives entails extending social benefits like maternity leaves and child care rather than changing gender roles. WUR rhetoric reflects a "biology is destiny" view of women as "natural" caretakers, as possessing distinctive qualities like greater patience and a greater commitment to compromise and to defending the weak and the elderly. While these characteristics are associated with women's traditional roles as mothers and wives, they also are cited as reasons why women must participate in the social, economic, and political life of the country. Women's presence is required to counterbalance men's more combative approach to decision making, relative lack of interest in social welfare issues, and so on.

WUR distances itself from feminism by engaging in oblique criticism of feminist and newer women's groups by calling itself closer to "real women." Feminists are regarded as people who ignore the realities of Russian life, who talk at a theoretical level, socialize with foreign journalists, and travel abroad, but who do not accomplish anything at home. Yet WUR does express positions that bring it closer to other women's groups. A particularly important point shared across major women's groups involves a heightened appreciation for the need to turn equal rights on paper into equal opportunity in practice, given the traditional penchant for empty rhetoric on women's rights.[9] It should be noted that the 1993 Russian Constitution departs from tradition by containing a clause guaranteeing "equal opportunities" as well as the more traditional phrase "equal rights," thanks to the work of legal scholar Liudmila Zavadskaia, who worked with WUR and served as a WOR deputy.

The Feminist Movement

Feminists reject the idea that Communism emancipated women and seek to advance the democratic ideals of individual and personal dignity. They note that Communism effectively "replaced the concept of the female personality with the female masses" (Aivazova 1994, 161). A Western-style women's movement that accentuates women as individuals runs up against patriarchal and Communist traditions that submerge women's identity in categories like motherhood and the working class. And they reject the mainstream emphasis on biological determinism in favor of socialization as the fundamental explanation for the distinctive patterns found in men's and women's lives.

From definitions of discrimination taken from the UN Convention on the Elimination of All Forms of Discrimination against Women (CEDAW) to feminist stances on sexual violence, the feminist movement has imported cultural frames and terminology unfamiliar to most Russians. That may isolate feminists from the larger society and slow the pace of change. For example, family planning (planirovanie sem'i) and reproductive rights (reproduktivnye prava) were translated into Russian, borrowed wholesale from abroad in an effort to join the world of "civilized" countries and more specifically allow the Russian Association of Family Planning, founded in the early 1990s, to easily interact with the international movement. But as Lakhova (as cited by Azhgikhina 1995b, 10) remarked, not only are these concepts unknown to the public, but she doubts whether even half of the Duma deputies understand them. In other words, it would have been more expedient to wrap new ideas in traditional attire. Reproductive rights and family planning could have been packaged as aspects of "safe motherhood" or the "protection of motherhood," more readily accepted frameworks in the Russian context.

On the other hand, the introduction of new language and "frames" may be part and parcel of the process of globalization, education, and innovation. For Russia, this is not a new development. Over the centuries the bulk of Russian political terms—including the words for "party" and "politics"—have come from foreign languages. There is a middle ground between all-out adoption of new cultural frames and sticking with traditional frameworks. One strategy involves what Armine Ishkanian (2004) describes as "talking gender": the way women's NGOs in Armenia use feminist/gender discourses to win grants from Western donors but employ more "traditional" discourses—caring, nurturing mothers working for the renewal of the nation—in the local context. Ishkanian refers to this approach as "practical," but Russian activists seem not as inclined to engage in this behavior as their Armenian counterparts. The reason seems clear: The Russian activists strongly embrace a feminist identity, and that commitment keeps them on a rather "purist" path. In addition, there can be problems with unhappy donors, who expect to see what they define as "progressive" in grantees' projects.

Movement of Women of Russia

While MWR's program shares many elements in common with WUR, there is a shift toward greater use of terms associated with democratization, like *civil society, rule of law,* and *human rights.* Although there is considerable emphasis on the family, there are departures from traditional thinking. The MWR views the family as the site where both men and women achieve self-realization and declares that men and women are equally responsible for raising children and that both should be equally eligible to take leaves to look after children. There also is strong support for the development of family planning services as well as a network of crisis centers for women and children (*Ustav Programma* 1996).[10] Positive references to international standards and practices, particularly with respect to UN conventions and Western European countries, are employed to back up MWR's positions and prod Russian society and government toward new ways of thinking about women's issues. Yet the MWR avoids the label "feminist" and favors strong government as a means of securing human rights, promoting economic growth, and guaranteeing social and national security. MWR, while supportive of reform within the Russian military, falls short of the antiwar (Chechnya) and antimilitarist approaches more associated with the Committees of Soldiers' Mothers (see Caiazza 2002).

Summary

According to Jo Freeman (1975, 12–13), the ideological basis for feminist sentiment in the Western world involves the logical extension to women of the rights and responsibilities of individuals. For the Russian women's movement, cultural frames place a greater stress on motherhood and the family. Olga Lipovskaya (1994, 275–76), a leading feminist activist in St. Petersburg, contends that Russia's collectivist mentality renders "it difficult to reach the level of individualism necessary to form a consciousness of gender comparable to that in the West." She expects Russian women to redefine or adjust Western feminism accordingly. The centrality of motherhood and family are reinforced by the "biology is destiny" explanation for gender differences, which are presumed to be natural and immutable. Those beliefs facilitate the acceptance of societal gender patterns as "women's fate" that might otherwise fuel a sense of injustice that could power a movement to overcome unjust discrimination. Yet these gender discourses did not restrict women to the private sphere or suggest that serious work and marriage were incompatible.

CONCLUSION

The contemporary women's movement in Russia is distinct from its American counterpart in several key respects. First, the dominant gender ideology in Russia makes the formation of gender consciousness a more formidable task. While American women could look at their male counterparts and ask why they should not enjoy the same opportunities, Russian women were more likely to accept that nature had given them a different mission in the family and in life. Rather than regarding male-dominated society as oppressive, Russian women emerged from a seventy-year history in which the gulf between the *nomenklatura* and the general populace overshadowed other considerations. Both men and women were victims. Indeed, in the Soviet case the kitchen table represented an island of freedom, the lone place where close friends could gather and talk freely, a far cry from the imagery of constrained opportunities associated with domesticity in the West.

Second, the global women's movement has played a significant role in spreading and sustaining feminist activities in Russia. Does this model of development work? The feminist movement is at a crossroads, where international assistance is likely to decline sharply. On the ground there is a domestic violence movement, many gender studies programs, an infrastructure of contacts between many women's organizations, and much more. It is unclear whether the movement is jump-started, whether it has enough momentum to thrive and grow in a context of greater dependence on its own resources. Or it may follow that the Russian women's movement develops more along the lines of WUR or MWR, reflecting more an amalgam of Russian traditions, the Communist legacy, post-Communist conditions, and international influences.

Third, the Russian women's movement faces great challenges in building cooperation and solidarity across women's groups. The lines of division with respect to political strategies and cultural frames appear more severe than in the United States and more troubling, given the weakness of women's voices in the halls of power in Russian society. Expanding the scope of the women's movement, bringing in more participants, also looms as a major issue, given the anemic state of civil society as a whole.

Finally, it should be noted that Russian society has undergone tremendous change, and the current period may be watershed years for the women's movement, perhaps similar to the 1970s in the United States, when public opinion about gender roles changed significantly. For example, public opinion has shifted toward a greater appreciation of the value of work in women's lives. A survey taken in 1995 and repeated in 2001 demonstrated that Russians from all demographic groups had become significantly more likely to name a good job over a successful marriage as a priority for an actual or would-be teenage daughter. Over a six-year period the respective priorities shifted from 46 percent to 27 percent favoring a successful marriage and from 36 to 64 percent mentioning a good job ("Public Opinion . . . " 2001). This fluidity suggests caution in assessing the future direction of the Russian women's movement—it is too early to state with any certainty how this movement will develop.

NOTES

1. A group of Leningrad women in 1979 founded an organization, Women and Russia, and published a *samizdat* (underground) almanac that advanced feminist ideals. The group split over differences regarding a feminism based on religious beliefs versus a Western style of political feminism. KGB persecution led to the leadership emigrating or being forced to emigrate. The efforts of these feminists received more attention abroad than in the Soviet Union or from the current generation of Russian feminists. See Morgan (1980); Ruthchild (1983); and Holt (1985).

2. The demand that women leave heavy physical labor did not come from the women who did such work. In many cases women preferred these positions because of earlier retirement, better pay, and other benefits. Political figures, including women deputies, in the USSR Congress of People's Deputies especially raised this issue in 1989; it was also a theme frequently picked up in the press.

3. This discourse actually originated in the late 1970s when the view began to be expressed that state policy should encourage women to place greater importance on their maternal and domestic roles and less emphasis on work outside the home (Attwood 1990, 4–6). In 1981 new state policies like increased family allowances were initiated with the aim of boosting birth rates, and 1984 marked the introduction of a new course on "The Ethics and Psychology of Family Life" for secondary students that sought to reinforce separate male and female roles and personality traits, or, as one advocate put it, raise girls to be "more feminine and housewifely, more kindly, neat and gentle" (see Attwood 1990, 184). This drift away from a concern with raising girls to be good citizens reflected a preoccupation with declining birth rates and secondarily with family tension and divorce.

4. ISEPP itself had been founded only in 1988, an indication of the growing importance of demography as a policy problem and research priority. At that time Rimashevskaia was one of only two women who headed a research institute in Moscow. She had been a friend of Gorbachev's when both had been students in the early 1950s in Moscow, a connection that provided some protection for her endeavors.

5. The US-NIS Consortium (after 1996 the Consortium of Women's Nongovernmental Associations) was a Western-funded coalition that funded numerous projects, including seminars, conferences, the publication of the first text treating the issue of sexual harassment, the distribution of a Russian-language version of *Our Bodies, Ourselves*, the development of e-mail networks for women's organizations, travel grants to attend the United Nations Fourth World Conference on Women in Beijing, etc.

6. Yet an approach that emphasizes humanitarian relief would provide so little money per person that it would not make a dent in the problem. An argument can be made that Western assistance geared toward human rights, greater transparency, accountability, and responsiveness on the part of Russian governments at all levels will ultimately aid all women's NGOs, including those indifferent to the agendas pushed by Western donors. See Squier 2003.

7. There also were low numbers of women in the eighty-nine regional legislatures of the Russian Federation—women held only 9 percent of those seats in 1997. Women held only a handful of leading executive positions at the regional or federal level.

8. Communal apartments became common with the onset of growing urban populations in the 1930s, World War II destruction, and the low priority until the late 1950s of building new apartment buildings on a massive scale. Because of an urban housing shortage, apartments that formerly housed one family were divided up, with families typically given one or more private rooms but sharing kitchen and bathroom facilities with other families.

9. Liudmila Zavadskaia, a scholar at the Institute of State and Law, participated in the constitutional conferences held in 1993 and worked to get "equal opportunities" included in the new Russian constitution. Zavadskaia is an interesting figure who worked with WUR, was elected to the State Duma in 1993 as part of the Women of Russia electoral bloc, and has worked over time with feminists as well.

10. The Children of Russia program, including the program on family planning, which WOR advanced between 1993 and 1995, was largely developed by Lakhova and the Commission on Women, Family, and Demography that she headed within the Yeltsin administration. Lakhova has been a firm advocate of reproductive rights, a stance that may stem from her own family background. Her mother had died from the complications of an illegal abortion. Abortion was illegal in the Soviet Union from 1936 to 1955.

10

Trends and Transformations in Women's Movements in Japan and the United States

Joyce Gelb

This chapter compares women's movements in Japan and the United States, the world's two leading economic powers, in the contemporary period. The relationships outlined by Banaszak in chapter 1, which combine resource mobilization, political opportunity structures, and culture and framing as essential to social movement development and impact, will be assessed to analyze the role of women's movements in these two very different contexts. The Gender Empowerment Measure of the United Nations Development Project (UNDP) ranks Japan forty-first and the United States eleventh. Taking into account such factors as income, percent of female administrators, and legislative seats (Gelb 2003, 2), this suggests that Japanese women are engaged in a more difficult struggle to gain equity. The role of international feminism, or indirect external pressure, *kansetsu gaiatsu,* in creating a basis for change through transnational actors such as the United Nations will be considered as a special force in Japanese policymaking related to gender. This is referred to as the "politics of externality" (see Gelb 2003, 4). In the United States, an initial world "standard bearer" with regard to gender equity policy, a "politics of insularity," which eschews interaction with international norms, has sometimes prevented the vigorous feminist movement from achieving new gains. Seen from this viewpoint, the historic international perspective and globalization of the U.S. women's movement, reported by Banaszak in chapter 1, at present has limited relevance to opportunities available to American women.

In both nations, advocacy coalitions involving increased women's political representation and activist women's mobilization have occasionally joined forces to achieve policy change. In the United States, the Congressional Caucus for Women's Issues (CCWI) has served as a force for women's policy advocacy in government. In Japan, in the Diet, cross-party coalitions of women representatives have played a role in advocating for women's policies through the phenomenon of *giin rippo*, or private members' bills.

Finally, women's movements in both nations have had to contend with "backlash," possibly limiting options for future advocacy and policy change.

A NOTE ON COMPARING POLITICAL
SYSTEMS AND OPPORTUNITY STRUCTURES

A brief overview of the ways in which the different structures of Japanese and American politics affect women's choices and options is necessary in order to understand movement development.

The U.S. political system is characterized by relatively fragmented government and a reluctant welfare state, a weak two-party system, and a major role for interest groups and social movements. Women have increased their representation in elective and appointive office (particularly the latter) but lag behind other, particularly Nordic, nations with regard to national legislative position. Women have incrementally increased their representation in Congress, now holding 13.6 percent of the seats in both houses (CAWP 2002b). The American women's movements are characterized by a significant national presence as interest groups and movements that combine national and local organizational structures (as outlined by Reger and Staggenborg in chapter 6), as well as increasing numbers of policymaking elites in the bureaucracy and courts. American feminists have a vast panoply of strategies at their disposal, from legal advocacy to campaign finance (à la EMILY's List) and lobbying before Congress and the executive branch to affect government policy. However, American feminists are adversely affected by the growing conservatism of the Republican Party, which, in a break with historic tradition after 1980, opposes abortion rights and other feminist goals. Organized feminism has faced several decades of right-wing rule and virulent opposition from antiabortion and antifeminist groups institutionalized politically (see Barakso chapter 5 for a discussion of the impact of these developments on NOW).

The Japanese political system is characterized by the political dominance of the Liberal Democratic Party (LDP) since 1955, though it now shares power with a coalition including two opposition parties. Significant political control is held by bureaucrats and the business community, arenas in which women have had little presence to date. It is widely felt that the Japanese system lacks transparency and openness, providing little space and opportunity for advocacy groups, such as women's groups, to operate effectively. Representation for women in government has increased, both in the first cabinet led by Koizumi Junichiro, with five female members out of seventeen after 2000, including the foreign minister (there were three women in his second cabinet as of 2004), and with better numbers in the Diet. In the less power-

ful Upper House (which uses proportional representation for some seat se-
lection), women comprise 15.4 percent of the total, compared to 7 percent
of the House of Representatives (Ichikawa Fusae 2001, 2).[1] Women have led
the Japanese Socialist Party, and the other third parties including the New
Sakigake and New Conservative parties, in recent years, as well.

Traditional roles and values in Japanese society continue to limit women's
opportunities for choice regarding occupations and political advocacy.
Women's lives have been and still are defined by child care, housework, and
care of the elderly (Liddle and Nakajima 2000, 312). Work outside the home
and political participation have been constrained by the gendered division of
labor, in which men dominate economic life. A widespread view has been that
"female emancipation is only partial. . . . Most Japanese females are not interested in politics. They make no effort through the ballot box to change Japan's
male oriented society, nor are they much concerned by the discrimination (illegal) which they suffer at work" (quoted in Liddle and Nakajima 2000, 320).
Others take a more positive stance toward the role of present-day Japanese
women, suggesting that it was the women's vote in part that ended the dominance of the LDP in Japanese politics in 1989 and also brought Doi Takako,
new head of the Socialist Party, to a more prominent role. This article will suggest that at least for some women, the process of legitimating women's rights
is underway, with women creating new feminine subjectivities, diversifying,
and transforming (see Liddle and Nakajima 2000, 324). As suggested above,
the assertion of rights has been aided by recourse to international feminism.

In the past, in contrast to the more structured and institutionalized movements in the United States, women's movements in Japan have been characterized by decentralization, fragmentation, and single-issue focus, partially as
a result of the lack of receptivity of the national political system. Increasing
indications of more inclusive networking and coalition building among feminist activists across issue lines, with an ability to pressure the central government, is explored below, although it is still difficult to discern an ongoing
women's movement presence at the national level. To provide a comprehensive view of all of the dimensions of the multifaceted efforts at mobilizing women in Japan, the analysis that follows emphasizes several different
aspects of Japanese women's movement organizing: feminist groups advocating for policy change, working women's groups who have mobilized
against discriminatory practices, and housewives active in local politics.

FEMINIST MOVEMENTS IN THE UNITED STATES: THE "MYTH" OF POSTFEMINISM

"The story of the women's movement in the US is one of transformation, expansion and diversification" (Wolfe and Tucker 1995, 436). In a similar vein,

Tarrow wrote that "the women's movement [is] among the most successful in American social history, effecting—among other things—a profound shift in political culture" (1994, 184). He points to a rich and varied repertoire, a network structure embedded in society and institutions, and electoral advantage in explaining what he perceives as extraordinary success. American feminist movements have been characterized by increasingly well-established and professional networks of national organizations, coordinating a national network of groups concerned with mainstream reform as well as goals of liberal equality (Gelb and Hart 1999, 151). The movement has also contained vigorous, though less visible, grassroots movements, which increasingly provide service delivery as well as advocacy. Increasingly, early dichotomies between radical and reformist feminists, or "older" and "younger" branches, or bureaucratic versus collectivist forms, have been left behind (Ferree and Martin 1995, 5) as the movements have become defined by coexistence between groups with sometimes differing goals and strategies that are all united in their commitment to feminism (Disney and Gelb 2000). Networks and coalition building have been emphasized across ideological and issue lines. At their most effective, as a result, feminists have been able to adapt with flexibility to changing conditions, pursuing varying goals and strategies.

Scholars writing about the women's movement in the United States since the second wave of feminism in the 1960s have emphasized the significance, political impact, and proliferation of feminist groups through at least the 1980s (Costain 1992; Ferree and Hess 2000; Gelb 2003; Minkoff 1995). Mayer Zald (1987, 19) wrote that "of all the social movements on the current scene . . . because of its specialized organizations and constituencies . . . the feminist movement appears to have the best chance for high levels of mobilization and activity." Addressing issues of movement change but not decline, Nancy Whittier suggests that in the 1980s individual feminists searched for new ways to be activists in the face of mounting opposition, financial difficulty, and their own aging, but contends that the women's movement has not only survived the 1990s but began to grow again in new and provocative ways in the 1990s (1995, 3). However, others view the current role of American feminism more skeptically. Anne Costain has contended that the "peak period" for feminist organization has passed, political opportunities have narrowed, consciousness has diminished, and organizations are preoccupied with just maintaining themselves (1992, 141). From an even more critical perspective, Burk and Hartmann argue that in a period of twenty years, women's organizations have lost "political power and came to be perceived as irrelevant (or even hostile) to the common woman" (1996, 19). This analysis may be more a reflection of problems of the U.S. political system than a true indictment of feminist advocacy. Nelson and Carver contend that "women's organizing—especially feminist organizing—had many voices but few vehicles for translating demand into sustained action. (1994, 739). None of these writers emphasizes the constraints that the forces of right-wing political reaction have placed on American feminists.

Political Representation by American Women

According to *Washington Representatives* (1997), a compilation of national lobbyists in the nation's capital, although the feminist presence decreased in the early 1990s, it began to grow again later in the decade. From 1982 to 1997, the number of active groups increased from 75 to 140. As many as forty-two political action committees (PACs) support increased electoral representation of women (Brenner 1996, 69, n.79). Since its establishment in 1977, the CCWI has been a force for policy reform on women's issues including violence against women and women's health, often with greater impact now that some women in Congress serve in more senior party and committee positions. Over 40 percent of all elected women belong to women's groups, according to one study, meaning that large numbers have inculcated many feminist values (Darcy, Welch, and Clark 1995, 37). Disney and Gelb (2000, 40) document the continued vitality of feminist movements in the United States, partially attributable to their "institutionalization" as national level lobbyists. At the same time, the range of groups described by Gelb and Palley in 1996 continues to flourish and grow: single-issue groups, staff-run groups, policy think-tanks, litigation groups, large-scale membership groups such as NOW, often with strong local branches, and campaign-related groups/PACs such as EMILY's List, Republican Wish List, and Voters for Choice (1996, xvi–xx). "Sub movements" have proliferated under the larger feminist umbrella, with such specializations as pro-choice, anti rape and domestic violence, and women's health (Ferree and Hess 2000, 183). Issue-focused coalitions reflecting specialization include the Coalition on Women and Job Training, Women's Health Action Mobilization, and National Network to End Domestic Violence (Disney and Gelb 2000, 53). Women's coalitions also continue to grow and develop, with tendencies toward fragmentation offset in part by such groups as the one-hundred-member Council of Presidents, which coordinates activity among Washington-based women's rights groups. In addition, feminist activists are involved in political party organizing, primarily in the Democratic Party in recent years given the hostility of Republicans and partisan polarization, for reasons outlined above (see Barakso chapter 5 for a discussion of this phenomenon).

Movement Changes and Challenges

Change is clearly in evidence, as an aging movement cannot remain static; however, far from being dead, the feminist movement has become more diffuse, organizing everywhere, often unobtrusively (Katzenstein 1998; Wolfe and Tucker 1995). New venues for feminist activism include the military, professional organizations, and other diverse institutions. It is the case that membership in feminist organizations tends to rise in periods of perceived crisis, for example, antiabortion court rulings, election of conservative presidents, and that many movement groups rely on "conscience constituencies," which provide resources rather than active membership (see Barakso chapter 5 for a similar point). Another cautionary note regarding American feminism relates to the significance of antifeminist political backlash, with "New Right" presidents occupying the White House for twelve years in the late twentieth century and again after 2000. Right-wingers also dominated both houses for six years during the earlier period, as well as after 2000. As Bashevkin has suggested, the virulence of the antifeminist movement institutionalized in the Republican Party after 1980 probably has no counterpart anywhere in the democratic world (1994, 670). This has resulted in the need for defensive adaptations and an emphasis on survival rather than growth in terms of new policy initiatives.

A major concern for American feminism in the future is how to move from this type of reactive stance to a more proactive vision of the future (Ferree and Hess 2000, 182). One response has been to turn to state politics; among the fifty states, many have been receptive to policy change (see Bernstein 1997). And even under New Right preeminence in politics, feminists have been able to achieve some positive change, for example, the Family and Medical Leave Act (FMLA) of 1993 and Violence Against Women Act (VAWA) of 1994, discussed below.

Fueled in part by women's studies programs and campus-based activism, younger women have organized as well. Groups such as Women's Action Coalition (WAC), Women's Health Action Mobilization (WHAM), and Third Wave are composed of twenty- and thirty-year-olds, who are not afraid to use dramatic confrontational tactics to dramatize their grievances regarding the system's inadequacy.

Policy Change

Movement success may be measured in several ways: through the continuation of movement mobilization, cultural change, or change in collective consciousness and discursive politics, which may create resources for further mobilization and change, and, of course, policy impact. Measured by the latter, in the policy sphere, a major contribution of American feminist movements has been to change local, state, and federal policy through legislative and judicial decisions. The movement has achieved recognition as a major participant in decision making.

Initial success for American feminists came in the context of the implementation of Title VII of the 1964 Civil Rights Act, which, via continued litigation and lobbying, created major educational and occupational advances. A major success for American women has been the economic mobility of American women; a huge 46.4 percent are in management and professional careers, perhaps the largest such group in the world (UNIFEM 2000). The contrast with Japanese women, discussed below, is clear.

Feminists have also been engaged in other activities. They have achieved significant success in policy areas related to violence against women, including domestic violence, at the state and national levels. In part under the leadership of the NOW Legal Defense and Education Fund, they were successful in passing the VAWA, part of an omnibus crime bill in 1994, four years after it was initially proposed (see Daniels 1997). Each of the fifty states and most municipalities also have legislation on domestic violence, in many instances mandating state intervention and providing for mandatory arrest of suspects (Schneider 2000, 186–87). At each level of government, there are provisions for training of police and judicial personnel, increased attention to protection for abused women, and additional support provided for shelters. The national legislation provided unprecedented monetary support for this struggle. Feminists have also been active in supporting efforts to end sexual harassment and other "women specific" policies. In the case of rape, increased public consciousness and new options for victims—including rape crisis centers and self-help strategies—have been the legacy of the antirape movement (Bevacqua 2000, 194). In addition, rape shield laws, need for corroboration of a complainant's story, and abandonment of the "rule of resistance" have been enacted in most state and local areas (Schneider 2000, 189).

Women's policy advocacy has been less effective in at least two other areas. With regard to abortion and reproductive choice, the context has been highly contentious and politicized since the 1973 Supreme Court decision in *Roe v. Wade*. The impact of a hostile environment continues to have a profound effect on limiting progress and furthering a proactive feminist agenda. Angered by the pro-choice decision, anti-choice groups coalesced against the decision and mobilized effectively in the fifty states, at the national legislative level, and in the courts. They have often been successful in limiting access to abortion provision, using violence against abortion providers, among other tactics. They have organized campaign-related strategies and probably gained their greatest legitimacy through their alliance with the Republican Party since 1980. The scope of conflict between the contending forces has been fierce. The pro-choice movement survives, as membership and protest figures suggest, but there has been a cost. Much energy has been consumed in trying to defend reproductive rights, a necessary battle, but one which has sometimes limited the movement's ability to develop new policy initiatives.

Another area that has proven difficult for American feminists has been comparing work and family life/motherhood. Increasingly, European and other democratic nations (including Japan, at least on paper) have moved to provide working women with special benefits, such as paid parental leave, state-supported child care, and the like. In the United States, however, a reluctant welfare state has not moved in this direction. Feminists did press for the adoption of the FMLA, signed into law by President Clinton in 1993 after two vetoes by George H. W. Bush. But although it does mark a national recognition of the need to balance work and family life, it is unpaid. Other supports for working women, including federally supported day care, have been ignored by the individualistic, market-based model employed by U.S. policymakers.

And a regressive policy, the Personal Responsibility and Work Opportunity Reconciliation Law, passed in 1996, creates punitive circumstances for poor women dependent on public support for their livelihood. It ends the federal entitlement to support for aid to families with dependent children, providing for time-limited aid and forced work requirements in order for aid to be forthcoming. This type of legislation has no parallel in other democratic nations. The result has been to exacerbate the differences between poor women and others; feminist activism has been unable to effectively address such fundamental barriers to equality—for working women and poor women (see Ferree and Hess 2000, 207).

JAPANESE WOMEN: MOVEMENTS, RIGHTS, AND POLICY CHANGE

The Japanese women's movement had its origins before the turn of the twentieth century, with women seeking suffrage, equality, socialist feminist goals, and reproductive freedom, much as in the United States and the West (Liddle and Nakajima 2000, 14–15). Working women's groups also formed in the nineteenth century. After a period of repression before and during World War II, women's activism resumed. Japanese women's movements, while active in many places in Japanese society, have tended to be localized, single-issue oriented, and fragmented. Nonetheless, several large-scale membership groups represent women's interests, if not feminism, including Chifuren (the League of Women's Regional Organizations) and Shufuren (the Housewives Association). Both have been involved in campaigns for consumer issues, often with considerable impact (Mackie 1996, 267–68). These groups often work in conjunction with local women and help to check industry and government, in a political context in which effective opposition is often difficult to achieve (Buckley 1994, 160).

As a result of the U.S. occupation after World War II, women gained the vote and right to run for office, and also new constitutional guarantees. Among them was Article 14, which promised equality in the family, education, employment, and political representation (Liddle and Nakajima 2000, 152). Civil Code reform removed the legal basis for women's subordination in the family, including the lack of the right to own family property and in-equality in marriage and divorce. Because many of the guarantees proved to have only symbolic as opposed to real meaning, a "second wave" of feminism emerged in the early 1970s among women who had been active in student peace movements, similar to mobilization in the United States. As the twentieth century drew to a close, several other strands of feminism developed in Japan, including efforts to increase women's numbers in politics, especially increasing national representation, and also working women's advocacy. A significant impact on Japanese women and feminists in particular has been international feminism, or *kansetsu gaitsu*, through which emerging international standards of gender equity have been used to prod a reluctant Japanese government into changing policy. These efforts began with the 1975 International Women's Year and continued at the 4th World Women's Conference in Beijing when Japanese women comprised the largest delegation (together with the United States and China) as well as at the Bejing + Five meeting in New York in 2000. These efforts include successful pressure on the Japanese government to sign the Convention on the Elimination of All Forms of Discrimination Against Women (CEDAW) in 1985, which the U.S. government has never done. The impact of the international human and women's rights movements on Japanese policy and mobilization cannot be overestimated (Fujieda and Fujimura-Fanselow 1995, 158). In the present era, some of the various strands of feminism and women's movements have joined forces, creating a potentially greater force on the political scene, sometimes working in conjunction with female legislators in the national parliament, the Diet, through advocacy coalitions.

Feminism in Japan

As in the United States, a feminist movement in Japan sprang up in the 1970s. Japanese movements were motivated both by goals of "sexual liberation" and dominant Japanese cultural values. *Uman ribu* (women's rib) groups attempted to establish collectives and mounted protests, for example, against the proposed revision of the Eugenic Protection Law, which provided easy access to abortion for women.

Founded in 1975, at the initiative of Ichikawa Fusae and Tanaka Sumiko, other Diet members, and other long-standing feminists, the International Women's Year Action Group still endures. Rather than making consciousness-raising key as was common among some American groups, they worked on issues such as education, employment, and representation. First comprising forty-eight, and now fifty-one, women's groups, this umbrella organization has applied domestic and international pressure, in a pattern that has now become well established (see Mackie 1996, 271). This group framed a set of demands for legislative change (discussed below), including the Equal

Employment Opportunity Law (EEOL) and Nationality Law (providing for assumption of citizenship through the mother as well as father), and pressing the Japanese government to sign CEDAW, partially by threatening embarrassment if ratification did not occur (Buckley 1994, 163).

Groups formed as well to contest women-only home economics courses in high school, to preserve abortion and the "pill,"[2] and against male sex tours and sexist court judgments (Buckley 1994, 163).

As in the United States and elsewhere, feminist activism has developed around issues of equal rights, domestic violence, abortion restrictions, and the like. The group Agora, founded in the 1960s by Saito Chiyo, helped to create child care facilities and provide opportunities for women to use their skills in the public sphere. It ultimately became a resource and training center for women, like many others in Japan, with centers evolving to meet the needs of local women (Mackie 1996, 269). It began to publish a journal in 1972, now the longest-running feminist journal in Japan (Buckley 1994, 157, 251).

Sexual harassment was first raised as a public issue through a widely publicized "poll of 10,000" conducted by suburban feminists in 1989, as well as a successful law suit in Fukuoka, Japan, in 1992 (Hada 1995, 266). Attention to harassment has advanced through litigation and the 1997 amendments to the Equal Employment Law, discussed below. The first rape crisis center, operated by feminists, was opened in 1983 (Hada 1995, 265). In 1992, feminists founded the Domestic Violence Action and Research Group, although there are still relatively few shelters available to Japanese women. Yayori Matsui helped to found the Asian Women's Association in the 1970s, which campaigns against sex tourism and exploitation of women and also campaigned for the revision of the Nationality Law, to remove sexist conditions for citizenship. Groups such as the Asian Women's Association have called attention to the role of Japan in creating a forced group of "comfort women" or military prostitutes to service their armed forces. Thus far they have not been able to press the Japanese government to provide compensation to the victims. Such movements do link Japanese women with their sisters in other Asian nations, as part of the effort to be a part of the international feminist community.

Japanese women often communicate through *minikomi,* or newsletters, which are handwritten or mimeographed, and relate individual stories and local news—providing alternatives to the bland mainstream national press (Buckley 1994, 253). These informal networks of women's communication, now supplemented by the Internet, have allowed the many and diverse feminist groups throughout the country to stay in close contact while remaining independent. Estimates of the numbers of such publications were around forty thousand by the end of the 1960s (Buckley 1994, 158).

Despite the characterization of Japanese feminism as localized and loosely organized, countertendencies to this model have been evident throughout the postwar period. In fact, a number of efforts, such as those to block change in abortion laws, gain free access to contraception, and produce change in equal employment policy, have demonstrated that seemingly disparate groups can be linked in a coherent way to affect Japanese institutions and policies, with varying degrees of success (see Mackie 1996, 278). Newer groups such as Peking JAC (Joint Accountability Coalition) have sought to develop a national presence, with the establishment of a center in Tokyo, though it is primarily a coalition of loosely structured groups with its "non-concrete" structure located in regional caucuses (interview with Nagai Yoshiko, Peking JAC, Tokyo, November 7, 2001). This organization holds an annual general meeting and meets with bureaucratic representatives twice a year, as is characteristic of many other women's groups.

Feminism appears to be a continuing force, albeit among a relatively small minority, as young women gather around the Asian Women's Association and Association for Japanese Women's Studies (Hashimoto Hiroko, personal communication, January 23, 2002).

Advocacy for Increased Political Representation

Efforts to increase women's representation in Japan have had some success in recent years. Doi Takako, a woman law professor who became leader of the Socialist Party of Japan after 1987, helped to galvanize women's greater interest in running for office. Doi campaigned for women candidates—even for nonmembers of the Socialist Party—in conjunction with networks of local feminists (Ling and Matsuno 1992, 62). In recent years, WIN WIN, modeled after the U.S.-based EMILY's List, has provided support to women candidates, including Domoto Akiko's successful campaign for the governorship of Chiba prefecture. This group supports candidates who have political experience and gender equality agendas (interview with Akamatsu Reiko, WIN WIN, Tokyo, October 16, 2001). Women's interests have been institutionalized to some extent in government, first in the Ministry of Labor Women's Bureau and now in the Council and Bureau for Gender Equality in the Prime Minister's Office, "national machinery" in accordance with Beijing directives, established in 1999. There have been increased numbers of women in the cabinet, three as of 2004 (including the foreign minister, Kawaguchi Yoriko), down from five in the first Koizumi cabinet.

In the Diet, as discussed below, female representatives have sometimes functioned as an informal nonpartisan bloc to support policies favorable to women's interests through the use of *giin rippo*, or private members' bills.

While a "gender gap" between male and female voters is not as visible in Japan as in the United States, in 1989 Japanese women, angered by sex scandals, corruption, and an increased consumption tax, helped to engineer a stunning defeat to the dominant LDP and increase the number of elected women representatives (Ling and Matsuno 1992, 58). There is some evidence for distinctive issue and partisan preferences among women, which may have consequences at the ballot box, including greater support for the Komeito (or Clean Government) Party, one of the LDP's present coalition partners (Patterson and Nishikawa 2002).

AFER, the Alliance of Feminist Representatives, was founded by Mitsui Mariko, who hoped to increase women's numbers to 30 percent (Morley 1999, 139). It had 250 members, 190 representing local assembly members; 20 national representatives; 40 activists (some former elected officials); and 10 male members as of 2002 (Kubo Kimiko, Director, FIMA, personal communication, December 5, 2002). It meets annually to exchange information and ideas. Other efforts to increase women's elective representation include that of the Fusae Ichikawa Memorial Association (FIMA), which conducts "*seiji*" (political) schools to train women for political office, while the short-lived New Japan Party in the 1990s offered a one-year political school to interested women. The Democratic Party, *Minshuto,* now the main opposition party in Japan, makes some special efforts to train and recruit women candidates.

Less Traditional Paths to Political Influence

Housewife Activists

For many women, conditions for men in the workplace are so difficult and subject to employers' strictures that they have no wish to enter the labor force full-time or bear economic responsibility. Their marginal workplace status is reinforced by tax laws, which provide an incentive to work part-time, tax free (below 1.2 million yen per year). These factors, together with the persistence of traditional roles, have meant that more women resist full-time employment and see their main role as being mothers and wives—for some, more private roles have been transformed into "housewife activism" (see Fujimura-Fanselow and Kameda 1995, xxviii). Middle-class, well-educated, relatively high status economically, and urban/suburban, local female activists "have excelled at organization and lobbying" (Ueno, in Buckley 1994, 275). Women have been the core of voluntarism, in consumer, antinuclear, peace, and antipollution, as well as cooperative, movements, beginning with their leadership of the anti-Minimata disease campaign during the 1960s (Morley 1999, 122; Ling and Matsuno 1992, 56). Women are also active in self-study groups and use local women's centers for political activity, as well as adult education centers. In addition to NWEC (National Women's Education Center), founded in the 1970s by the Ministry of Education, Science and Culture (Morley 1999, 123), which provides meeting space and resources, women's centers are government supported in prefectures, cities, and local communities. Among the most active have been the Yokahama and Kitakyushu Women's forums, the Dawn Center in Osaka, Wings/Kyoto, and the Tokyo Women's Plaza. All provide meeting space, workshops, and training of various kinds, and provide resource materials (Fujieda and Fujimura-Fanselow 1995, 176). The support of local and prefectural governments for women's resource and community centers has led to unforeseen and potentially more radical outcomes than initially intended by the funders as the "politics of these centers has been renegotiated" (Buckley 1994, 180).

The vigor of activism is impressive, given the sex-based stereotypes that continue to prevail in Japan (Morley 1999, 141). Working and nonworking women participate in local community activities, and, as is true elsewhere, women gain citizenship and access to politics in a manner different from men (Le Blanc 1999, 123). As suggested below, they may represent a new kind of citizens' movement in local Japanese politics.

Initially many women became active in "soap movements"—purchasing cooperatives. They embraced activism, decrying the evil effects of synthetic products and pollution, including waste disposal, clean water, and other environmental and consumer issues. They founded recycling clubs and mounted campaigns to get signatures to protest the side effects of Japan's rapid industrialization. The Seiktatsu (or Daily Life) Clubs, founded in 1965 by leftist men, are among the most interesting of the numerous cooperative groups in any given locale. They have a huge membership in Kanagawa, Tokyo, and elsewhere—47,000 in Kanagawa alone in 1997, and a total membership of almost 250,000 (Er 1999, 114; Morley 1999, 129; Sato 1995, 367), almost all of whom are women.

The groups have now moved into supervision and management of welfare activities, providing service provision through care for the elderly and children, and have developed economic enterprises through workers' collectives, catering to "niche" markets by selling vegetables, organic pastry, and jam. They have also entered political office through the "Network" (*Netto*) movement and even joined movements for gender equality. The Networks have been surprisingly successful in electing women to local office (Ling and Matsuno 1992, 60). In the early 1990s, they proved their vote-getting ability, making particular strides in larger cities like Yokohama and Kawasaki, as well as Tokyo. They have been unusually effective in recruiting and mobilizing women locally, in community and electoral politics, doubling their representation in 1995. In 1995, they comprised eleven of eighteen local assemblywomen in Yokohama City and 40 of 106 in Kanagawa prefecture (Gelb and Estevez Abe 1998, 270). As of the end of October 2001, the group had sixty-one women serving in Tokyo-area town and city assemblies, including six at the Metropolitan level (Ogai Tokuko, personal communication, November 15, 2001). Network members comprise 3.8 percent of the 6.4 percent female local assembly representatives (Ogai Tokuko, personal communication, February 1, 2002).

While many members are antipathetic to gender equality issues, for a small minority, values and goals have been dramatically transformed and they have developed a greater sense of gender consciousness (Er 1999, 163; Gelb and Estevez Abe 1998, 264, 268). Seikatsu is one of the few independent political groups to gain any foothold in local politics, perhaps representing a new type of female-based citizens' mobilization.

Working Women's Groups

At work, women's roles have tended to be limited to clerical and low-level jobs, and even in the early 1990s, the traditional function of female tea pouring was in practice in almost all companies, with over 90 percent reporting that only women poured tea (Morley 1999, 74)!

Within this context, a little-studied phenomenon in Japan (at least in English-language publications) has been the emergence of working women's advocacy groups in the late 1990s and into the second millennium. Some of these groups were motivated to mobilize by their attendance at international women's forums such as the 4th UN Women's Conference in Beijing in 1995.[3] There are at least three types of working women's social movement groups: 1) working women's advocacy groups protesting discriminatory policies by employers, related to unequal pay, failure to promote women, and the institutionalization of the gender-biased, two-track employment system; 2) support groups for plaintiffs in sex discrimination litigation; and 3) women's unions, which represent a new approach, seeking resolution of work-related disputes related to women's workplace issues.

Women's groups advocating for change in their workplace and other areas are important contributories to the civil society networks that are emerging in Japan. While many nongovernmental organizations (NGOs) in Japan have been small and localized, working women's advocacy may be developing a more national presence and potentially larger policy impact. Their mobilization also emphasizes the role played by international feminism and conferences in galvanizing advocacy efforts among Japanese working women. This chapter concentrates on the most "political" of the working women's groups, those that emphasize workplace discrimination.

A Note on Women's Unions

Women's unions represent a new development in Japan: combining "new social movements" linked to feminism with labor union organizing, but established in opposition to male-dominated, hierarchical, enterprise-based organization (Kotani 1999, 4). They differ from American women's unions, which are usually organized within labor unions themselves (although the group Nine to Five was initially developed outside the union, it ultimately merged with it). There are presently seven women's unions in Japan—two in Osaka and one each in Tokyo, Niigata, Sendai, Kanagawa, and Sapporo. The first was founded in Osaka in 1987 (Kotani 1999, 1). Some are derived from general unions, from which they split off or were created; this is true of the Tokyo-based union and one in Osaka. Others developed out of consultation groups on domestic violence and sexual harassment; when they received many complaints about labor-related problems, they transformed into labor unions.

In the Tokyo area, women wanted to create something different from the male-dominated unions, hence the Tokyo Union (known as the *Josei*, or Women's, Union), founded in 1995, which, unlike its counterparts, recognizes the individual membership of women (Kotani 1999, 2). Working women have been acting as intermediaries through the organization, essentially representing women in collective bargaining proceedings. At present, the Tokyo group claims a volunteer membership of about 250. The process is to have former complainants remain in the group and assist others who need help. For a number of women, the experience of empowerment and autonomy has been especially valuable in keeping them involved. Volunteers take phone calls, help to consult, and provide vigorous "genki" power (interview with Ito Midori, Tokyo, November 6, 2001). Lawyers who specialize in labor cases are affiliated with the group.

Of the two hundred complaints processed through 2002, such issues as unwanted dismissal (forced early retirement, "restructuring"), sexual harassment, and bullying, as well as overwork, have been dealt with. In 63 percent of the cases undertaken, total resolution has been achieved—either through continued employment or financial restitution (Kotani 1999, 11). In addition to acting as negotiator on behalf of the female complainants, the union has used other tactics such as picketing if companies are recalcitrant, although these have rarely been invoked (interview with Ito Midori).

A second group, the Tokyo Union, established in 1979, organizes part-time workers, who are primarily female, in order to attempt to gain new legislation to protect such workers and to notify international organizations such as the ILO of treaty infringements, as well as supporting litigants in court (interview with Sakai Kazuko, Tokyo, November 6, 2001). Galvanized by a favorable court ruling in the *Maruko* case in 1993, now with over nine hundred members, the Tokyo Union is seeking to amend the 1993 part-timers law, which they see as ineffective. The union responds to over two thousand complaints a year (Gottfried 2002).

Women Organized to Fight Company Sex Discrimination in Corporate Japan; Plaintiffs in Lawsuits and Their Supporters

Other groups active in the struggle for working women include plaintiffs and their supporters. They represent women who are opposing discrimination against themselves and also support the efforts of others to end discriminatory employment practices, including gender-based two-track systems, which place women in the lower, clerical track; inequitable promotion and salary patterns; and indirect discrimination. Activists within specific companies hold workshops and try to recruit members, pursuing pressure-group tactics and legal advocacy. Perhaps the most successful group is one that operates outside of a company base—the Working Women's Network (WWN)—now with an international branch (WWIN) composed of over seven hundred members, led by Koedo Shizuko. This group has litigated cases in the courts, particularly lawsuits against various parts of the Sumitomo companies (e.g., Electric, Chemical, etc.), rejecting unsatisfactory rulings from the bureaucratic administrative process, and has both recruited and supported the plaintiffs in these cases. The group seeks to "pack" the courtroom with supporters—Japanese and foreign—and holds rallies and protests when adverse decisions are handed down. The WWIN has good media access and, win or lose in the courts, is usually assured of a hearing and publicity in the press. It also seeks to change public opinion through the dissemination and sale of booklets and informational pamphlets. After an unfavorable judicial ruling, a "human chain" demonstration was mounted, with over two hundred participants, to protest an Osaka District Court decision and set the stage for their appeal. The WWIN seeks to negotiate with the Japanese government and to bring pressure to bear on it through international testimony at the International Labor Organization (ILO), Commission on the Status of Women (CSW) at the UN, and CEDAW by filing critical reports and embarrassing the government for failing to live up to its commitments.

Other recent efforts related to working women involve new alliances among feminists from different backgrounds. One example is the Women's Labor Issue Research Group, comprising two-thirds researchers and one-third working women. They conduct research and gather data on discriminatory practices. In a sex discrimination lawsuit against the Shell company, a group called the Equal Opportunity Network was created, which also combined scholars, workers, lawyers, and researchers.

Policy Impact

The numerous activities undertaken by women in social movements in Japan have produced some policy change.

It has been suggested that access to international feminism has called attention to discriminatory practices in employment and lack of political representation (Morley 1999, 177). Policy change has tended to be based in "insider/outsider" tactics—appeals to *gaiatsu* or international pressure coupled with domestic activism. (Norgren 2001, 77).

Women activists pressed for the passage of the EEOL in 1986 and, dissatisfied with its weak enforcement provisions, helped to gain amendments to the law in 1997 that strengthen it a bit. Litigation has helped to keep issues of gender discrimination and harassment in the public arena, as women have brought a number of lawsuits in normally nonlitigious Japan. While in a number of cases (e.g., *Sharp Electronics* in 2000) women have been awarded monetary compensation for discrimination in promotion and salaries, this is not necessarily the norm. Japanese courts have been loathe to find that placing women in subsidiary positions without access to promotion and higher pay is discriminatory, ruling recently that such practices are "not against public order and standards of decency" (WWIN *Newsletter* 2001, 10, 1). A key test of judicial willingness to rule more broadly and demonstrate greater sensitivity to gender discrimination issues was evident in the outcome of the *Shiba Shinyo Credit* case. In 2002, the Supreme Court found that women's failure to gain management-level positions was a violation of a contract specifying that there should be no gender-based discrimination; promotion, damages, and compensation were ordered to the plaintiff. However, in another case, *Nomura Shoken*, a gendered two-track employment system was upheld by the courts, suggesting continued ambivalence about legal change in the employment arena. The EEOL continues to be a weak law, with few sanctions for disobedience, as control of this policy remains largely in the hands of politically strong Japanese employers. The limited impact is seen in the failure of Japanese women to gain access to managerial and professional positions; they comprise only 2.1 percent of department heads and are segregated into low-level clerical and part-time jobs (see Gelb 2003, 52, for more discussion of their limited economic gains).

There is some sense among activists that the present economic downturn may have a depressing effect on future litigation. Women continue to lobby for more changes in the EEOL, including efforts to gain serious attention for issues of part-time work and indirect discrimination.

Sexual harassment policy has been more positively affected by the 1997 EEOL amendments, and the number of successfully prosecuted cases dealing with this behavior has risen significantly.

Women's groups have been active in protecting the right of easy access to abortion, although the right was not initially gained through women's activism. Twice, in 1973 when right-wing groups sought to tighten the Eugenic Protection Law and again in the 1983, they mounted a broad coalition to defend the existing law. They were unable to stop bureaucratic efforts in 1989 to cut abortion access from twenty-four to twenty-two weeks, although protest did occur after this decision (Buckley 1997, 335). They successfully attained their goal of changing the name of the Eugenic Protection Law to the Maternal Protection Law (*Botai Hogo Ho*) in 1996 and finally gained legalization of low-dose birth control pills in 1999, after the rapid approval of Viagra (Norgren 2001, 130).[4] Groups representing women's interests gained a larger "voice" in reproductive policymaking as the twentieth century drew to a close (Norgren 2001, 137).

Women's groups also lobbied to pressure the Japanese government for improved access to child care facilities and laws to provide for child care and parental leave, as well as aid to part-time workers (Buckley 1994, 165). Child care facilities, while inadequate in terms of hours and with long waiting lists for admission, are in the process of expansion. Partially paid parental leave is available, as well as improved maternity benefits. Given the conservative bent of the Japanese government, these reforms are quite remarkable (and apparently far more supportive of working women than is true in the United States). They are born out of deep current concern over low birth and marriage rates among discontented women, rather than any explicit feminist agenda.

One of the most interesting trends in Japanese policymaking relates to the role of the increased number of female Diet representatives. An informal, all-party group was crucial in the passage of the Law for the Prevention of Spousal Violence and the Protection of Victims (Domestic Violence or DV) in 2001, long a demand of feminist activists. Similar groups have also sponsored other legislation, including antistalking laws, anti–child pornography and prostitution, and the Basic Law on Gender Equal Society, passed in 1999. This law also established a Council for Gender Equality in the Cabinet Office, in accordance with Beijing directives for "national machinery," creating an agency devoted to women's issues that has no U.S. counterpart. Women who serve in the Diet, working in conjunction with the networks of women activists described above, have similarly increasingly engaged in nonpartisan efforts to permit women to retain their surnames after marriage, decriminalize abortion, and equalize and individualize pensions. In Japan, even the modest policy gains that have been made have been greeted by a "backlash," which seeks to restore traditional values and roles for women. Of course, in the United States, policy change is also constrained by values and ideology, largely related to the limited role of the state in social provision.

CONCLUSION

While systemic and cultural differences affect the strategic choices available to feminist advocates in both nations examined here, the array of tactics employed is remarkably similar, including lobbying, litigation, and protest, as well as coalition building. Japanese women have networked across issue lines far more successfully in recent years. American women have a far greater presence in national policymaking than their Japanese counterparts, the result of decades of mobilization. In the United States, multiple entry points permit more extensive policy intervention, also attributable to greater transparency and bureaucratic openness. However, these same factors have also permitted countermobilization, which has placed women's movements on the defensive.

While lawsuits have been utilized by American feminists to benefit women collectively, through class action suits and a history of important decisions, litigation has been employed on behalf of women's rights advocacy in Japan as well, albeit often with less dramatic and precedent-setting results. In Japan, "insider/outsider" approaches, litigation, and other rights assertion through the legislative process (employed as well by American feminists) have been further buttressed by international feminism and the development of new transnational gender equity norms. Advocacy coalitions or policy communities involving elected officials (and sometimes "femocratic" bureaucrats) in office in both countries have helped to create a more conducive atmosphere for policy change, as increased female representation has occurred incrementally in each country over the past decades. In Japan, these have been propelled by *giin rippo*, private members' bills, sponsored by nonpartisan groups of female Diet representatives. In the United States, the CCWI, together with feminist groups, has been a force for policy change. These similarities suggest that while culture plays a significant political role, it by no means makes Japanese politics related to gender unique.

Despite these apparent similarities, Japanese policy initiatives on behalf of women are often limited by meager resource allocation. For example, in 2001 domestic violence initiatives received the equivalent of $1 million dollars in Japan, in contrast to over $3.3 billion in the United States (Gelb 2003). In addition, weak or nonexistent implementation may be a concern. Many policies are left to virtually voluntary enforcement, suggesting the limitation of laws without teeth or punishment for noncompliance. It appears that victim protection laws, which involve only a limited outlay of funds but do invoke criminal procedures, are more likely to succeed politically, as opposed to reforms that challenge the core of Japanese mores (such as equal employment and surname retention). Policy change in both countries is most successful if it is "framed" to appeal to prevailing ideology, such as "family values" in the United States. Despite increased attention to women's issues in recent Japanese politics, often only symbolic policy change may result, as the history of the EEOL suggests. Nonetheless, even symbolic law can lead to increased consciousness and "feedback" that results in enhanced mobilization for extensive policy reform. However, in some instances noted above, such as access to abortion in a far less confrontational environment and policies to assist working mothers, the Japanese system may provide positive models for the United States.

This analysis has also pointed to the significance of international feminism for Japanese women, as they have turned to the "politics of externality" to support rights advocacy. In the United States, the real policy gains and leadership of an earlier era may have been limited by the "politics of insularity," or refusal to engage with emerging international gender norms, exemplified by the failure to ratify CEDAW and establish "national machinery" for women's issues. In addition, as noted, American women are beset by hostility from right-wing forces, limiting their policy options. Japanese women at the present time confront a similar "backlash," suggesting that even the modest but significant policy gains they have made may be in danger.

In both Japan and the United States, women's movement mobilization and policy advocacy are here to stay, but the path to positive change will not be easy or smooth.

NOTES

1. All Japanese names are referred to with last name first, in Japanese style.

2. There was division among Japanese feminists about licensing and disseminating the pill for many years, as they feared its health consequences. The absence of unity on this issue contributed to retarding the legalization of the pill until 1999.

3. This section is largely based on interviews conducted in Japan in 2000 and 2001.

4. As noted above, this issue had divided Japanese feminists for many years.

11

Transnational Framing of Access to Abortion in the United States, England, and Ireland

Deana A. Rohlinger and David S. Meyer

Since at least 1848, when activists held an international conference on women's rights in Seneca Falls, New York, large elements of the women's movement have seen the sources of—and solutions to—women's oppression as extending beyond the boundaries of the nation-state. Even as transnational efforts at organizing have a long history prior to enthusiastic social science interest in transnationalism or "global civil society," coordination has been stalled by cross-national inequalities of resources, differing national political and cultural contexts, and different legal challenges. The extent to which women globally share a common identity that could be represented by a common program remains an issue contested not only by states, but by activists as well.

The notion of cultivating and expressing a transnational identity, including a common analysis, set of goals, and program, is one that has recently captured social science attention, as part of the wave of interest in globalization. Eased international travel and communication, and increased political and economic integration, have increased both the capacity and the incentives for transnational coordination of social movements. Movement actors now *can* more easily mobilize extranational resources in national conflicts, build shared social and communication networks, share information and strategies, cultivate a collective identity that crosses national boundaries, and generate transnational constituencies. The extent to which they do so, and what this means, remains an unanswered and contested empirical question. On one side of the debate, scholars contend that the nature of social movement politics has fundamentally changed as a "global civil society" has emerged, producing increased homogeneity of interests and actions around the world (Coy 1997; Smith, Pagnucco, and Chatfield 1997; Keck and Sikkink 1998a; Keck and

Sikkink 1998b; Smith 1998; Keck and Sikkink 1999; Smith 1999; Guidry, Kennedy, and Zald 2000; Mato 2000). Others, however, while acknowledging increased transnational possibilities, stress the predominance of the nation-state in shaping the constellation of political opportunities available and maintaining the capacity to redress grievances through policy reform (Imig and Tarrow 2001b; Tarrow 1996, 2001; Koopmans 1999; Krasner 1995; Risse-Kappen 1995; della Porta and Kriesi 1999; Ferree and Gamson 1999; Lahusen 1999).

Through close empirical examination of the framing processes of explicitly transnational opposing movements, we can see the extent to which transnational identities and movements have emerged (e.g., Atwood 1997; Cortright and Pagnucco 1997; Hovey 1997; Ferree and Gamson 1999). Framing is a dynamic activity in which movement actors strategically create shared understandings of the world and of their actions, offering shorthand understandings of identity, grievances, and political programs (McAdam 1996b; Benford and Snow 2000; Gamson and Modigiliani 1989; Gamson et al. 1992; Snow et al. 1986). Because frames are strategically crafted both to mobilize and define a constituency and its claims (Gamson and Meyer 1996), they provide a useful window into how activists see the relative importance of national and supranational targets and audiences (McCarthy 1997). Recent research looks for convergence or divergence among frames in the transnational arena (cf. Ferree and Gamson 1999), but at least two important variables have so far escaped scholarly attention: the activities of oppositional movements and the nature of the relationship among transnational movement organizations (but see Smith 1999).

In this chapter, we seek to illuminate the factors that affect how organizations frame the abortion issue at the national level. We expect that frames are affected by 1) the relationship between international and affiliated national organizations, 2) the nature of past national policies, 3) the structure of the political system, and 4) national political contingencies. In other words, we expect the national context to weigh more heavily than either the international organization or transnational identity.

DATA AND METHODS

To investigate the strategic shaping of messages, we compare the framing of abortion discourse by national branches of abortion-rights and pro-life groups in three advanced industrial, English-speaking countries where international coordination exists: the United States, England, and Ireland. Abortion is a useful issue to examine because its definition and attendant policy options are relatively narrow, particularly compared to other transnational issues like environmental protection. As a result, abortion is an issue on which convergence in discourse is most likely.

While a common language makes the diffusion of frames less compli-
cated, the three nations vary in terms of state structure, political system, and
abortion policy. The United States has the least restrictive abortion policy,
along with the most contested debate. The multiplicity of venues for policymaking seem to encourage volatile debate (Meyer and Staggenborg 1996,
1998). Access to the political system on abortion in England is more limited,
and the unitary polity, coupled with a responsible party system, have allowed the debate to be largely depoliticized (Cohan 1986; Lovenduski and
Outshoorn 1986). Parliament makes policy, and activists' routes to influence
are limited. Ireland's abortion policy is the most restrictive of the three cases.
Because abortion is covered within the Constitution under the Eighth
Amendment, which prohibits abortion (Randall 1986; Gallagher 1999), there
are very limited ways in which activists can affect policy change. Policy
change on abortion can only be achieved through Parliament, which has depoliticized the issue, a constitutional initiative, or judicial review (Chubb
1992). This range of policies, politics, and polities provides a good window
into which to look for an emerging transnational identity on women's issues.

We examine International Planned Parenthood Federation (IPPF) and the
International Right to Life Federation (IRLF). Both organizations began in the
United States and then went global, establishing international and affiliate organizations around the world. Both are single-issue organizations that focus
on issues of reproduction, particularly abortion. IPPF seeks to make abortion
a safe and legal alternative in every country, while IRLF seeks to ban abortion globally. IPPF's affiliate organization in the United States is Planned Parenthood Federation of America (PPFA), in England the United Kingdom
Family Planning Association (UKFPA), and in Ireland the Irish Family Planning Association (IFPA). IRLF's affiliate organization in the United States is
the National Right to Life Committee (NRLC), in England the Society for the
Protection of Unborn Children (SPUC), and in Ireland the Pro-Life Campaign
(PLC).

To compare abortion framing by these organizations, we read all the articles relating to the abortion issue in each organization's newsletters from
2000 and 2001, assessing the preferred messages used to discuss the abortion issue. We also examined organizational press releases, position papers,
action alerts, and other web-based documents to analyze organizational
strategies and activities, paying attention to metaphors, catch phrases, slogans, visuals, moral appeals, and other symbolic devices (Gamson 1992).[1]
We constructed a master list of abortion frames and packages used by the different organizations (at the different levels) and coded the nature of the discourse.[2] Frames are a central organizing idea that tells an audience what is at
issue and outlines the boundaries of a debate. Organizational leaders present frames as a way to define a situation as problematic, identify the responsible party or structure, articulate a reasonable solution, and call individuals

to action (Snow and Benford 1988; Gamson 1992; Benford and Snow 2000). Packages are a set of ideas that are related to the frame and are used to structure and negotiate an issue's meaning over time (Ryan 1991; Gamson 1992). Packages are "chunks" of information that "hang" on a frame. Because packages may change over time, packages may appear, disappear, and reappear in response to political happenings in the larger environment (Rohlinger 2002). Activists on both sides of the abortion debate, for example, frame the issue in terms of "rights," with the pro-life organizations advocating for the rights of the unborn child and pro-choice organizations advocating for the rights of women to make their own reproductive decisions. Activists have several arguments, or packages, that are related to the rights frame. Pro-life activists often buttress their claims regarding the rights of unborn children by drawing on scientific evidence that maps fetal development and illustrates that abortion kills an unborn child (the *abortion kills a child* package). Pro-choice activists reinforce their claims regarding a woman's right to an abortion by pointing to incidents in which women are maimed and killed because safe abortion procedures were unavailable, unaffordable, or illegal (the *abortion is a fact of life* package).

In addition to examining organizational documents, we interviewed representatives from the organizations in order to understand the formal relationship between the national and international levels as well as the construction of frames and the sharing of information. Interviews were conducted with the current president of the IRLF (Respondent A); the national director of the SPUC (Respondent B); a representative for the PLC (Respondent C); a representative from the IPPF (Respondent D); a representative from the UKFPA (Respondent E); and a representative from the IFPA (Respondent F). The identities of all respondents are confidential. We also consulted secondary historical accounts of the abortion issue in each of these national contexts, including the role of international and affiliate organizations.

ABORTION IN THE UNITED STATES

The Supreme Court has provided the primary motor for abortion policy in the United States, as well as a frequent target for activists. The polarization of the major parties on the abortion issue has prevented resolution of the issue through legislative compromise and thrown the issue back to the court repeatedly (Cohan 1986; Hershey 1986; Meyer and Staggenborg 1998; Staggenborg 1991; Craig and O'Brien 1993; O'Connor 1996). Because the abortion issue remains salient and divisive, activists have an opportunity to access the political system, frame the issue, and affect policy change at both the federal and state levels.

Because many women's organizations believed that *Roe* had settled the abortion issue politically and legally (Craig and O'Brien 1993; O'Connor 1996; Staggenborg 1991), they were caught off guard by the massive pro-life mobilization. This meant that the pro-choice movement repeatedly found itself not only on the defensive but losing ground on abortion policy. The movement employed three reactive strategies in response to pro-life tactics, including pressuring the Democratic Party and party elites to support abortion rights, challenging the constitutionality of restrictive state laws, and mobilizing pubic opinion through mass media (Barker-Plummer 1997; Woliver 1998a, 1998b). In contrast, the pro-life movement largely assumed the offensive following *Roe* and employed a four-pronged strategy to limit abortion in the United States, including lobbying Republican legislators and party elites (Merton 1982; Conway 1986; O'Connor 1996; Woliver 1998b), pressuring state governments to restrict abortion (Woliver 1998a, 1998b; Cohen and Barrilleaux 1993; Day 1995; Segers and Byrnes 1995; O'Connor 1996; Ginsburg 1998), defending the constitutionality of state laws (Cohan 1986; Staggenborg 1991; Craig and O'Brien 1993; Bashevkin 1994; O'Connor 1996; Woliver 1998a), and protesting abortion through direct action tactics (Staggenborg 1991; Guth et al. 1994; Ginsburg 1998). We now discuss the key organizations involved in these debates.

The National Right to Life Committee

The NRLC is the largest organization on either side of the abortion debate, with more than eleven million active supporters in three thousand chapters nationwide and a $3 million budget (Gelb and Palley 1996; Ginsburg 1998). The NRLC argues that life, as stated in the U.S. Constitution, is an unalienable right and requires legal protection (NRLC website). It seeks to make incremental gains for the legal protection of the unborn (Kelly 1994).

The NRLC employs eight main packages in the abortion debate (packages are noted in italics). First, it discusses the consequences of legal and available abortion for women and American culture. The NRLC argues that there are health risks associated with abortions (*health risks of abortion*), and, in fact, posits that scientific research shows the abortion rate is correlated with an increased murder rate and that women who obtain abortions are at a higher risk of depression, other psychological problems, and breast cancer. In addition to the health risks, abortion either *kills a child* or *maims women and babies*. Women who believe the "false promise of 'easy' abortions" not only put their babies in harm's way, but also unknowingly subject themselves to painful side effects. These consequences are linked to the state of contemporary American civic culture, which, the NRLC contends, "has lost its moral anchor." A society cannot nurture children when it aborts babies and supports euthanasia (*cultural decay*). To battle cultural decay, NRLC uses mass media to show the mainstream that pro-life activists are not irrational terrorists (*over-coming the stereotypes*) and engages in conscience-raising to educate the public about abortion and defeat the "culture of death" (*conscience-raising activism*).

Finally, the organization discusses the progress of the pro-life movement. It examines *organizational actions* and *oppositional activities,* often in a historical perspective to highlight a pattern of dishonesty by "abortion advocates." For example, Norma McCorvey (the infamous Jane Roe) and Sandra Cano (Jane Doe) recount how they were "used" by the movement to advance a "pro-abortion agenda." In addition, NRLC seeks to *debunk the rhetoric* by unmasking the dishonesty spread by "abortion advocates" and by educating society on abortion alternatives such as adoption. The NRLC carefully *monitors the movement* at the local, national, and global levels as well as the positions of various religious denominations on the abortion issue. Specifically, NRLC monitors voting records of elected officials; provides an update on abortion legislation; watches U.S. abortion rates; discusses public opinion, organizational strategies, and the role of African Americans in the movement; and provides testimonials and stories to motivate activists.

Planned Parenthood Federation of America

Established in 1916, PPFA is the world's largest and oldest family planning organization, with affiliate organizations and health centers in each of the fifty states and the District of Columbia. PPFA believes that "reproductive self-determination must be voluntary and preserve the individual's right to privacy" (PPFA website). Thus, reproductive freedom is a reaffirmation of the principle of individual liberty and "abortion must always be a matter of personal choice" (PPFA website).

PPFA employs eleven main packages in the abortion debate. PPFA argues that people must be aware of their rights and must make informed decisions regarding their reproductive health options, which include emergency contraception, surgical abortion, and chemical abortion (*public awareness*). In addition to public awareness, there must be *education* on abortion and reproductive health so that the public, pharmacists, and other health care professionals understand the risks and realities of abortion. To inform the larger public and health care professionals about reproductive services, PPFA uses scientific fact to *unmask the rhetoric* of the opposition. "Anti-choicers" use scientific, medical, and legal inaccuracies to frighten women and deny democracy by clouding the abortion debate with "supposed health risks." It argues that elective abortion does not pose a risk to the mental or physical health of most women, and that countless physical, emotional, and social benefits have accrued since the legalization of abortion in the United States (*abortion is safe*). PPFA also contends with *anti-abortion zealots,* who stop at nothing to win their cause and often encourage fanaticism and violence. This is most apparent in the murder of abortion providers, the establishment of fake clinics that "misinform" and "intimidate" women seeking abortions, and the creation of a website that identifies pro-choice supporters and encourages violence against them and their families. Finally, it reminds the public that *abortion is a fact of life.* The *Roe* decision did not invent abortion; it just made it safe for women so that "back alley butchers" did not take advantage of them.

PPFA examines the progress of the pro-choice movement. It *monitors the movement* by discussing legislative and judicial activities as well as drug approvals on a local, national, and global scale. In addition, it discusses *organizational actions* and monitors *oppositional activities* at the local and national levels as well as on college campuses. It analyzes the role of the United States in global abortion politics and argues that George W. Bush's *global gag rule is undemocratic* because it denies the free speech of American and other citizens. Finally, PPFA *evaluates the health care system.* It conducts studies to assess the type and quality of services and information available to patients and the training and education of providers and identifies the barriers that exist to the abortion procedure the world over.

INTERNATIONAL ORGANIZATIONS: U.S. NATIONAL ORGANIZATIONS GO GLOBAL

The International Right to Life Federation (IRLF)

The NRLC was critical to the formation of the International Right to Life Federation (IRLF), providing the bulk of its funds and an experienced leadership. In fact, both organizations had the same president from 1984 (the year IRLF was founded) to 1991 (Respondent A, the current president of IRLC). Much like NRLC, the IRLF is a secular, nonpartisan organization that recognizes the right to life of all humans and seeks to legally protect life from conception to natural death. IRLF welcomes international affiliates who can commit to the very small $100 annual affiliation fee and uphold the IRLF's commitment to being a single-issue organization focused on the protection of human life. The IRLF depends on volunteer labor from staff and provides newsletters, mailings, press releases, and expertise to its affiliates, but not financial support. The organization is structured in a senatorial fashion with a president and affiliate representatives from the North Pacific Rim, the South Pacific Rim, Australia, India, Africa, Western Europe, Eastern Europe, Central America, the United Kingdom, and the United States determining federation policy. The IRLF holds an annual board meeting, has quarterly conference calls with board members, and cosponsors meetings around the world at which it attempts to harness national resources and target its influence on supranational policy. IRLF employs lobbyists in the United Nations (UN), where it holds five nongovernmental organization (NGO) slots (Respondent A).

IRLF employs five packages in the abortion debate. Much like NRLC, IRLC discusses the psychological and physical affects of abortion on women (*health risk of abortion*) and argues that abortion either *kills a child* or *maims a baby*. IRLF also focuses on the pro-life movement globally. It tracks global victories and the activities of politicians who are working to advance a pro-life agenda (*monitoring the movement*) as well as "pro-abortion" activities and the legislative, judicial, and tactical obstacles the movement faces. It *debunks the rhetoric* of the "pro-abortion" forces. For example, IRLF argues that the language of "reproductive health" veils abortion advocates' real intent: to impose abortion on developing countries.

The International Planned Parenthood Federation (IPPF)

PPFA was instrumental in the creation of the IPPF. IPPF was founded in 1952 at a conference in Bombay by the volunteer leaders of national family planning associations (FPAs) in eight countries and has grown since then sufficiently to support member organizations in developing countries. IPPF links national autonomous family planning associations in over 180 countries worldwide and currently provides more than ninety member associations with grants (IPPF website; Respondent D, a representative from IPPF). The federation itself is supported by financial contributions from more than twenty governments as well as by donations from both individuals and private foundations (IPPF website) and was structured after the already successful PPFA (Suitters 1973). IPPF and its affiliate members are committed to reproductive health, which includes "access to family planning and safe abortion services [as well as] equal rights for women" (IPPF website). Affiliated FPAs raise funds for their programs and operate within their own cultural, social, and legal setting but are linked to the federation by common standards and objectives, which they can influence by participating in governance. IPPF has Category I consultative status at the UN and works closely with other voluntary, intergovernmental, and UN agencies that share its concerns (IPPF website).

IPPF employs ten packages in the abortion debate. IPPF believes that citizens must be aware of their rights and make informed decisions regarding their reproductive health options (*public awareness*) based on extensive *education* on abortion and reproductive health. In order to inform the larger public and health care professionals about reproductive services, IPPF has to *unmask the rhetoric* of the opposition, which seeks to deny the rights of individuals by "imposing a pro-life culture" on the rest of the world. The global gag rule is an example of "pro-life imperialism" that denies basic freedoms to a global citizenry. IPPF reminds the public that *abortion is safe* and *a fact of life,* and that outlawing it compromises women's safety when abortion occurs. IPPF also stresses the necessity of establishing effective links between abortion and family planning services so that abortion is one accessible means of family planning but not used as a form of contraception (*beyond legalization*).

IPPF also tracks the progress of the pro-choice movement. It *monitors the movement* by tracking legislation and judicial rulings on a global scale. In addition, it evaluates access to reproductive health services, watches public opinion, offers stories and testimony to motivate global activism, and discusses the new generation of pro-choicers and their activities. It highlights the global support for emergency contraception among providers and clients in developing countries (*global support for EC*) and discusses *organizational actions* and monitors *oppositional activities* worldwide.

ABORTION IN ENGLAND

Abortion in England is regulated by the 1967 Abortion Act, which allows a doctor to perform an abortion on a woman whose life is at mental or physical risk prior to the twentieth-eighth week with the support of two physicians. Thus, general practitioners are the ultimate arbiters over abortion practices (Cohan 1986; Lovenduski and Outshoorn 1986; Sheldon 1998; Lovenduski 1998). The medicalization of abortion allows politicians to avoid the issue with little political consequence (Cohan 1986; Lovenduski and Outshoorn 1986; Paintin 1998; Sheldon 1998) and leaves social movement activists with very limited routes to pursue policy change. Activists can try to influence abortion policy by either encouraging a private members' bill, which is the only alternative source of initiative in Parliament (Cohan 1986; Crewe 1993), or by lobbying bureaucratic agencies (Wilson 1993). Over the last decades, social movement organizations on both sides have focused on lobbying Parliament for incremental changes in policy and on educational campaigns to mobilize a larger public.

The Society for the Protection of Unborn Children (SPUC)

The SPUC is a lobby and advocacy organization founded in 1967, after parliamentary reform of abortion laws. Supported by the Catholic Church and sympathetic U.S. pro-life organizations, it made several attempts at policy reform throughout the 1970s and 1980s (Cohan 1986; Lovenduski 1986b; Read 1998).[3] Currently, SPUC has more than forty-five thousand members and offices throughout the United Kingdom and depends on grassroots support to promote its position in political parties, trade unions, educational institutions, and religious groups (Respondent B, national director of SPUC; SPUC website).

SPUC is a major player in the IRLF, where a representative sits on the board, representing the UK (Respondent A). While IRLF does not provide financial resources to SPUC, its national director noted that the IRLF provides invaluable experience and insight to their efforts in England. The director of the organization explained, "We are colleagues that keep in close touch with each other and we each know how our respective organizations work. And hearing each other's experience and expertise is what it is all about."

SPUC employs seven main packages in the abortion debate. Much like NRLC and IRLC, SPUC argues that *abortion kills a child* and that there are serious *health risks associated with abortion*. In addition to the health risks, there are cultural consequences for a society that tolerates abortion; abortion encourages a "Kleenex culture" that degrades the value of human life by making some lives "disposable," often those of people with disabilities, in a vegetative state, or unborn (*cultural decay*). SPUC also monitors the movement's progress at the local, national, and global level, as well as positions of different religious denominations on relevant issues (*monitoring the movement*). The organization focuses on *educating* the larger public and school-age children on pro-life issues, discusses *organizational action* in the political realm, and monitors *oppositional activities* and policy gains. Finally, it supports the *role of general practitioners* in abortion decisions, arguing that physicians, who have a woman's best interest in mind, can dissuade a woman from obtaining an abortion.

The United Kingdom Family Planning Association (UKFPA)

The UKFPA runs high-profile campaigns and lobbies decision makers at every level in an effort to ensure that sexual health is a priority in public health legislation. It does not, however, operate family planning clinics, as its allies elsewhere do. After providing family planning services for over forty years, it successfully lobbied for the National Health Service (NHS) to take on this role in 1974 (UKFPA website). The UKFPA is a "pro-choice" organization that supports a woman's right to confidential, unbiased, and accurate information on abortion services and is a member of the Pro-Choice Alliance in England. The organization largely focuses its efforts on ensuring that women using the NHS receive the "choice" and "quality" in fertility options they deserve in a country where private clinics are overregulated and the NHS is underfunded (Respondent E, a representative of UKFPA; UKFPA website).

Relations with the IPPF are loose, although UKFPA was a founding member of IPPF and continues as an affiliate. A spokesperson for UKFPA reported that the organization does not receive funding or other resources from IPPF, nor does the UKFPA have a representative on any IPPF board. The UKFPA representative indicated that the organization is autonomous and does not regularly send staff to meetings or conferences at the international level (Respondent E).

UKFPA employs eight packages in the abortion debate. UKFPA monitors progress on abortion, discusses public opinion on the issue, tracks legislation and judicial rulings, analyzes barriers to sexual health services, and examines the confusion of the public regarding the 1967 Act in practice (*monitoring the movement*). However, unlike PPFA and IPPF, it does not directly discuss oppositional activities in the country. Instead, the organization focuses on educating the public on the abortion issue. It argues that abortion is essential to *fertility control* and must be available through the NHS. In addition to access to services through the NHS, *women need a choice* of both contraceptive methods and abortion services.

UKFPA advocates several steps to improve sexual health services in the UK. First, the 1967 Abortion Act must be revised to constrain general practitioners from serving as "gatekeepers" to services, including abortion (*revising the act*). Second, the United Kingdom needs to develop a national health strategy to provide *equal access* to services by increasing funding and the number and dispersion of health centers. Current funding levels for the NHS leads to long waiting lists, which effectively encourages women to seek private treatment; for less-privileged women this can mean unsafe abortions. Third, women need to be aware of their rights and options, which requires access to reliable information (*public awareness*). Finally, in order for the public to be informed, the organization must *unmask the rhetoric* of the opposition.

ABORTION IN IRELAND

In March 2002 voters in Ireland narrowly defeated a constitutional referendum that would have toughened abortion laws. Referenda and the Supreme Court have sporadically engaged the issue of abortion, but formal law has diverged widely from actual practice in a country where the Roman Catholic Church is particularly influential (Randall 1986; Gallagher 1999). The liberalization of abortion laws in surrounding countries, beginning in the 1960s, made abortion more accessible by travel, and the Supreme Court has whittled away at the strong influence of the church on practice by allowing, first, the distribution of contraceptives to married people, then information about abortion, and finally exceptions to the strict prohibitions on abortion in the case of maternal health (Barry 1988; Randall 1986; Rossiter 1993; Smyth 1993; Coliver 1995; Scheppele 1996; Fahey 1998; Murphy-Lawless and McCarthy 1999). Nonetheless, the sheer size, resources, and bureaucratic organization of the church enable it to affect public discourse on abortion, such that there is not popular support for the legalization or liberalization of abortion even within the emerging women's movement (Randall 1986; Scheppele 1996; Whelan 1994).

In the wake of controversial Supreme Court decisions in the 1990s, organizations on both sides of the issue have mobilized and urged the government to clarify and reshape the state's position on abortion, emphasizing venues in which each thinks it has an advantage (see Meyer and Staggenborg 1996). The PLC has successfully pushed for referenda on abortion policy, while the IFPA has advocated more conventional legislative reforms, based on Supreme Court decisions (Murphy-Lawless and McCarthy 1999).[4]

Neither side has been able to win decisive victories. The nature of abortion politics in Ireland has encouraged members of parliament to depoliticize the issue (Randall 1986; Girvin 1996; Chubb 1992), and abortion rights organizations have followed by focusing on services rather than "rights."

The Pro-Life Campaign (PLC)

The PLC, the only pro-life lobbying organization in Ireland, was established in 1981 to support a constitutional amendment banning abortion. Located in Dublin with branches in each of the forty-one constituencies, PLC focuses on engaging politicians on pro-life issues, formulating legislation and referenda that protect a child's right to life, and educating the country on pro-life issues through seminars, debates, and newspaper articles (Respondent C, a representative from PLC).

The PLC has a tenuous relationship with the IRLF. While it has been an affiliate of IRLF for several years and attends the international conferences and seminars, a spokesperson suggested that IRLF was a "counter-resource." Its frustration with IRLF surrounds a recent piece of legislation; after spending three days with criminal and constitutional lawyers, the PLC approved the wording of legislation in 2001 that included the word "implantation," which the IRLF president immediately criticized. According to the PLC respondent, the president of the IRLF wanted the word "fertilization" instead, which would have risked threatening the law allowing access to contraceptives, undermining support. Despite this tension, PLC adheres to the IRLF's mission statement guidelines. Unlike SPUC, however, PLC does not sit on the board of directors, have regular contact with IRLF leadership, or enjoy the same level of regular access to organizational resources and expertise (Respondent C).

PLC employs eight packages for a pro-life Ireland. First, PLC exposes the reality of abortion: *it kills a child* and presents a *health risk* for women. It also monitors politicians who are not representing the "will" of the people on the abortion issue, especially at the European level, and calls attention to the fact that government is purposely undermining Irish democracy by failing to address abortion adequately (*democracy denied*). PLC posits that the pro-life position is embedded in *medical ethics*, which place the duty to preserve life and promote health in the hands of doctors, and that in order to have an honest discussion about abortion in Ireland, the *opposition must be exposed*. The PLC does not discuss pro-choice organizations in Ireland, focusing instead on the founders of the "abortion movement," which included eugenicists. The PLC also monitors the progress of the movement, particularly its European dimensions, as European Community policies will influence Irish law (*monitoring the movement*). In addition, it highlights its activities at the national and regional level (*organizational action*).

The Irish Family Planning Association (IFPA)

The IFPA, founded in 1969 as a provider of family planning, education, and political advocacy, is the leading "pro-choice" organization in Ireland (Coliver 1995). As a national voluntary organization and a registered charity, the organization focuses on lobbying politicians and raising public awareness of the need for comprehensive and worldwide sexual and reproductive health services (IFPA website). The organization states three goals: 1) to provide universal and free access to all services required for the exercise of reproductive choice, 2) to achieve the changes necessary to ensure the ability of individuals to exercise their reproductive rights, and 3) to develop and sustain a strong association (IFPA website). While IFPA clearly advocates a "woman's right to choose" and has been central to the abortion debate and activism in Ireland, it focuses more generally on services and "hard cases" than on legal reform (Respondent F, a representative of IFPA; IFPA website).

Unlike UKFPA, IFPA receives financial and other assistance from IPPF for certain projects. IPPF has made information, advocacy materials, and professional assistance available to IFPA, and IFPA representatives attend IPPF conferences and events. While IFPA regards IPPF as a tremendous resource, it generally seeks autonomy on the abortion issue, recognizing the differences between Ireland and other European countries. Although IFPA is more clearly linked to the international organization than UKFPA, it frames the abortion issue in ways that work best in the Irish context (Respondent F).

IFPA employs six packages in the abortion debate. The organization argues that *Ireland needs the abortion alternative* because the evidence clearly shows that Irish women travel to England to obtain abortions. IFPA posits that there is a demand for abortion in the country and women should be provided services at home rather than abroad. IFPA emphasizes that there is a need to discuss forms of contraception, institute more crisis pregnancy centers across the country, and create postabortion counseling and checkup services for women returning from England (*beyond abortion*).

IFPA condemns the discussion of a referendum that is not supported by the people, would ultimately divide the public, and would not prevent women from obtaining abortions in England. In addition, it criticizes the government for its continued avoidance of the abortion issue, which hinders civilized debate (*democracy denied*). IFPA *monitors the movement*, educates the public on its own activities (*organizational actions*), and *unmasks the rhetoric* of the opposition. For example, it posits that the "anti-choice" movement abroad is filled with hypocrisy and ultimately clouds the abortion debate in Ireland.

FRAMING THE ABORTION DEBATE: CONTENTION AND DISCOURSE IN THE NATIONAL AND INTERNATIONAL CONTEXT

Abortion policy, despite variance in funding and access, presents a more easily comparable terrain for activists across borders than virtually any other issue. At base, pro-life activists want to reduce the number of abortions, using both legal restrictions and public discourse, and abortion rights activists want to limit obstacles preventing women from getting abortions, including legal restrictions and funding. Despite differences in national political structures and cultures, "rights talk" (Glendon 1991) animates rhetoric on both sides. In some ways, this plays out cross-nationally in predictable ways. Generally, the pro-life organizations emphasize the "unborn child's" right to life, while the "abortion rights" organizations stress the right of a woman to make choices about her body, health, and life. Such rights talk, characteristic of the abortion debate, and, indeed, many contemporary issues, is inherently divisive and difficult to manage (Glendon 1991; Scheppele 1996; Bridgeman 1998). Contested rights, articulated as moral, legal, and political trumps, cannot readily be ranked, balanced, or compromised without antagonizing one side—or both (Meyer and Staggenborg 1996). Moreover, "rights talk" trivializes the concerns of the opposition, constraining both sides. Opponents of abortion rights criticize the defenders of choice as defending morally irresponsible decisions about not only abortion but also sexuality and birth control (Bridgeman 1998). Advocates of abortion rights criticize their opponents for placing the life, health, and autonomy of women below that of the "fetus."

To avoid this rights contest, some pro-life groups have tried to inject nuance into their position, allowing for distinctions between "induced abortion" and those necessary to save the life of the mother. While the pro-life organizations have adopted a similar use of the rights frame, the packages, or ideational material used to support the rights frame, vary according to national context; in fact the organizations have only three packages in common: *the health risks of abortion, abortion kills a child*, and *monitoring the movement*—two of which rely on scientific findings that can easily be oriented to a global audience. (See table 11.1.)

Table 11.1. Comparison of Pro-Life Packages

Package	IRLF	NRLC	SPUC	PLC
Abortion Kills a Child	X	X	X	X
Conscience-Raising Activism		X		
Cultural Decay		X	X	
Debunking the Rhetoric	X	X		X
Democratic Ireland				X
Education			X	
Exposing the Opposition				X
Health Risks of Abortion	X	X	X	X
Maiming Women and Babies	X	X		
Medical Ethics				X
Monitoring the Movement	X	X	X	X
Oppositional Activities	X	X	X	
Organizational Action		X	X	X
Overcoming the Stereotypes		X		
Role of GPs			X	

Note that the IRLF shares more packages with the NRLC than with its other allies, likely the result of the strong U.S. influence on the international, which the NRLC helped create. The tighter the organizational ties among these groups, the more extensive the sharing of frames; thus, it is not surprising that SPUC has more packages in common with NRLC than with the other organizations or that PLC varies the most in its packages. PLC is less tied into the same transnational information and organizational network, and its packages are largely oriented to the particulars of the national context. For example, *medical ethics, Democratic Ireland,* and *exposing the opposition* are specific to Ireland. Still, the ideological foundation of the pro-life movement leads to considerable similarities in framing.

Pro-choice organizations vary more in their discourse. While "rights" are at the heart of each of the pro-choice organizations' arguments (Bashevkin 1996; Bridgeman 1998; Hardiman and Whelan 1994), the organizations frame this theme in ways that resonate with national politics and culture. For example, PPFA and IPPF emphasize a "woman's right to choose" an abortion, whereas UKFPA and IFPA focus much more on a woman's right to services. In England, a woman's right to services is more resonant than the right to choose an abortion because discourse and politics on abortion is medicalized: It is a doctor's choice (Paintin 1998; Sheldon 1998). Similarly, it makes strategic sense for IFPA to embrace the consensus position advocated by the political parties, which focuses on the need for reproductive health services.

It is not surprising, then, that the pro-choice organizations have few packages in common across contexts (table 11.2). Like the rights frame, the common packages are oriented toward the national rather than global context.

Table 11.2.   Comparison of Pro-Choice Packages

Package	IPPF	PPFA	UKFPA	IFPA
Abortion Essential to Fertility Control			X	
Abortion Is a Fact of Life	X	X		
Abortion Is Safe	X	X		
Antiabortion Zealots		X		
Beyond Abortion				X
Beyond Legalization	X			
Democracy Denied				X
Education	X	X		
Equal Access			X	
Evaluating Health Care		X		
Global Gag Rule Is Undemocratic		X		
Global Support for EC	X			
Ireland Needs Abortion				X
Monitoring the Movement	X	X	X	X
Oppositional Activities	X	X		
Organizational Actions	X	X	X	X
Public Awareness	X	X	X	
Revising the Act			X	
Unmasking the Rhetoric	X	X	X	X
Women Need Choices			X	

The two organizations with the greatest overlap are the international and U.S. offices of Planned Parenthood. As are its opponents, the U.S. organization is a strong force within the international. UKFPA, as an "autonomous affiliate" of IPPF, has limited contact with the international organization. Even when the organization has more extensive contact with the international, as is the case with IFPA, the particulars of the national context ultimately determine strategic framing.

In summary, the nature of the relationship between the international and affiliate organizations affects the framing of the abortion issue. If the organizations have a relationship beyond affiliation and share tactics and expertise, they are more likely to converge on frames and packages. This is most visible among pro-life organizations. IRLF, NRLC, and SPUC are part of a larger organizational network that shares strategies and information across borders and as a result have overlap among the packages used in the abortion debate. In contrast, the existence of a cohesive organizational network is much less clear among pro-choice organizations, which have a great deal of divergence in the ways abortion is packaged for a national audience. In fact, most of the overlap in abortion discourse exists between IPPF and PPFA. This is not only a result of PPFA being a major founder of the international organization but a logical consequence of its effort to cultivate a global partnership with IPPF. It is interesting to note that U.S. organizations on both sides of the issue are much more globally oriented in their discourse than their other affiliates. The entrepreneurial nature of campaigns and fund-raising in the United States encourages activists to seek additional issues and additional venues in which to make claims, such that abortion outside the United States becomes a volatile political issue inside—and the U.S. government funds international agencies that affect the availability of abortion globally (Pine and Fischler 1995).

CONCLUSION

We began this study to speak to the growing debate about women's movements internationally and intimations of an emerging global civil society. We were curious about the relationship between international organizations and their national affiliates and whether these relationships cultivated a cohesive, transnational discourse on the problems of and solutions to abortion. In order to investigate the strategic shaping of messages, we compared the framing of abortion discourse by national branches of pro-life and pro-choice groups in three advanced industrial, English-speaking countries. This is the sort of issue and sorts of contexts in which similarities among organizations and strategies are most likely cross-nationally.

We found that how each organization discusses abortion varies according to both national context and its relationship with the international organization. The national context ultimately determines the strategies an organization uses to instigate policy change, even as it may draw upon resources and discourse of allies elsewhere. This sharing is more extensive when there is more interorganizational contact. Although international coordination matters, state policies and national political culture still dominate the field on which activists struggle.

The abortion issue, by providing a window into the configuration of both social movements and women's identities, suggests that even as globalization of culture and communications continues, national context—and indeed the changing nation-states (Banaszak, Beckwith, and Rucht 2003b)—is still the appropriate place to start any analysis. To the extent that supranational or transnational organizations make new claims about women, national actors have additional resources to use in forging identities and making claims, but resources whose value is still bounded by national borders.

NOTES

1. All web-based documents were collected between October 2000 and December 2001.

2. Because Ireland's PLC does not issue a newsletter, we relied on press releases, position papers, and other web-based documents to ascertain their frames, packages, strategies, and tactics. To ensure that we accurately represented the organization's position on abortion, we also examined two regional affiliates of the PLC, Galway for Life and Offaly for Life. Both organizations had extensive websites that included additional press releases, position papers, and organizational information.

3. Since 1967, abortion law has been amended only once. The Human Fertilization and Embryology Act of 1990, in line with national consensus, reduced the abortion time frame from twenty-eight to twenty-four weeks and removed any time limit for abortion where there is a risk to the mother's health or serious fetal abnormality (Lovenduski and Randall 1993; Read 1998; Sheldon 1998).

4. European Community law, binding on Ireland, also complicates abortion law and politics. See Reid 1992; Gardiner 1993; Girvin 1996; and O'Brien 1998 for a detailed discussion of the European dimension.

12

Conclusion: The U.S. Women's Movement and Beyond

Lee Ann Banaszak

On April 25, 2004, feminists from throughout the United States ranging in age from college students to Social Security recipients filled the National Mall of Washington, D.C. The *Washington Post* labeled the protest "among the largest demonstrations ever held on the Mall" (April 26, 2004), with estimates ranging from five hundred thousand to over one million participants. Feminist organizations continued high levels of mobilization throughout 2004, with many feminist organizations developing extensive "get out the vote" campaigns for the November election. Despite these high levels of mobilization, feminists had suffered several major policy defeats in the last two years. The adoption of legislation banning "partial birth" abortions represented a significant blow to women's reproductive rights and a major political victory for the pro-life movement. And although 2004 began with a court ruling allowing gays and lesbians to marry in Massachusetts, voters in thirteen states passed referenda defining marriage as between a man and woman only. Thus, the U.S. women's movement appears to be in a phase characterized both by high mobilization and serious policy defeats.

The chapters in this book have explored the dynamics of women's movements over the past four decades. Yet equally important is the trajectory of women's movements into the twenty-first century. While we cannot predict the future, our understanding of the past can help us speculate about what the future will bring. That is the purpose of this chapter.

Three large themes that emerge from the contributions to this book inspire questions about the future of the U.S. women's movement. First, many of the authors examine issues of mobilization. In discussing mobilization we are concerned both about the ability of the movement to mobilize women to activism (such as participating in demonstrations or other important events) and the ability of activists to sustain their organizations. These issues lead to the question: How effectively will feminists be able to mobilize women in the future? Second, several of the chapters throughout this book analyze divisions that exist within the women's movement. Given what we know, what role will intramovement divisions play in the future of the women's movement? Third, discussions of the U.S. women's movement in a comparative perspective point to the role of the U.S. women's movement in the global community. What role is the U.S. women's movement likely to play in the coming decades? And what will the international feminist community look like in the future? In proposing some tentative answers to these questions, I follow the organization of this volume, speaking first specifically about the U.S. women's movement and then about women's movements globally.

MOBILIZING THE U.S. WOMEN'S MOVEMENT

In June 1998, *Time* magazine's cover asked "Is Feminism Dead?" Social movement scholars rarely put the issue in such stark terms, because they recognize the ability of movements to demobilize and still survive (see, e.g., Rupp and Taylor 1987). Nevertheless we may ask if the U.S. women's movement will be stronger or weaker in the coming decades. In chapter 3, Nancy Whittier demonstrates that new generations of women are entering into the women's movement on college campuses and major cities, although the issues that mobilize them and the experiences that have molded them differ from those of previous generations. The March for Women's Lives of April 2004 also indicates that great numbers of women are still mobilizing around issues of reproductive rights. Can we anticipate that such mobilization will continue?

One important factor in determining future mobilization is the political context around the women's movement. While both political parties provided some access to women's movements during the early years of the women's movement, the current party structure is much more divided, with feminists having few allies within the Republican Party on the issues of reproductive rights and equal rights. Thus, the 2004 election resulted in a Congress and president who will not be open to the issues of the women's movement. Even Democratic Party leaders have begun to back away from their support of abortion rights since the 2004 election (Kirkpatrick 2005). The issue of gay marriages has also clearly resulted in the rise of a countermovement in many local communities, emboldening antifeminist Republicans and giving pause to sympathetic Democrats. Feminist activists continue to have better access to the Democratic Party than the Republican Party and have found openings on the state and local level. Nevertheless, opportunities for access have shrunk considerably in recent years, and movements counter to the U.S. women's movements are very strong in some issue areas.

The rise of countermovements and the shrinking opportunities are likely to have different overall effects on movement mobilization. As Meyer and Staggenborg (1996) suggest, movements mobilize in the face of strong countermovements. Indeed, the increased activity of women's organizations in 2004 reflects a concern about reproductive rights in the face of the antiabortion movement's success in passing the Partial Birth Abortion Ban Act. On the other hand, if the shrinking opportunities on the national level result in repeated defeats, this will make mobilization more difficult. There are two major issues that will undoubtedly mobilize the feminist movement. One will be the stance on abortion rights of future Supreme Court justice nominees, and the other will be the Democratic Party's willingness to nominate and support pro-life candidates. Failure to halt openly pro-life candidates in either the Supreme Court or the electoral arena would likely demoralize and demobilize the movement, especially if other venues for opportunities remain closed.

As opportunities for effecting change on the national level close, local and state venues are likely to become more important for mobilizing feminists. The discussions of the U.S. women's movement in this volume point to multiple sites of mobilization for the women's movement. As Freeman describes (in chapter 2), women have mobilized in local communities and on the national level from the origins of the movement. Reger and Staggenborg (chapter 6) and Whittier (chapter 3) describe vibrant activism in local communities, although Reger and Staggenborg note that the resources of national organizations as well as local conditions temper the ability of groups to organize locally. Barakso (chapter 5) and Ryan (chapter 4), on the other hand, focus on national level mobilizing, although they also note the influence of local mobilization on national campaigns. The current vitality of the women's movement lies both in the local areas and in national organizations and networks, with their ability to coordinate local pockets of feminist strength, as Reger and Staggenborg have so aptly illustrated. If national political opportunities remain closed, we may see a decrease in national level activity (as social movement theory predicts). Yet we would also expect that local forms of mobilization might continue to be important (or even grow in strength).

Thus, both the continued threat to the feminist agenda and the fluidity and strength of women's movement mobilization show that feminism is not dead as predicted by the news media in the late 1990s. Yet whether the movement's strength will lie at the local level or at the national level depends in large part on both the Democratic Party and the success of social conservatives in achieving policy agendas in the Republican-controlled Congress, White House, and federal courts.

DIVISIONS WITHIN THE MOVEMENT

Divisions among women's movement activists occur along many dimensions. Both Ryan's chapter on the campaign for the Equal Rights Amendment and Freeman's chapter on the origins of the women's movement argue that issues of tactics and ideology have divided the movement, particularly between the early 1960s and the early 1980s. Social characteristics, particularly sexuality, race, and class, have also created a number of "feminisms" that differ in their goals and ideology. The activists associated with these feminisms differ in their collective identity and views of appropriate collective action strategies. Both activists and scholars have long wondered if differences among feminists impede the movement's ability to mobilize feminists for action and to achieve social, economic, or political change, and whether the movement represents the viewpoints of all feminists or merely those of middle-class, white feminists.

Both the chapters in this volume and recent events suggest that the diversity of the women's movement does not necessarily imply discord. Along those lines, Ryan's chapter argues that one important factor in mobilizing the women's movement is the existence of an issue that unites all groups regardless of ideology and identity. Diversity can flourish in an active movement, Ryan concludes, as long as there is agreement on the basic issue. Whittier also argues that the diversity of the third and second waves together provides strength by allowing the movement to take advantage of any openings in political opportunities and creating a multiplicity of collective identities and frames with each being persuasive to different constituencies. The example of the March for Women's Lives seems to support these ideas; one important characteristic of the march was the diversity of race, sexuality, age, and occupation of people united in support of women's reproductive rights.

However, unity behind a single issue often comes at a cost. When diverse feminists focus on any particular issue, they may narrow the field of issues being advocated. Unity within the women's movement has traditionally occurred around issues relevant to middle-class, white feminists. For example, in the first wave of the women's movement, when suffrage was the "unity" issue, minimum wages and working conditions and even suffrage for black women were ignored by suffrage activists. Similarly, Mary Katzenstein (2003) argues that unity behind economic equality has served middle-class women better than poor women, particularly since the 1980s. The issue of who benefits from unity in a movement is not limited to the women's movement. Belinda Robnett (in chapter 7) argues that unity behind traditional movement repertoires in the 1990s inhibits the emergence of a strong African American movement, because it ignores gender differences in the movement. Thus, even where unity brings diverse feminists (or other social movement activists) together, it may in the end further divide the movement, creating larger differences in the future.

The issue of unity versus diversity is to some extent artificial. The U.S. women's movement has never focused solely on a single issue even in those periods when one issue like suffrage or the Equal Rights Amendment has dominated the public agenda. Rather, women's movements activists are better characterized as splintered along multiple policy interests. The wide array of issues that feminists advocate has led to a variety of *policy networks* within the feminist community on both the local and national levels. While some of today's feminist organizations are multi-issue, as Barakso describes in her chapter on the national NOW, many feminist organizations erupt around specific issues.

A good illustration of policy networks comes from efforts to enforce and strengthen Title IX, part of the Education Amendments of 1972, which prohibited sexual discrimination in educational programs receiving federal assistance. While national feminist organizations like NOW and Feminist Majority have concerned themselves with issues of Title IX, a number of movement organizations have been created with a single focus on the issue (e.g., Association for Gender Equity Leadership in Education, Educational Equity Concepts, and the National Coalition for Women and Girls in Education). Within a single issue like Title IX, feminist activism revolves around a specific policy network, and education specialists form the core of the policy network. While some feminists within this issue network have ties with multi-issue organizations or feminists in other networks, information and activism on current controversies often remains concentrated within the network. Thus, while these groups are still tied together with an overarching belief in "feminism," in most of their day-to-day activities they act as semi-autonomous units.

These feminist policy networks may occasionally need to mobilize larger groups of activists to preserve existing gains (as occurred around the recent attempt to scuttle Title IX) or to gain new outcomes. In these cases, feminists within the policy network will activate connections to other movement groups to try to mobilize larger groups of feminists. Whether they can mobilize other feminists extensively outside of their own network depends on two things: the general ability of the movement to mobilize women, and whether the movement itself is focused on a single "unity" issue. Unity issues can suppress the willingness of feminists to mobilize around other issues.

These feminist policy networks have mixed effects on the movement. On the one hand, specializing in a particular issue allows feminist activists to gain extensive expertise in the area and develop strong ties to government officials. Indeed, many such feminists enter government agencies and are able to influence the government from within. As a result, these feminists are able to work successfully on multiple issues within the movement even as other issues gain primary focus. On the other hand, policy networks may become institutionalized, failing to innovate at critical times, retreating into a focus on formal organizations, forging ties with government officials, and losing the connections to a mass base or a larger network of feminists. The result is that when important issues come to the fore, particularly in times when the political opportunities for gaining success are few or countermovements are strong, feminists in these policy networks may be less able to mobilize outside of their narrow circle. Similarly, these policy networks may also be unable or unwilling to mobilize for other feminist issues, weakening the unity of the larger feminist movement.

The future of the U.S. women's movement in the coming years thus depends on how it deals with these different types of diversity. For the movement to be able to mobilize in the coming years, particularly in the face of an increasingly hostile environment, it must avoid the push into a single issue that alienates the multiple feminists under its roof. Yet it must also avoid the splintering into institutionalized policy networks that might dilute the ability of different feminists and feminisms to mobilize together when needed.

THE U.S. MOVEMENT IN THE GLOBAL COMMUNITY

International organizations and international issues have been a part of the women's movement agenda since the first wave of the women's movement in the late 1800s (DuBois 1994; Keck and Sikkink 1998a). Yet, international activity has been increasingly important to the goals and mobilization of the U.S. women's movement, as feminist activists have looked to international organizations as a means of affecting politics at home as well as attempting to voice support for sister movements in other countries. Globalization in the form of increasing economic ties between countries, technological advances that facilitate international communication among individuals, and the development of international forums has encouraged activists in the United States to work with or work for feminist causes around the world. The result has been a dramatic increase in the number of U.S. women's organizations focusing on international issues at all levels of activism. Perhaps most interesting has been the rise of local organizations with ties to groups in other countries without the use of an intermediate national organization. For example, the organization Manavi was created by Asian Indian feminists in New Jersey to raise money for women's development projects and other women's collectives in South Asia (Shukla 1997).

The dramatic increase in international activism and international issues within the United States corresponds with an increase in political constraints at home. Yet despite the conservative social values advanced by the Bush administration, its current emphasis on extending democratic values also creates some opportunities for feminists in the United States to support women's issues in other countries. For example, the Bush administration has become a supporter of women's education and formal political rights for women in Afghanistan. Such a policy provides allies (albeit strange bedfellows), legitimacy in the American political arena, and resources for U.S. feminists to support international feminist action.

While U.S. feminist action in the international realm clearly brings resources and allies to feminist movements overseas, it also creates and exacerbates existing problems within countries. As Carol Nechemias notes (chapter 9) in discussing the Russian women's movement, external support has created a domestic feminist movement that is often at odds with the demands of women on the ground (see also Richter 2002). Moreover, Uma Narayan (2005) suggests that even well-meaning support ends up buttressing the economic and social structures that are at the root of the problem. Narayan argues, for example, that providing microcredit as a way of supporting poor women in developing countries (something encouraged by numerous feminist organizations in the United States) actually reinforces their marginal economic position, as well as the global economic system that created the problem.

Thus, while we see an increase in U.S. feminist activity in the global community, the few studies on the effects of such activism suggest that healthy skepticism is needed about what U.S. feminists, no matter how well meaning, can and should do. Most important, it suggests a need for evaluating both the intended and unintended effects of U.S. activism in the global community.

WHITHER THE WOMEN'S MOVEMENT AROUND THE GLOBE?

The chapters in part II of this volume examine the United States in comparison with five different countries around the globe. Extrapolation from these countries to other countries or continents is dangerous, yet there are a few themes common to these chapters. These themes have also appeared in other comparative analyses of women's movements (see, e.g., Beckwith 2000 and Nelson and Chowdury 1994).

First, there is evidence of a flourishing women's movement in all of the countries studied here. While none of these movements directly mirrors the U.S. feminist movement, in each case women have mobilized around women's gendered experiences and issues.[1] In general terms, the concerns of women's movements in all the countries studied here overlap to a great extent; attempts to alleviate women's poverty and enshrine human rights for women in law and praxis are among the commonalities. Another common concern in all of these countries has been a focus on women moving into political institutions. Movement activists in Chile, Russia, and Japan have all demanded the incorporation of women and women's interests into state institutions, most often by pushing women into elective office but also by encouraging the creation of government agencies charged with representing women's issues.

Yet the consequences of a focus on entering political institutions remain largely unexamined in most countries.[2] While extensive studies of women in elected office in the United States show that women do make a difference (Carroll 2001; Swers 2002), the U.S. political system is in many ways unique. A weak candidate-centered party system, the alliance between the Democratic Party and feminists, and other aspects of the political context may create the ideal setting for women elected to political office to provide substantive representation of women's issues. Moreover, the culture and philosophy of government bureaucracies remain very different in each of the countries analyzed in this volume. Such system-level factors may have large consequences for how women may act as women in any situation. Thus, there remain many questions about how the focus on gender mainstreaming into parties, legislatures, and bureaucracies will affect women's movements in each country. Not only do we not know whether "insider" women can make a difference, but we have also not yet examined *which women* are advantaged by a focus on increasing women's representation in institutions. Quota laws and gender mainstreaming, even if they produce concrete gains for women in countries with different cultural heritages, historical precedents, and economic positions in a global economy, are likely to most benefit middle-class women.

The second theme to emerge from part II suggests that any generalization about women's movements worldwide should be tempered with skepticism. Historical legacies, specific cleavage structures, cultural norms, and social and political practices all create major differences in the issues and interests of the women's movements studied here. In Chile, as Baldez and Montoya note in chapter 8, the movement was in part a response to Pinochet's authoritarian regime. In Japan a housewives' movement that focuses on consumer and environmental issues complements a feminist movement (see chapter 10 by Joyce Gelb), and in Russia grassroots organizations often focus on children and motherhood (see chapter 9 by Carol Nechemias). While providing a unique set of interests for the women's movement, country- (or region-) specific institutions also constitute additional political constraints, limiting the potential allies and issues that can be addressed. In Russia, for example, women were faced with a political opening with the transition from authoritarianism, but one limited by a conservative view of women as belonging in a private sphere (see chapter 9 by Carol Nechemias). The cultural arguments that underlie *perestroika* reduced the ability of the women's movement to ally with other opponents of authoritarianism and to raise the feminist issues of equality found in the United States. At the same time, the transition to market capitalism greatly increased the need to deal with issues of women's poverty and need for employment.

What is the implication for a global women's movement? Keck and Sikkink (1998a), analyzing women's transnational networks, highlight the development of a transnational consensus opposed to violence against women, which, they argue, transcends cultural and national boundaries. Certainly, this volume notes similar common themes among national women's movements. Yet Rohlinger and Meyer's contribution (chapter 11) speaks also to the limits of this consensus. The authors find that international women's movement organizations (or, for that matter, international antifeminist movement organizations) remain an amalgam of local organizations adapted to and focused on their own political circumstances. In this sense, the global women's movement is and must continue to be a movement of many women's movements, each with its own identity and issues. In many ways this parallels the movement in the United States, where local feminists often negotiate different local conditions with national coordination (as Reger and Staggenborg note in chapter 6) and where the intersection of race, class, and sexuality creates diverse groups of feminists, each with different interests and identities. The history of feminism in the United States suggests that it is important that local interests drive the mobilization of the movement, with a particular eye to which groups of women benefit. Yet it also provides hope for the future. A global feminist network can successfully mobilize and create substantial social, political, and economic change for women, even as each group remains grounded in its own particular set of interests and political opportunities.

NOTES

1. Indeed, as we move outside of the United States, women's movements take on a different character, focused less on a specific agenda of equality for women, the elimination of women's subordination, and the destruction of patriarchal institutions and more on "the primacy of women's gendered experiences, women's issues, and women's leadership and decision-making" (see Beckwith 2000, 437).

2. Although the existence of insiders has been well documented, fewer works have been able to track the effects that feminist activists have had in political parties and government institutions (for example, in Western Europe, see Beckwith 2000, 1987; della Porta 2003; Lovenduski and Randall 1993; Valiente 2003).

References

Abubikirova, N. I., T. A. Klimenkova, E. V. Kotchkina, M. A. Regentova, and T. G. Troinova. 1998. *Directory of Women's Non-Governmental Organizations in Russia & the NIS.* Moscow: Aslan Publishers.

ACLU. n.d. *ACLU Position Paper: Affirmative Action,* at www.aclu.org (accessed December 10, 2003).

Act NOW. 1974. *Act NOW (Newsletter of the Chicago Chapter of the National Organization for Women)* 6, no. 3 (March).

Addams, Jane. 1917. "Why Women Should Vote." In *The Blue Book, Woman Suffrage: History, Arguments and Results,* edited by F. Bjorhmand and A. Porritt, 110–29. New York: National Woman Suffrage Publishing.

Adorno, L. W., et al. 1950. *The Authoritarian Personality.* New York: Harper.

Aivazova, Svetlana. 1994. "Feminism in Russia: Debates from the Past." In *Women in Russia: A New Era in Russian Feminism,* edited by Anastasia Posadskaya, 154–63. London: Verso Press.

Alvarez, Sonia E. 1990. *Engendering Democracy in Brazil: Women's Movements in Transition Politics.* Princeton, NJ: Princeton University Press.

Alvarez, Sonia, Elisabeth J. Friedman, Ericka Beckman, and Maylei Blackwell. 2002. "Encountering Latin American and Caribbean Feminisms." *Signs: Journal of Women in Culture and Society* 28, no. 2: 537–79.

Andersen, Kristi. 1996. *After Suffrage: Women in Partisan and Electoral Politics before the New Deal.* Chicago: University of Chicago Press.

Anderson, Bonnie S. 2000. *Joyous Greetings: The First International Women's Movement, 1830–1860.* New York: Oxford University Press.

Arnold, Gretchen. 1995. "Dilemmas of Feminist Coalitions: Collective Identity and Strategic Effectiveness in the Battered Women's Movement." In *Feminist Organizations: Harvest of the New Women's Movement,* edited by Myra Marx Ferree and Patricia Yancey Martin, 276–90. Philadelphia: Temple University Press.

Arrington, Theodore S., and Patricia A. Kyle. 1978. "Equal Rights Amendment Activists in North Carolina." *Signs: Journal of Women in Culture and Society* 3: 666–80.

Attwood, Lynne. 1990. *The New Soviet Man and Woman: Sex-Role Socialization in the USSR.* Bloomington: Indiana University Press.

Atwood, David. 1997. "Mobilizing Around the United Nations Special Sessions on Disarmament." In *Transnational Social Movements and Global Politics: Solidarity Beyond the State,* edited by J. Smith, C. Chatfield, and R. Pagnucco, 141–58. New York: Syracuse University Press.

Azhgikhina, Nadezhda. 1995a. "A Movement Is Born." *The Bulletin of the Atomic Scientists* 51 (July): 47–53.

———. 1995b. "Reproduktivnye prava kak zerkalo obshestva." *Vy i My* 11: 10–12.

———. 2000."Empowering Russia's Women: Will Their Potential Be Tapped?" *We/My, The Women's Dialogue, Millenium Issue,* at www.we-myi.org/issues/millenium/index.html.

Baldez, Lisa. 2002. *Why Women Protest: Women's Movements in Chile.* New York: Cambridge University Press.

Bambara, Toni Cade. 1970. "On the Issue of Roles." In *The Black Woman: An Anthology,* edited by Toni Cade Bambara. New York: New American Library.

Banaszak, Lee Ann. 1996a. *Why Movements Succeed or Fail: Opportunity, Culture, and the Struggle for Woman Suffrage.* Princeton, NJ: Princeton University Press.

———. 1996b. "When Waves Collide: Cycles of Protest and the Swiss and American Women's Movements." *Political Research Quarterly* 49 (December): 837–60.

———. 1996c. "The Use of the Initiative by the Swiss and American Woman Suffrage Movements." In *Social Movements and American Political Institutions,* edited by Anne Costain and Andrew McFarland, 99–114. Boulder: Rowman & Littlefield.

Banaszak, Lee Ann, Karen Beckwith, and Dieter Rucht. 2003a. "When Power Relocates: Interactive Changes in Women's Movements and States." In *Women's Movements Facing a Reconfigured State,* edited by Lee Ann Banaszak, Karen Beckwith, and Dieter Rucht, 1–29. Cambridge: Cambridge University Press.

———. 2003b. *Women's Movements Facing a Reconfigured State.* Cambridge: Cambridge University Press.

Barakso, Maryann. 2004. *Governing NOW: Grassroots Activism in the National Organization for Women.* Ithaca, NY: Cornell University Press.

Barbie Liberation Organization. n.d. "Official Barbie Liberation Organization Barbie/G.I.Joe Home Surgery Instructions," at users.lmi.net/~eve/download/barbiedir.pdf (accessed January 6, 2003).

Barker-Plummer, Bernadette. 1997. "News as a Political Resource? A Case Study of the Media Strategies and Media Representation of the National Organization for Women, 1966–1980." Ph.D. dissertation, University of Pennsylvania (UMI# 9727190).

Barry, Ursula. 1988. "Women in Ireland." *Women's Studies International Forum* 11: 317–22.

Bashevkin, Sylvia. 1994. "Facing a Renewed Right: American Feminism and the Reagan/Bush Challenge." *Canadian Journal of Political Science* 27, no. 4: 669–98.

———. 1996. "Tough Times in Review: The British Women's Movement During the Thatcher Years." *Comparative Political Studies* 28, no. 4: 525–52.

———. 1998. *Women on the Defensive*. Chicago: University of Chicago Press.

Basler, Barbara. 1984. "Mondale Effort in Florida Hinges on Little and Big NOW Chapters." *New York Times,* March 6, A13.

Baumgardner, Jennifer, and Amy Richards. 2000. *Manifesta: Young Women, Feminism, and the Future*. New York: Farrar, Straus & Giroux.

Beal, Frances. 1970. "Double Jeopardy: To Be Black and Female." In *The Black Woman: An Anthology,* edited by Toni Cade Bambara, 90–100. New York: New American Library.

Becker, Susan D. 1981. *The Origins of the Equal Rights Movement: American Feminism Between the Wars*. Westport, CT: Greenwood Press.

Beckwith, Karen. 1987. "Response to Feminism in the Italian Parliament: Divorce, Abortion, and Sexual Violence Legislation." In *The Women's Movements of the United States and Western Europe,* edited by Mary Fainsod Katzenstein and Carol McClurg Mueller, 153–71. Philadelphia: Temple University Press.

———. 1996. "Lancashire Women against Pit Closures: Women's Standing in a Men's Movement." *Signs* 21, no. 4 (Summer):1034—68.

———. 2000. "Beyond Compare? Women's Movements in Comparative Perspective." *European Journal of Political Research* 37, no. 4 (June): 431–68.

Belin, Laura. 2000. "Fewer Women to Serve in New Duma." *RFE/RL Russian Election Report* 8 (January 7), at www.rferl.specials/russianelection/archives/08-070100.asp (accessed May 6, 2005).

Benford, Robert, and David Snow. 2000. "Framing Processes and Social Movements: An Overview and Assessment." *Annual Review of Sociology* 26: 611–39.

Bennetts, Leslie. 1978. "Feminist Drive Is Likely to Persist Even If Rights Amendment Fails: Fighting the Incumbents Women's Rights." *New York Times,* May 31, A1.

Bernstein Anya. 2001. *The Moderation Dilemma: Legislative Coalitions and the Politics of Family and Medical Leave*. Pittsburgh, PA: University of Pittsburgh Press.

Bernstein, Mary. 1997. "Celebration and Suppression: The Strategic Uses of Identity by the Lesbian and Gay Movement." *American Journal of Sociology* 103, no. 3: 531–65.

Berry, Jeffrey. 1984. *The Interest Group Society*. 2d ed. Glenview, IL: Scott, Foresman/Little, Brown.

Berry, Mary Frances. 1986. *Why ERA Failed: Politics, Women's Rights, and the Amending Process of the Constitution*. Bloomington: Indiana University Press.

Bevacqua, Maria. 2000. *Rape on the Public Agenda*. Boston: Northeastern University Press.

Beyer, Janice M. 1981. "Ideologies, Values, and Decision Making in Organizations." In *Handbook of Organizational Design,* edited by P. C. Nystrom and W. H. Starbuck. New York: Oxford University Press.

Bird, Caroline. 1968. *Born Female: The High Cost of Keeping Women Down*. New York: David McKay.

Blanchard, Dallas A. 1994. *The Anti-Abortion Movement and the Rise of the Religious Right*. New York: Twayne.

Blumer, Herbert. 1951. "Social Movements." In *New Outline of the Principles of Sociology,* edited by A. M. Lee. New York: Barnes & Noble.

———. 1957. "Collective Behavior." In *Review of Sociology: Analysis of a Decade,* edited by Joseph B. Gittler. New York: Wiley.

Boles, Janet K. 1979. *The Politics of the Equal Rights Amendment*. New York: Longman.

———. 1980. "Feminists as Agents of Social Change: Lobbying for the Equal Rights Amendment." *Peace and Change* 6: 1–19.

———. 1991. "Form Follows Function: Evolution of Feminist Strategies." *Annual of American Academy of Political and Social Science* 515: 38–49.

Bond, Jean Carey, and Patricia Perry. 1970. "Is the Black Male Castrated?" In *The Black Woman: An Anthology*, edited by Toni Cade Bambara, 113–18. New York: New American Library.

Brenner, Joanna. 1996. "The Best of Times, The Worst of Times: Feminism in the United States." In *Mapping the Women's Movement*, edited by Monica Threlfall, 17–72. London: Verso.

Bridgeman, Jo. 1998. "A Woman's Right to Choose?" In *Abortion Law and Politics Today*, edited by Ellie Lee, 76–94. London: Macmillan Press.

Bridger, Sue, Rebecca Kay, and Kathryn Pinnick. 1996. *No More Heroines? Russia, Women and the Market*. London: Routledge.

Brown, Elaine. 1992. *A Taste of Power: A Black Woman's Story*. New York: Pantheon Books.

Brownmiller, Susan. 1999. *In Our Time*. New York: Dial Press.

Buck, Solon J. 1920. *The Agrarian Crusade*. New Haven, CT: Yale University Press.

Buckley, Sandra. 1994. "A Short History of the Feminist Movement in Japan." In *Women of Japan and Korea*, edited by Joyce Gelb and Marian Lief Palley, 150–88. Philadelphia: Temple University Press.

———. 1997. *Broken Silence: Voices of Japanese Feminism*. Berkeley: University of California Press.

Buechler, Steven M. 1990. *Women's Movements in the United States: Woman Suffrage, Equal Rights, and Beyond*. New Brunswick, NJ: Rutgers University Press.

Buhle, Mari Jo, and Paul Buhle, ed. 1978. *The Concise History of Woman Suffrage: Selections from the Classic Work of Stanton, Anthony, Gage and Harper*. Urbana: University of Illinois Press.

Bunce, Valerie. 2002. "Then and Now, Us and Them." *NewsNet: The Newsletter of the AAASS* 42, no. 1 (January): 1–5.

Bunster, Ximena. 1993. "Surviving Beyond Fear: Women and Torture in Latin America." In *Surviving Beyond Fear: Women, Children and Human Rights in Latin America*, edited by Marjorie Agosin and Monica Bruno, 98–125. Fredonia, NY: White Pine Press.

Burk, Martha, and Heidi Hartmann. 1996. "Beyond the Gender Gap." *Nation* (June 10): 18–21.

Butler, Judith. 1990. *Gender Trouble: Feminism and the Subversion of Identity*. New York: Routledge.

———. 1997. "Merely Cultural." *Social Text* 15, no. 3–4: 265–77.

Button, James W. 1989. *Blacks and Social Change: Impact of the Civil Rights Movement in Southern Communities*. Princeton, NJ: Princeton University Press.

Bystydzienski, Jill. 1995. *Women in Electoral Politics: Lessons from Norway*. Westport, CT: Praeger.

Caiazza, Amy. 2001. "Women's Union of Russia or WUR (Soiuz zhenshchin Rossii) (1990–)." In *Encyclopedia of Russian Women's Movements*, edited by Norma Corigliano Noonan and Carol Nechemias, 366–69. Westport, CT: Greenwood Press.

———. 2002. *Mothers and Soldiers: Gender, Citizenship, and Civil Society in Contemporary Russia*. New York: Routledge.

Califia, Pat. 1997. *Sex Changes: The Politics of Transgenderism*. San Francisco: Cleis Press.

Cantril, Hadley. 1941. *The Psychology of Social Movements*. New York: Wiley.

Carabillo, Toni, Judith Meuli, and June Bundy Csida. 1993. *Feminist Chronicles, 1953–1993*. Los Angeles: Women's Graphics.

Carden, Maren Lockwood. 1974. *The New Feminist Movement*. New York: Russell Sage Foundation.

———. 1978. "The Proliferation of a Social Movement: Ideology and Individual Incentives in the Contemporary Feminist Movement." *Research in Social Movements, Conflicts and Change* 1:179–96. Greenwich, CT: JAI Press.

Carroll, Susan J., ed. 2001. *The Impact of Women in Public Office*. Bloomington: Indiana University Press.

Cassell, Joan. 1977. *A Group Called Women*. New York: David McKay.

Catt, Carrie Chapman. 1929. "Letter to A. Leusch, president of the Schweizerischer Verband für Frauenstimmrecht." Found in uncataloged materials from the Schweizerischer Verband für Frauenstimmrecht (Sozialarchiv Zürich).

Cella, Carrie. 2001. "Pay Day." *See It? Tell It. Change It! Third Wave Foundation Newsletter* (Summer): 5, at www.thirdwavefoundation.org (accessed January 14, 2002).

Center for American Women and Politics (CAWP). 2002a. "Women in the U.S. Senate 1922–2002." Fact Sheet from the National Information Bank on Women in Public Office, Eagleton Institute of Politics, Rutgers University.

———. 2002b. "Women in the U.S. Congress 2002." Fact Sheet from the National Information Bank on Women in Public Office, Eagleton Institute of Politics, Rutgers University.

Centro de Estudios de la Mujer. 1988. *Mundo De Mujer: Continuidad Y Cambio*. Santiago: Ediciones CEM.

Chafetz, Janet Saltzman, and Anthony Gary Dworkin. 1986. *Female Revolt: Women's Movements in World and Historical Perspective*. Totowa, NJ: Rowman & Allanheld.

Chubb, Basil. 1992. *The Government and Politics of Ireland*. 2d ed. London: Longman Press.

Chuchryk, Patricia. 1994. "From Dictatorship to Democracy." In *The Women's Movement in Latin America*, edited by Jane S. Jaquette, 65–108. Boulder: Westview.

Civil Rights Coalition for the 21st Century, The. "Affirmative Action Court Decisions of the Supreme Court," at www.civilrights.org.

Clemens, Elisabeth. 1996. "Organizational Form as Frame: Collective Identity and Political Strategy in the American Labor Movement, 1880–1920." In *Comparative Perspectives on Social Movements: Political Opportunities, Mobilizing Structures, and Cultural Framings*, edited by Doug McAdam, John D. McCarthy, and Mayer N. Zald, 205–26. Cambridge: Cambridge University Press.

———. 1997. *The People's Lobby: Organizational Innovation and the Rise of Interest Group Politics in the United States, 1890–1925*. Chicago: University of Chicago Press.

Cleveland NOW Newsletter. August 1990. Files of the Cleveland NOW chapter.

CNN, at www.CNN.com/US/9510/megamarch/whowasthere.html.

Cockburn, Cynthia. 1991. "'Democracy Without Women Is No Democracy': Soviet Women Hold Their First Autonomous National Conference." *Feminist Review* 39: 141–48.

Cohan, Alvin. 1986. "Abortion as a Marginal Issue: The Use of Peripheral Mechanisms in Britain and the United States." In *The New Politics of Abortion,* edited by Joni Lovenduski and Joyce Outshoorn, 27–47. London: Sage Publications.

Cohen, Jeffrey, and Charles Barrilleaux. 1993. "Public Opinion, Interest Groups, and Public Policy Making: Abortion Policy in the American States." In *Understanding the New Politics of Abortion,* edited by Malcolm Goggin, 203–21. Newbury Park, CA: Sage Publications.

Coleman, James. 1957. *Community Conflict.* Glencoe, IL: Free Press.

Coliver, Sandra. 1995. "Ireland." In *The Right to Know: Human Rights and Access to Reproductive Health Information,* edited by Sandra Coliver, 159–80. London: Article 19, and Philadelphia: The University of Pennsylvania Press.

Constable, Pamela, and Arturo Valenzuela. 1991. *A Nation of Enemies: Chile under Pinochet.* New York: W. W. Norton.

Conway, M. Margaret. 1986. "PACs and Congressional Elections in the 1980s." In *Interest Group Politics,* 2d ed., edited by Allan J. Cigler and Burdett A Loomis, 70–90. Washington, DC: Congressional Quarterly Press.

Cook, Linda, and Carol Nechemias. 2004. "Women in the Russian Duma, 1993–2004." Paper presented at the Conference on Women in East European Politics, Co-sponsored by the Kennan Institute, the Watson Institute for International Studies of Brown University, and George Washington University, Washington, DC, April 23–24.

Cordero, Joseph. 1997. "Major U.S. Court Cases." *Institutional Diversity & Equal Opportunity, CSUSM,* at www.csusm.edu/affirm_action/court.htm (accessed December 10, 2003).

Cortright, David, and Ron Pagnucco. 1997. "Limits to Transnationalism: The 1980s Freeze Campaign." In *Transnational Social Movements and Global Politics: Solidarity Beyond the State,* edited by J. Smith, C. Chatfield, and R. Pagnucco, 159–74. New York: Syracuse University Press.

Costain, Anne N. 1992. *Inviting Women's Rebellion: A Political Process Interpretation of the Women's Movement.* Baltimore: Johns Hopkins University Press.

Cott, Nancy F. 1987. *The Grounding of Modern Feminism.* New Haven, CT: Yale University Press.

———. 1990. "Historical Perspectives: The Equal Rights Amendment Conflict in the 1920s." In *Conflicts in Feminism,* edited by Marianne Hirsch and Evelyn Fox Keller, 44–59. New York: Routledge.

Courier-Tribune. 1972. "To Celebrate Vote Birthday." July 22.

Coy, Patrick. 1997. "Cooperative Accompaniment and Peace Brigades International in Sri Lanka." In *Transnational Social Movements and Global Politics: Solidarity Beyond the State,* edited by Jackie Smith, Charles Chatfield, and Ron Pagnucco, 81–100. Syracuse, NY: Syracuse University Press.

Craig, Barbara, and David O'Brien. 1993. *Abortion and American Politics.* Chatham, NJ: Chatham House Publishers.

Cress, Daniel, and David Snow. 1998. "Mobilization at the Margins: Organizing by the Homeless." In *Social Movements and American Political Institutions,* edited by Anne Costain and Andrew McFarland, 73–98. Lanham, MD: Rowman & Littlefield.

Crewe, Ivor. 1993. "Parties and Electors." In *The Developing British Political System: The 1990s*, 3d ed., edited by Ian Budge and David McKay, 66–82. London: Longman Group UK Unlimited.

Currie, Elliott, and Jerome H. Skolnick. 1970. "A Critical Note on Conceptions of Collective Behavior." *Annals of the American Academy of Political and Social Science* 391 (September): 34–45.

Curtis, Russell L., and Louis A. Zurcher Jr. 1973. "Stable Resources of Protest Movements: The Multi-organizational Field." *Social Forces* 52: 53–61.

Dahlerup, Drude. 1986. *The New Women's Movements, Feminism and Political Power in Europe and the USA*. Belmont, CA: Sage Publications.

Dahrendorf, Ralf. 1959. *Class and Class Conflict in Industrial Society*. Palo Alto, CA: Stanford University Press.

Daly, Mary. 1978. *GynEcology: The Metaethics of Radical Feminism*. Boston: Beacon Press.

Daniels, Cynthia. 1997. *Feminists Negotiate the State: The Politics of Domestic Violence*. Latham, MD: University Press of America.

Darcy, Robert, Susan Welch, and Janet Clark. 1995. *Women, Elections and Representation*. Lincoln: University of Nebraska Press.

Davies, James C. 1962. "Toward a Theory of Revolution." *American Sociological Review* 27, no. 1: 5–19.

Davis, Angela Y. 1974. *Angela Davis: An Autobiography*. New York: Random House.
———. 1981. *Women, Race and Class*. New York: Random House.

Davis, Flora. 1999. *Moving the Mountain: The Women's Movement in America Since 1960*. Champaign: University of Illinois Press.

Dawson, C. A., and W. E. Gettys. 1929. *An Introduction to Sociology*. New York: Ronald.

Day, Christine. 1995. "Louisiana: Religious Politics and the Pro-Life Cause." In *Abortion Politics in the American States*, edited by Mary Segers and Timothy Byrnes, 69–83. New York: M. E. Sharpe.

de Beauvoir, Simone. 1952. *The Second Sex*. New York: Vintage Books.

della Porta, Donatella. 1995. *Social Movements: Political Violence and the State*. New York: Cambridge University Press.
———. 2003. "The Women's Movement, the Left and the State: Continuities and Changes in the Italian Case." In *Women's Movements Facing a Reconfigured State*, edited by Lee Ann Banaszak, Karen Beckwith, and Dieter Rucht, 48–68. Cambridge: Cambridge University Press.

della Porta, Donatella, and Hanspeter Kriesi. 1999. "Social Movements in a Globalizing World: An Introduction." In *Social Movements in a Globalizing World*, edited by Donatella della Porta, Hanspeter Kriesi, and Dieter Rucht, 3–39. London: Macmillan.

Deutchman, Iva E., and Sandra Prince-Embury. 1982. "Political Ideology of Pro and Anti-ERA Women." *Women and Politics* 2 (March): 39–55.

Dill, Bonnie Thornton. 1983. "Race, Class and Gender: Prospects for an All-Inclusive Sisterhood." *Feminist Studies* 9: 131–50.

Dill, Kim. 1989. "'Qualified Feminism' and its Influence on Identification with the Women's Movement." Undergraduate honors thesis, Ohio State University.

Dionne, E. J., Jr. 1989. "Women's Caucus is Focusing on Abortion Rights." *New York Times*, August 6, Section 1:18.

Disney, Jennifer Leigh, and Joyce Gelb. 2000. "Feminist Organizational 'Success': The State of U.S. Women's Movement Organizations in the 1990s." *Women & Politics* 21, no. 4: 39–76.

DuBois, Ellen. 1978. *Feminism and Suffrage: The Emergence of an Independent Women's Movement in America, 1848–1869.* Ithaca, NY: Cornell University Press.

———. 1981. *Elizabeth Cady Stanton, Susan B. Anthony: Correspondence, Writings, Speeches.* New York: Schocken Books.

———. 1994. "Woman Suffrage Around the World: Three Phases of Suffragist Internationalism." In *Suffrage and Beyond: International Feminist Perspectives,* edited by Caroline Daley and Melanie Nolan, 252–74. New York: New York University Press.

Duerst-Lahti, Georgia. 1989. "The Government's Role in Building the Women's Movement." *Political Science Quarterly* 104, no. 2: 249–68.

Dyson, Michael. 1995. "African American Women and the Million Man March." *Christian Century* 112, no. 34: 1100–1.

Echols, Alice. 1989. *Daring to Be Bad: Radical Feminism in America, 1967–1975.* Minneapolis: University of Minnesota Press.

Edelsberg, Herman. 1965. "N.Y.U. 18th Conference on Labor." *Labor Relations Reporter* 61 (August): 253–55.

Edut, Tali, with Dyann Logwood and Ophira Edut. 1997. "HUES Magazine: The Making of a Movement." In *Third Wave Agenda,* edited by Leslie Heywood and Jennifer Drake, 83–98. Minneapolis: University of Minnesota Press.

Eighth Annual National Young Women's Day of Action. 2002, January 23, at hamp.hampshire.edu/~clpp/NYWDA/nywda.html.

Eisenstein, Zillah. 1982. "Some Thoughts on the Patriarchal State and the Defeat of the ERA." *Journal of Sociology and Social Welfare* 9 (September): 388–90.

Epstein, Cynthia Fuchs. 1993. *Women in Law.* Urbana: University of Illinois Press.

Er, Lam Peng. 1999. *Green Politics in Japan.* London: Routledge.

Evans, Sara. 1979. *Personal Politics: The Roots of Women's Liberation in the Civil Rights Movement and the New Left.* New York: Random House.

Evans, Sara, and Harry C. Boyte. 1986. *Free Spaces: The Source of Democratic Change in America.* New York: Harper & Row.

"EW=EW" Tokyo Circle. 1995. "We are Fighting for Equality in the Japanese Workplace." Handout, August 15.

Ezekiel, Judith. 2002. *Feminism in the Heartland.* Columbus: Ohio State University Press.

Fahey, Tony. 1998. "The Catholic Church and Social Policy." In *Social Policy in Ireland: Principles, Practice, and Problems,* edited by Sean Healy and Brigid Reynolds, 411–30. Dublin: Oak Tree Press.

Feminist View. 1981. Untitled, Ohio National Organization for Women archives, Box 1, Lake-Geauga newsletters, 1977–1982, The Ohio Historical Society, Columbus, Ohio (May).

Ferguson, Kathy. 1984. *The Feminist Case Against Bureaucracy.* Philadelphia: Temple University Press.

Ferree, Myra Marx, and William Gamson. 1999. "The Gendering of Abortion Discourse: Assessing Global Feminist Influence in the United States and Germany." In *Social Movements in a Globalizing World,* edited by Donatella della Porta, Hanspeter Kriesi, and Dieter Rucht, 40–56. London: Macmillan.

Ferree, Myra Marx, William Gamson, Jürgen Gerhards, and Dieter Rucht, eds. 2002. *Shaping Abortion Discourse: Democracy and the Public Sphere in Germany and the United States.* Cambridge: Cambridge University Press.

Ferree, Myra Marx, and Beth B. Hess. 1985. *Controversy and Coalition: The New Feminist Movement.* Boston: Twayne Publishers.

———. 1994. *Controversy and Coalition: The New Feminist Movement.* Rev. ed. New York: Twayne Publishers.

———. 2000. *Controversy and Coalition: The New Feminist Movement Across Three Decades.* 3d ed. New York: Routledge.

Ferree, Myra Marx, and Patricia Yancey Martin, eds. 1995. *Feminist Organizations: Harvest of the New Women's Movement.* Philadelphia: Temple University Press.

Ferree, Myra Marx, and Frederick D. Miller. 1985. "Mobilization and Meaning: Toward an Integration of Social Psychological and Resource Perspectives on Social Movements." *Sociological Inquiry* 55: 38–61.

Ferriss, Abbott L. 1971. *Indicators of Trends in the Status of American Women.* New York: Russell Sage.

Findlen, Barbara. 1995. *Listen Up: Voices from the Next Feminist Generation.* 1st ed. Seattle: Seal Press.

———. 2001. *Listen Up: Voices from the Next Feminist Generation.* 2d ed. Seattle: Seal Press.

Firestone, David. 1993. "While Barbie Talks Tough, G.I. Joe Goes Shopping." *The New York Times,* December 31—Late Edition, A12.

Firestone, Shulamith. 1971. *Dialectics of Sex.* New York: Morrow.

Fishman, Walda Katz, and Georgia E. Fuller. 1981. "Unraveling the Right Wing Opposition to Women's Equality." Paper available from Interchange Resource Center, New York.

Flexner, Eleanor. 1968. *Century of Struggle: The Woman's Rights Movement in the United States.* New York: Atheneum.

———. 1975 [1959]. *Century of Struggle: The Woman's Rights Movement in the United States.* Rev. ed. Cambridge, MA: Belknap Press.

Foley, Michael W., and Bob Edwards. 1999. "Is it Time to Disinvest in Social Capital?" *Journal of Public Policy* 19: 219–31.

Foner, Philip S. 1979. *Women and the American Labor Movement: From the First Trade Unions to the Present.* New York: Free Press.

Ford, Linda G. 1991. *Iron-Jawed Angels: The Suffrage Militancy of the National Woman's Party, 1912–1920.* Lanham, MD: University Press of America.

Franceschet, Susan. 2004. "Explaining Social Movement Outcomes: Collective Action Frames and Strategic Choices in First- and Second- Wave Feminism in Chile." *Comparative Political Studies* 37, no. 5: 499–530.

Franzen, Trisha. 1993. "Differences and Identities: Feminism and the Albuquerque Lesbian Community." *Signs: Journal of Women in Culture and Society* 18: 891–906.

Freeman, Jo. 1973. "The Tyranny of Structurelessness." In *Radical Feminism,* edited by Anne Koedt, E. Levine, and Anita Rapone, 285–99. New York: Quadrangle Books.

———. 1975. *The Politics of Women's Liberation: A Case Study of an Emerging Social Movement and Its Relation to the Policy Process.* New York: David McKay.

———. 1986. "The Quest for Equality: The ERA vs. Other Means." In *Ethnicity and Women,* edited by Winston A. Van Horne, 46–78. Milwaukee: University of Wisconsin System.

——. 1987. "Whom You Know versus Whom You Represent: Feminist Influence in the Democratic and Republican Parties." In *The Women's Movements of the United States and Western Europe: Feminist Consciousness, Political Opportunity, and Public Policy*, edited by Mary Fainsod Katzenstein and Carol McClurg Mueller, 215–44. Philadelphia: Temple University Press.

——. 2000. *A Room at a Time: How Women Entered Party Politics*. Lanham, MD: Rowman & Littlefield.

Friedan, Betty. 1963. *The Feminine Mystique*. New York: Dell.

——. 1967. "N.O.W.: How It Began." *Women Speaking* (April): 4, 6.

——. 1977. *It Changed My Life: Writings on the Women's Movement*. New York: Dell Publishing.

Friedman, Debra, and Doug McAdam. 1992. "Collective Identity and Activism: Networks, Choices and the Life of a Social Movement." In *Frontiers in Social Movement Theory*, edited by Aldon D. Morris and Carol McClurg Mueller, 156–73. New Haven, CT: Yale University Press.

Frohmann, Alicia, and Teresa Valdés. 1995. "Democracy in the Country and in the Home." In *The Challenge of Local Feminisms*, edited by Amrita Basu and C. Elizabeth McCrory, 276–301. Boulder: Westview.

Fujieda, Mioko, and Kumiko Fujimura-Fanselow. 1995. "Women's Studies: An Overview." In *Japanese Women*, edited by Kumiko Fujimura-Fanselow and Atsuko Kameda, 155–82. New York: Feminist Press.

Fujimura-Fanselow, Kumiko, and Atsuka Kameda. 1995. "Introduction." In *Japanese Women*, edited by Kumiko Fujimura-Fanselow and Atsuko Kameda, xvii–xxxviii. New York: Feminist Press.

Gabin, Nancy. 1990. *Feminism and the Labor Movement: Women and the United Auto Workers, 1935–1975*. Ithaca, NY: Cornell University Press.

Galey, Margaret E. 1995. "Forerunners in Women's Quest for Partnership." In *Women, Politics and the United Nations*, edited by Anne Winslow, 1–10. Westport, CT: Greenwood Press.

Galway for Life, at www.galwayforlife.ie.

Gallagher, Michael. 1999. "The Changing Constitution." In *Politics in the Republic of Ireland*, 3d ed., edited by John Coakley and Michael Gallagher, 71–98. New York: Routledge.

Gamson, Joshua. 1997. "Messages of Exclusion: Gender, Movements, and Symbolic Boundaries." *Gender and Society* 11 (April): 178–99.

Gamson, William A. 1975. *The Strategy of Social Protest*. Homewood, IL: Dorsey Press.

——. 1992. *Talking Politics*. Cambridge: University of Cambridge Press.

Gamson, William, David Croteau, William Hoynes, and Theodore Sasson. 1992. "Media Images and the Social Construction of Reality." *Annual Review of Sociology* 18: 373–93.

Gamson, William A., and David S. Meyer. 1996. "Framing Political Opportunity." In *Comparative Perspectives on Social Movements: Political Opportunities, Mobilizing Structures, and Cultural Framings*, edited by Doug McAdam, John D. McCarthy, and Mayer N. Zald, 275–90. Cambridge: Cambridge University Press.

Gamson, William, and Andre Modigliani. 1989. "Media Discourse and Public Opinion on Nuclear Power: A Constructionist Approach." *American Journal of Sociology* 95, no. 1: 1–37.

Gardiner, Frances. 1993. "Political Interest and Participation of Irish Women 1922–1992: The Unfinished Revolution." In *Irish Women's Studies Reader*, edited by Ailbhe Smyth, 45–78. Dublin: Attic Press.

Gardner, Marilyn. 1988. "Former US First Ladies Provide Launch Pad for New ERA Drive." *The Christian Science Monitor*, February 16, A5.

Garretón, Manuel Antonio. 1995. "The Political Opposition and the Party System under the Military Regime." In *The Struggle for Democracy in Chile*, edited by Paul Drake and Ivan Jaksic, 211–50. Lincoln: University of Nebraska Press.

Gelb, Joyce. 1989. *Feminism and Politics: A Comparative Perspective*. Berkeley: University of California Press.

———. 1995. "Feminist Organization Success and the Politics of Engagement." In *Feminist Organizations: Harvest of the New Women's Movement*, edited by M. M. Ferree and P. Y. Martin, 128–36. Philadelphia: Temple University Press.

———. 2003. *Gender Policies in Japan and the United States: Comparing Women's Movements, Rights and Politics*. New York: Palgrave Macmillan.

Gelb, Joyce, and Margarita Estevez Abe. 1998. "Political Women in Japan: A Case Study of the Seikatsusha Network Movement." *Social Science Japan Journal* 1, no. 2 (October): 263–80.

Gelb, Joyce, and Vivien Hart. 1999. "Feminist Politics in a Hostile Environment: Obstacles and Opportunities." In *How Social Movements Matter*, edited by Marco Giugni, Doug McAdam, and Charles Tilly, 149–81. Minneapolis: University of Minnesota Press.

Gelb, Joyce, and Marian Lief Palley. 1996. *Women and Public Policies: Reassessing Gender Politics*. Charlottesville: University Press of Virginia.

Gialey, Phil. 1985. "NOW Chief Describes Plans to Fight 'Fascists and Bigots." *New York Times*, September 6.

Gilmore, Stephanie. 2001. "Rethinking the Liberal/Feminist Divide: Dynamic Feminism in a Southern U.S. City." Unpublished paper.

Ginsburg, Faye. 1998. *Contested Lives: The Abortion Debate in an American Community*. Los Angeles: University of California Press.

Girvin, Brian. 1996. "Ireland and the European Union: The Impact of Integration and Social Change on Abortion Policy." In *Abortion Politics: Public Policy in Cross-Cultural Perspective*, edited by Marianne Githens and Dorothy McBride Stetson, 165–84. New York: Routledge.

Glendon, Mary Ann. 1991. *Rights Talk: The Impoverishment of Political Discourse*. New York: Free Press.

Gorbachev, Mikhail. 1987. *Perestroika: New Thinking for Our Country and the World*. New York: Harper & Row.

Gottfried, Heidi. 2002. "Network Organizations: A New Face of Union Representation in Japan." *Critical Solidarity* 2, no.1: 5–6.

Greater Cleveland Coordinating Council. 1976. Meeting minutes. National Organization for Women archives, Lana Moretsky Papers, Box 4, Folder 102, Western Reserve Historical Society, Cleveland, Ohio, January 22.

Greater Cleveland NOW newsletter. 1974. Untitled, National Organization for Women archives, Lana Moretsky Papers, Box 12, Folder 271, Western Reserve Historical Society, Cleveland, Ohio, July.

Griffiths, Martha. 1966. Speech of June 20, *Congressional Record*.

Gross, Jane. 1992. "NOW; Patricia Ireland, President of NOW: Does She Speak for Today's Women?" *New York Times,* March 1, SM 16.

Guidry, John, Michael Kennedy, and Mayer Zald. 2000. *Globalizations and Social
Movements: Culture, Power, and the Transnational Public Sphere.* Ann Arbor:
University of Michigan Press.

Gurr, Ted. 1970. *Why Men Rebel.* Princeton, NJ: Princeton University Press.

Gusfield, Joseph R. 1970. *Symbolic Crusade: Status Politics and the American Temperance Movement.* Chicago: University of Illinois Press.

Guth, James, Lyman Kellstedt, Corwin Smidt, and John Green. 1994. "Cut from the
Whole Cloth: Antiabortion Mobilization among Religious Activists." In *Abortion
Politics in the United States and Canada: Studies in Public Opinion,* edited by Ted
Jelen and Marthe Chandler, 107–30. Westport, CT: Praeger.

Gutterman, Steve. 2002. "AP: USAID Shifts Focus in Russia from National Level to
Grass-Roots Programs in Provinces." *Johnson's Russia List* 6348 (July 11), at www
.cdi.org/johnson/6348-1.cfm (accessed May 6, 2005).

Haas, Liesl. 2000. "Legislating Equality: Feminist Policymaking in Chile." Ph.D. dissertation, University of North Carolina.

Hada, Aiko. 1995. "Domestic Violence." In *Japanese Women,* edited by Kumiko
Fujimura-Fanselow and Atsuko Kameda, 265–70. New York: Feminist Press.

Handlin, Amy. 1998. *Whatever Happened to the Year of the Woman? Why Women
Are Still Not Making it to the Top in Politics.* Denver, CO: Arden Press.

Hardiman, Niamh, and Christopher Whelan. 1994. "Politics and Democratic Values."
In *Values and Social Change in Ireland,* edited by Christopher Whelan, 100–35.
Dublin: Gill & Macmillan.

Harrison, Cynthia E. 1980. "A New Frontier for Women: The Public Policy of the
Kennedy Administration." *The Journal of American History* 67 (December): 630–46.

———. 1988. *On Account of Sex: The Politics of Women's Issues 1945–1968.* Berkeley: University of California Press.

Hayden, Casey, and Mary King. 1966. "A Kind of Memo." *Liberation* (April): 35–36.

Heberle, Rudolph. 1951. *Social Movements.* New York: Appleton-Century-Crofts.

Hemment, Julie. 2004. "Strategizing Development: Translations, Appropriations, Responsibilities." In *Post-Soviet Women Encountering Transition: Nation-Building,
Economic Survival, and Civic Activism,* edited by Kathleen Kuehnast and Carol
Nechemias, 313–33. Baltimore: Woodrow Wilson Press and Johns Hopkins University Press.

Henderson, Sarah. 2001. "Foreign Funding and the Women's Movement in Russia (ca.
1991–)." In *Encyclopedia of Russian Women's Movements,* edited by Norma
Corigliano Noonan and Carol Nechemias, 254–57. Westport, CT: Greenwood Press.

———. 2003. *Building Democracy in Contemporary Russia: Western Support for
Grassroots Organizations.* Ithaca, NY: Cornell University Press.

Herbers, John. 1982. "Women Turn View to Public Office." *New York Times,* June 28.

Hershey, Majorie Randon. 1986. "Direct Action and the Abortion Issue: The Political
Participation of Single-Issue Groups." in *Interest Group Politics,* 2d ed., edited by
Allan J. Cigler and Burdett A Loomis, 27–45. Washington, DC: Congressional Quar-
terly Press.

———. 1993. "The Congressional Elections." In *The Election of 1992,* edited by Ger-
ald M. Pomper. Chatham, NJ: Chatham House Publishers.

Heywood, Leslie, and Jennifer Drake, eds. 1997a. *Third Wave Agenda*. Minneapolis: University of Minnesota Press.

———. 1997b. "Introduction." In *Third Wave Agenda*, edited by Leslie Heywood and Jennifer Drake, 1–20. Minneapolis: University of Minnesota Press.

Hoffer, Eric. 1951. *The True Believer*. New York: Harper.

Hoff-Wilson, Joan, ed. 1986. *Rights of Passage: The Past and Future of the ERA*. Bloomington: Indiana University Press.

Hole, Judith, and Ellen Levine. 1971. *Rebirth of Feminism*. New York: Quadrangle Books.

Holt, Alix. 1985. "The First Soviet Feminists." In *Soviet Sisterhood*, edited by Barbara Holland, 237–65. Bloomington: Indiana University Press.

Holzman, Abraham. 1963. *The Townsend Movement: A Political Study*. New York: Bookman.

hooks, bell. 1981. *Ain't I a Woman: Black Women and Feminism*. Boston: South End Press.

Hovey, Michael. 1997. "Interceding at the United Nations: The Human Right of Conscientious Objection." In *Transnational Social Movements and Global Politics: Solidarity Beyond the State*, edited by J. Smith, C. Chatfield, and R. Pagnucco, 214–24. New York: Syracuse University Press.

Hyde, Cheryl. 1995. "Feminist Social Movement Organizations Survive the New Right." In *Feminist Organizations: Harvest of the New Women's Movement*, edited by M. M. Ferree and P. Y. Martin, 306–22. Philadelphia: Temple University Press.

Ichikawa Fusae Memorial Association. 2001. *Japanese Women* 1 (September): 86.

Imig, Doug, and Sidney Tarrow, eds. 2001a. *Contentious Europeans: Protest and Politics in an Emerging Polity*. New York: Rowman & Littlefield.

———. 2001b. "Studying Contention in an Emerging Polity." In *Contentious Europeans: Protest and Politics in an Emerging Polity*, edited by Doug Imig and Sidney Tarrow, 3–26. New York: Rowman & Littlefield.

Inglehart, Ronald. 1990. *Culture Shift in Advanced Industrial Society*. Princeton, NJ: Princeton University Press.

International Planned Parenthood Federation, at www.ippf.org.

Irish Family Planning Association, at www.ifpa.ie.

Ishiyama, John T., and Sarah Kuntz. 2000. "Social Identity and Party Development in Post-Soviet Politics: The Case of the 'Women of Russia'." *The American Review of Politics* 21: 43–67.

Ishkanian, Armine. 2004. "Working at the Local-Global Intersection: The Challenges Facing Women in Armenia's NGO Sector." In *Post-Soviet Women Encountering Transition: Nation-Building, Economic Survival, and Civic Activism*, edited by Kathleen Kuehnast and Carol Nechemias, 262–87. Baltimore: Woodrow Wilson Press and Johns Hopkins University Press.

Jackson, Maurice, Eleanora Petersen, James Bull, Sverre Monsen, and Patricia Richmond. 1960. "The Failure of an Incipient Social Movement." *Pacific Sociological Review* 3, no. 1 (Spring): 40.

Jenkins, J. Craig. 1983. "Resource Mobilization Theory and the Study of Social Movements." *American Review of Sociology* 9: 527–53.

Jenkins, J. Craig, and Charles Perrow. 1977. "Insurgency of the Powerless: Farm Worker Movements (1946–1972)." *American Sociological Review* 42 (April): 249–68.

Jenson, Jane. 1987. "Changing Discourse, Changing Agendas: Political Rights and Reproductive Policies in France." In *The Women's Movements of the United States and Western Europe*, edited by Mary Fainsod Katzenstein and Carol McClurg Mueller, 64–88. Philadelphia: Temple University Press.

Johnson, Sonia. 1987.*Going Out of Our Minds: The Metaphysics of Liberation*. Freedom, CA: Crossing Press.

———. 1989. *Wildfire: Igniting the She/Volution*. Albuquerque, NM: Wildfire.

Johnston, Hank. 2002. "Verification and Proof in Frame and Discourse Analysis." In *Methods of Social Movement Research*, edited by Bert Klandermans and Suzanne Staggenborg, 62–91. Minneapolis: University of Minnesota Press.

Johnston, Hank, and Bert Klandermans, eds. 1995. *Social Movements and Culture*. Minneapolis: University of Minnesota Press.

Johnston, Hank, and David Snow. 1998. "Subcultures of Opposition and Social Movements." *Sociological Perspectives* 41, no. 3: 473–98.

Johnston, Jill. 1973. *Lesbian Nation: The Feminist Solution*. New York: Simon & Schuster.

Kahn, Kim Fridkin, and Edie N. Goldenberg. 1991. "The Media: Ally or Obstacle of Feminists?" *The Annals of the American Academy of Political and Social Science* 515: 104–13.

Kaplan, Gisela. 1992. *Contemporary Western Feminism*. London: Allen and Unwin.

Kaplan, Laura. 1995. *The Story of Jane*. Chicago: University of Chicago Press.

Katzenstein, Mary. 1998. *Faithful and Fearless*. Princeton, NJ: Princeton University Press.

———. 2003. "'Redividing Citizens'—Divided Feminisms: The Reconfigured U.S. State and Women's Citizenship." In *Women's Movements Facing a Reconfigured State*, edited by Lee Ann Banaszak, Karen Beckwith, and Dieter Rucht, 203–18. Cambridge: Cambridge University Press.

Katzenstein, Mary Fainsod, and Carol McClurg Mueller, eds. 1987. *The Women's Movements of the United States and Western Europe: Feminist Consciousness, Political Opportunity, and Public Policy*. Philadelphia: Temple University Press.

Kay, Diana. 1987. *Chileans in Exile: Private Struggles, Public Lives*. Houndmills, Basingstoke, Hampshire: Macmillan.

Kay, Rebecca. 2004. "Meeting the Challenge Together? Russian Grassroots Women's Organizations and the Shortcomings of Western Aid." In *Post-Soviet Women Encountering Transition: Nation-Building, Economic Survival, and Civic Activism*, edited by Kathleen Kuehnast and Carol Nechemias, 241–61. Baltimore: Woodrow Wilson Press and Johns Hopkins University Press.

Keck, Margaret E., and Kathryn Sikkink. 1998a. *Activists Beyond Borders: Advocacy Networks in International Politics*. Ithaca, NY: Cornell University Press.

———. 1998b. "Transnational Advocacy Networks in the Movement Society." In *The Social Movement Society: Contentious Politics for a New Century*, edited by David S. Meyer and Sidney Tarrow, 217–38. New York: Rowman & Littlefield.

———. 1999. "Transnational Advocacy Networks in International and Regional Politics." *International Social Science Journal* 51, no. 1: 89–101.

Kelly, James. 1994. "Seeking a Sociologically Correct Name for Abortion Opponents." In *Abortion Politics in the United States and Canada: Studies in Public Opinion*, edited by Ted Jelen and Marthe Chandler, 15–40. Westport, CT: Praeger.

Kessler-Harris, Alice. 1992. "The View from Women's Studies." *Signs: Journal of Women in Culture and Society* 17: 794–805.

Khotkina, Z. 2000. "Zhenskaia bezrabotnitsa i neformal'naia zaniatnost' v Rossii [Women's Unemployment and Informal Employment]." *Voprosy ekonomiki* 3: 85–93.

Khudiakova, Tat'iana. 1993. "Alevtina Fedulova: Nasha dvizhenie sledovalo by nazvat' 'Zhenshchiny dlia Rossii' [Alevtina Fedulova: Our Movement Should Be Called 'Women For Russia']." *Izvestiya*, December 2, 4.

Killian, Lewis M. 1964. "Social Movements." In *Handbook of Modern Sociology*, edited by R. E. L. Faris. Chicago: Rand McNally.

King, C. Wendell. 1956. *Social Movements in the United States*. New York: Random House.

King, Martin Luther, Jr. 1958. *Stride toward Freedom*. New York: Harper.

Kirkpatrick, David D. 2005. "For Democrats, Rethinking Abortion Position Meets with Mix of Reactions in Party." *New York Times,* February 16, A:18.

Kirkwood, Julieta. 1986. *Ser Política En Chile: Las Feministas Y Los Partidos*. Santiago, Chile: FLACSO.

Kissinger, C. Clark, and Bob Ross. 1968. "Starting in '60: Or From SLID to Resistance." *New Left Notes* (June 10).

Kitschelt, Herbert. 1986. "Political Opportunity Structures and Political Protest." *British Journal of Political Science* 16: 57–85.

Klandermans, Bert. 1984. "Mobilization and Participation: Social-Psychological Expansions of Resource Mobilization Theory." *American Sociological Review* 49: 583–600.

———. 1992. "The Social Construction of Protest and Multi-Organizational Fields." In *Frontiers in Social Movement Theory*, edited by A. D. Morris and C. M. Muller, 77–103. New Haven, CT: Yale University Press.

Klatch, Rebecca. 1999. *A Generation Divided*. Berkeley: University of California Press.

Klemesrud, Judy. 1985. "New Head of NOW Prefers Activism." *New York Times*, July 22.

Koopmans, Ruud. 1999. "A Comparison of Protest against the Gulf War in Germany, France, and the Netherlands." In *Social Movements in a Globalizing World*, edited by Donatella della Porta, Hanspeter Kriesi, and Dieter Rucht, 57–70. London: Macmillan.

Kornhauser, William. 1959. *The Politics of Mass Society*. Glencoe, IL: Free Press.

Kotani, Sachi. 1999. "Women's New Labor Movement: A Case Study of the Women's Union Tokyo." *Journal of Labor Sociology* 1, no.1: 3–25.

Krasner, Stephen. 1995. "Power Politics, Institutions, and Transnational Relations." In *Bringing Transnational Relations Back In: Non-state Actors, Domestic Structures, and International Institutions*, edited by Thomas Risse-Kappen, 257–79. Cambridge: Cambridge University Press.

Kriesi, Hanspeter, Ruud Koopmans, Jan Willem Duyvendak, and Marco G. Guigni. 1995. *New Social Movements in Western Europe: A Comparative Analysis*. Minneapolis: University of Minnesota Press.

Labaton, Vivien. 2000. "Looking Back, Looking Ahead." *See It? Tell It. Change It! Third Wave Foundation' Newsletter* 1 (Spring–Summer) at www.thirdwave foundation.org (accessed January 14, 2002).

Lader, Lawrence. 1973. *Abortion II: Making the Revolution*. Boston: Beacon Press.

Lahusen, Christian. 1999. "International Campaigns in Context: Collective Action between the Local and Global." In *Social Movements in a Globalizing World*, edited by Donatella della Porta, Hanspeter Kriesi, and Dieter Rucht, 189–205. London: Macmillan.

Lang, Kurt, and Gladys Engle Lang. 1961. *Collective Dynamics*. New York: Cromwell.

Langolis, Karen. 1982. "An Interview with Sonia Johnson." *Feminist Studies* 8 (Spring): 22–28.

Lapidus, Gail Warshofsky. 1978. *Women in Soviet Society: Equality, Development, and Social Change*. Berkeley: University of California Press.

Larson, Katie. 1972. "Some Organizations Formed, Changed, Dissolved." *Courier-Tribune*, December 31.

Le Blanc, Robin. 1999. *Bicycle Citizens*. Berkeley: University of California Press.

Leidner, Robin. 1991. "Stretching the Boundaries of Liberalism: Democratic Innovation in a Feminist Organization." *Signs: Journal of Women in Culture and Society* 16: 263–89.

Lemons, J. Stanley. 1973. *The Woman Citizen: Social Feminism in the 1920s*. Chicago: University of Illinois Press.

Lesbian Avengers. 2002. *Lesbian Avengers Handbook,* at www.lesbian.org/chicago-avengers/avengerhandbook.html (accessed January 20, 2002).

Liddle, Joanna, and Sachiko Nakajima. 2000. *Rising Suns, Rising Daughters*. London: Zed Books.

Ling Yuriko, and Azusa Matsuno. 1992. "Women's Struggle for Empowerment in Japan." In *Women Transforming Politics*, edited by Jill Bystydzienski, 51–66. Bloomington: Indiana University Press.

Lionberger, Herbert F. 1960. *Adoption of New Ideas and Practices*. Ames: Iowa State University Press.

Lipovskaya, Olga. 1994. "Sisters or Stepsisters: How Close Is Sisterhood?" *Women's Studies International Forum* 17, no. 2–3: 273–76.

Lipset, Seymour M. 1959. *Agrarian Socialism*. Berkeley: University of California Press.

Lovenduski, Joni. 1986a. *Women and European Politics: Contemporary Feminism and Public Policy*. Amherst: University of Massachusetts Press.

———. 1986b. "Parliament, Pressure Groups, Networks, and the Women's Movement: The Politics of Abortion Law Reform in Britain (1967–1983)." In *The New Politics of Abortion*, edited by Joni Lovenduski and Joyce Outshoorn, 49–66. London: Sage.

———. 1998. "Gender Dynamics in Congressional Elections." *Party Politics* 4: 408–10.

Lovenduski, Joni, and Joyce Outshoorn. 1986. "Introduction: The New Politics of Abortion." In *The New Politics of Abortion*, edited by Joni Lovenduski and Joyce Outshoorn, 1–4. London: Sage.

Lovenduski, Joni, and Vicky Randall. 1993. *Contemporary Feminist Politics: Women and Power in Britain*. New York: Oxford University Press.

Lowi, Theodore J. 1971. *The Politics of Disorder*. New York: Basic.

Luker, Kristin. 1984. *Abortion and the Politics of Motherhood*. Berkeley: University of California Press.

Lunardini, Christine. 1986. *From Equal Suffrage to Equal Rights: Alice Paul and the National Woman's Party, 1910–1928*. New York: New York University Press.

Lynn, Morgan. 2001. "(In)Visible Privilege: An Examination of Whiteness in Social Movement Organizations." Honors thesis, Smith College.

Mackie, Vera. 1996. "Feminist Critiques of Modern Japanese Politics." In *Mapping the Women's Movement*, edited by Monica Threlfall, 260–87. London: Verso.

Malveaux, Julianne. 1995. "A Woman's Place Is in the March: Why Should I Stand by My Man, When He's Trying to Step Over Me?" *Washington Post*, October 8, C3.

Manegold, Catherine S. 1992. "No More Nice Girls: Growing Wave of Radical Feminists Do Not Just Want to Have Fun." *New York Times*, July 12, 25, 31.

Mann, Judy. 1979. "Women Understanding Power Structure Better." *Washington Post*, May 2, C1, 2.

———. 1982. "Here to Stay." *Washington Post*, March 24, A3.

Mannheim, Karl. 1952 [1928]. "The Problem of Generations." In *Essays on the Sociology of Knowledge*, edited by P. Kecskemeti, 276–332. London: Routledge and Kegan Paul.

Mansbridge, Jane J. 1986. *Why We Lost the ERA*. Chicago: University of Chicago Press.

Marsh, Rosalind. 1996. "The Russian Women's Movement: Anastasiia Posadskaia, the Dubna Forum, and the Independent Women's Movement in Russia." In *Women in Russia and Ukraine*, edited by Rosalind Marsh, 286–97. Cambridge: Cambridge University Press.

Marshall, Susan E. 1984. "Keep Us on the Pedestal: Women Against Feminism in Twentieth-Century America." In *Women: A Feminist Perspective*, 3d ed., edited by Jo Freeman, 568–81. Palo Alto, CA: Mayfield Publishing.

———. 1990. "Equity Issues and Black-White Differences in Women's ERA Support." *Social Science Quarterly* 71: 299–314.

———. 1995. "Confrontation and Cooptation in Antifeminist Organizations." In *Feminist Organizations: Harvest of a New Women's Movement*, edited by Myra Marx Ferree and Patricia Yancey Martin, 323–35. Philadelphia: Temple University Press.

Marx, Gary, and Doug McAdam. 1996. "Social Movements and the Changing Structure of Political Opportunity in the European Union." *West European Politics* 19, no. 2: 249–78.

Matear, Ann. 1996. "Desde La Protesta a La Propuesta." *Democratization* 3: 246–63.

Mathews, G. Donald, and Jane Sherron De Hart. 1990. *Sex, Gender, and the Politics of ERA: A State and the Nation*. New York: Oxford University Press.

Mato, Daniel. 2000. "Transnational Networking and the Social Production of Representations of Identities by Indigenous Peoples' Organizations of Latin America." *International Sociology* 15, no. 2: 343–60.

Matthews, Nancy. 1995. *Confronting Rape: The Feminist Anti-Rape Movement and the State*. London: Routledge.

McAdam, Douglas. 1982. *Political Process and the Development of Black Insurgency: 1930–1970*. Chicago: University of Chicago Press.

———. 1988. *Freedom Summer*. Oxford: Oxford University Press.

———. 1996a. "Conceptual Origins, Current Problems, Future Directions." In *Comparative Perspectives on Social Movements: Political Opportunities, Mobilizing Structures, and Cultural Framings,* edited by Doug McAdam, John D. McCarthy, and Mayer N. Zald, 23–40. Cambridge: Cambridge University Press.

———. 1996b. "The Framing Function of Movement Tactics: Strategic Dramaturgy in the American Civil Rights Movement." In *Comparative Perspectives on Social*

Movements: Political Opportunities, Mobilizing Structures, and Cultural Framings, edited by Doug McAdam, John D. McCarthy, and Mayer N. Zald, 338–55. Cambridge: Cambridge University Press.

McAdam, Doug, John D. McCarthy, and Mayer N. Zald, eds. 1996. *Comparative Perspectives on Social Movements: Political Opportunities, Mobilizing Structures, and Cultural Framings*. New York: Cambridge University Press.

McAdam, Doug, Sidney Tarrow, and Charles Tilly. 1996. "To Map Contentious Politics." *Mobilization* 1: 17–34.

———. 2001. *The Dynamics of Contention*. Cambridge: Cambridge University Press, 2001.

McBride Stetson, Dorothy. 1995. "The Oldest Women's Policy Agency: The Women's Bureau in the United States." In *Comparative State Feminism*, edited by Dorothy McBride Stetson and Amy Mazur. Thousand Oaks, CA: Sage Publications.

McCammon, Holly J. 2001. "Stirring Up Suffrage Sentiment: The Formation of the State Woman Suffrage Organizations, 1866–1914." *Social Forces* 80, no.2: 449–80.

McCammon, Holly J., Karen Campbell, and Ellen Granberg. 2001. "How Movements Win: Gendered Opportunity Structures and U.S. Women's Suffrage Movements, 1866 to 1919." *American Sociological Review* 66, no. 1: 49–70.

McCarthy, John. 1997. "The Globalization of Social Movement Theory." In *Transnational Social Movements and Global Politics: Solidarity Beyond the State*, edited by Jackie Smith, Charles Chatfield, and Ron Pagnucco, 243–59. Syracuse, NY: Syracuse University Press.

McCarthy, John, and Mark Wolfson. 1996. "Resource Mobilization by Local Social Movement Organizations: Agency, Strategy, and Organization in the Movement against Drunk Driving." *American Sociological Review* 61: 1070–88.

McCarthy, John D., and Mayer N. Zald. 1973. *The Trend of Social Movements in America*. Morristown, NJ: General Learning Press.

———. 1977. "Resource Mobilization and Social Movements: A Partial Theory." *American Journal of Sociology* 82, no.6: 1212–41.

McClachlen, Patricia. 2002. *Consumer Politics in Post War Japan*. New York: Columbia University Press.

McGlen, Nancy E., and Karen O'Connor. 1988. "Toward a Theoretical Model of Counter Movements and Constitutional Change: A Case Study of the ERA." *Women & Politics* 8: 45–71.

McKay, Nellie Y. 1993. "Acknowledging Differences: Can Women Find Unity Through Diversity?" In *Theorizing Black Feminisms: The Visionary Pragmatism of Black Women*, edited by Stanlie M. James and Abena P. A. Busia, 267–82. New York: Routledge.

McNeil, Kenneth, and James D. Thompson. 1971. "The Regeneration of Social Organizations." *American Sociological Review* 36: 624–37.

Melucci, Alberto. 1985. "The Symbolic Challenge of Contemporary Movements." *Social Research* 52: 789–816.

———. 1988. "Getting Involved: Identity and Mobilization in Social Movements." In *International Social Movement Research, Vol. 1: From Structure to Action*, edited by Bert Klandermans, Hanspeter Kriesi, and Sidney Tarrow, 329–48. Greenwich, CT: JAI Press.

——. 1989. *Nomads of the Present: Social Movements and Individual Needs in Contemporary Society.* Philadelphia: Temple University Press.

Merton, Andrew. 1982. *Enemies of Choice: The Right-to-Life Movement and Its Threat to Abortion.* Boston: Beacon Press.

Meyer, David S., and Suzanne Staggenborg. 1996. "Movements, Countermovements, and the Structure of Political Opportunity." *American Journal of Sociology* 101, no. 6: 1628–60.

——. 1998. "Countermovement Dynamics in Federal Systems: A Comparison of Abortion Politics in Canada and the United States." *Research in Political Sociology* 8: 209–40.

Meyer, David S., and Sidney Tarrow. 1998a. "A Movement Society: Contentious Politics for a New Century." In *The Social Movement Society,* edited by David S. Meyer and Sidney Tarrow. Lanham, MD: Rowman & Littlefield.

——, eds. 1998b. *The Social Movement Society.* Lanham, MD: Rowman & Littlefield.

Meyer, David S., and Nancy Whittier. 1994. "Social Movement Spillover." *Social Problems* 41, no. 2: 277–98.

Meyer, David S., Nancy Whittier, and Belinda Robnett, eds. 2002. *Social Movements: Identity, Culture, and the State.* New York: Oxford University Press.

Mikhaleva, Galina. 2002. "Pochetnaia forma discriminatsii vmesto ravnopraviia [An Honorable Form of Discrimination Instead of Equal Rights]." *Nezavisimaia gazeta* (March 7): 2.

Miller, Margaret I., and Helene Linker. 1974. "Equal Rights Amendment Campaigns in California and Utah." *Sociology* 11: 40–53.

"Million Woman March—10.25.97, The," at www.mwmsisters.com/the march.html.

Million Woman March Platform Issues, at members.aol.com/lilbitz/platform.htm.

Minkoff, Debra. 1995. *Organizing for Equality.* New Jersey: Rutgers University Press.

——. 1999. "Bending with the Wind: Strategic Change and Adaptation by Women's and Racial Minority Organizations." *The American Journal of Sociology* 104, no. 6 (May): 1666–1703.

——. 2002. "Walking a Political Tightrope: Responsiveness and Internal Accountability in Social Movement Organizations." In *Exploring Organizations and Advocacy: Governance and Accountability. Nonprofit Advocacy and the Policy Process,* Issue 2, edited by Elizabeth Reid and M. Montilla, 33–48. Washington, DC: The Urban Institute.

Moghadam, Valentine M., ed. 1994. *Identity Politics and Women: Cultural Reassertions and Feminisms in International Perspective.* Boulder, CO: Westview.

——. 2000. "Transnational Feminist Networks: Collective Action in an Era of Globalization." *International Sociology* 15, no. 1: 57–85.

Moraga, Cherrie, and Gloria Anzaldua, eds. 1983. *This Bridge Called My Back: Writings by Radical Women of Color, 2nd edition.* New York: Kitchen Table, Women of Color Press.

Morgan, Robin. 1978. "Women Disrupt the Miss America Pageant." In *Going to Far,* edited by Robin Morgan. New York: Vintage.

——. 1980. "The First Feminist Exiles from the U.S.S.R." *Ms.* (November): 49–56, 80–83, 102, 107–108.

Morgan, Tracy. 2002. "From WHAM! to ACT UP." In *From ACT UP to the WTO,* edited by Benjamin Shepard and Ronald Hayduk, 141–49. New York: Verso.

Morley, Patricia. 1999. *The Mountain Is Moving: Japanese Women's Lives*. New York: New York University Press.

Morris, Aldon D. 1984. *The Origins of the Civil Rights Movement: Black Communities Organizing for Change*. New York: Free Press.

Morris, Aldon D., and Carol McClurg Mueller, eds. 1992. *Frontiers in Social Movement Theory*. New Haven, CT: Yale University Press.

Mueller, Carol McClurg, ed. 1988. *The Politics of the Gender Gap: The Social Construction of Political Influence*. Thousand Oaks, CA: Sage Publications.

Mueller, Carol, and Thomas Dimieri. 1982. "The Structure of Belief Systems Among Contending ERA Activists." *Social Forces* 60 (March): 657–75.

Murphy-Lawless, Jo. 2001. "Fertility, Bodies, and Politics: The Irish Case." On the Global Reproductive Health Forum at Harvard Library, at www.hsph.harvard.edu/Organizations/healthnet/reprorights/docs/murphy.html.

Murphy-Lawless, Jo, and James McCarthy. 1999. "Social Policy and Fertility Change in Ireland: The Push to Legislate in Favour of Women's Agency." *The European Journal of Women's Studies* 6: 69–96.

Myron, Nancy, and Charlotte Bunch, eds. 1975. *Lesbianism and the Women's Movement*. Baltimore: Diana Press.

Naples, Nancy. 1998. *Grassroots Warriors: Activist Mothering, Community Work and the War on Poverty*. New York: Routledge.

Narayan, Uma. 2005. "Colonialism, Capitalism, Gender and Informal Sector Work." Paper presented at the Feminist Scholars Lecture Series, Women's Studies Program, The Pennsylvania State University, University Park, PA, February 25.

National NOW Times. 1980–1981. "Women Vote Differently than Men: Feminist Bloc Emerges in 1980 Elections." (December/January).

———. 1982. "ERA Countdown Ends: Spurs Renewed Fight for Equality." (August).

National Organization for Women. 1977. National Board Meeting Minutes, July 30–31.

———. 1982. "A Salute to NOW President Ellie Smeal, 1977–1982." *National NOW Times* 9, no. 8: 3.

———. 2001. "NOW Bylaws," at www.now.org/organiza/bylaws.html.

National Right to Life Committee, at www.nrlc.org.

Nechemias, Carol. 1991. "The Prospects for a Soviet Women's Movement: Opportunities and Obstacles." In *Perestroika From Below: Social Movements in the Soviet Union*, edited by Judith B. Sedaitis and Jim Butterfield, 73–96. Boulder, CO: Westview.

———. 2000. "Politics in Post-Soviet Russia: Where Are the Women?" *Demokratizatsiya* 8, no. 2: 199–218.

———. 2001. "Moscow Center for Gender Studies (MCGS) [Moskovskii Tsentr gendernykh Issledovanii] (1990–)." In *Encyclopedia of Russian Women's Movements*, edited by Norma Corigliano Noonan and Carol Nechemias, 294–97. Westport, CT: Greenwood Press.

———. 2003. "Russia." In *The Greenwood Encyclopedia of Women's Issues Worldwide: Europe*, edited by Lynn Walter, 545–75. Westport, CT: Greenwood Press.

Nelson, Barbara, and Katherine Carver. 1994. "Many Voices but Few Vehicles." In *Women and Politics Worldwide*, edited by Barbara Nelson and Nazma Chowdbury, 738–57. New Haven, CT: Yale University Press.

Nelson, Barbara, and Najma Chowdhury, eds. 1994. *Women and Politics Worldwide*. New Haven, CT: Yale University Press.

Nelson, Barbara J., and Nancy J. Johnson. 1991. "Political Structures and Social Movement Tactics: Feminist Policy Agendas in the United States in the 1990s." *NWSA Journal* 3 (March): 199–212.

New York City NOW Document. 1986. Correspondence between State President and Bronx NOW President, National Organization for Women—New York State Records 1966–88, Series 2, Box 7, President's Subject Files, May 10. From the Eugene P. Link Papers, Archives of Public Affairs and Policy, University of Albany, State University of New York.

New York Times. 1991. "NOW Urges a New Party." September 16:B10.

Norgren, Tiana. 2001. *Abortion Before Birth Control.* Princeton, NJ: Princeton University Press.

NOW Foundation. 2002. "*Young Feminist Summit Information,*" at www.now foundation.org/yfsummit97/ (accessed January 14, 2002).

NOW NYC News. 1987. "State President Connell to Challenge Smeal." Files of the New York City NOW chapter, May/June.

———. 1989. "Hundreds of Thousands March on Washington for Pro-Choice." Files of the New York City NOW chapter, May/June.

———. 1992. "NOW-NYC Donor Campaign." Files of the New York City NOW chapter, September/October.

———. 1993. "The Move." Files of the New York City NOW chapter, May/June.

NOW York Woman. 1977. "Banquet to End all Banquets: A Report." National Organization for Women–New York State Records 1966–1988, Series 6, Box 1, New York City newsletters 1975–1986, May. From the Eugene P. Link Papers, Archives of Public Affairs and Policy, University of Albany, State University of New York.

———. 1987. "Eat, Drink and Be Generous." Files of the New York City NOW chapter, February/March.

Oberschall, Anthony. 1973. *Social Conflict and Social Movements.* Englewood Cliffs, NJ: Prentice Hall.

———. 1996. "Opportunities and Framing in the Eastern European Revolts of 1989." In *Comparative Perspectives on Social Movements,* edited by Douglas McAdam, John McCarthy, and Mayer Zald, 93–121. Cambridge: Cambridge University Press.

Oberschall, Anthony, and Hyojoung Kim. 1996. "Identity and Action." *Mobilization* 1: 63–65.

O'Brien, Tony. 1998. "Abortion Law in the Republic of Ireland." In *Abortion Law and Politics Today,* edited by Ellie Lee, 110–15. London: Macmillan.

O'Connor, Karen. 1996. *No Neutral Group? Abortion Politics in an Age of Absolutes.* Boulder, CO: Westview.

off our backs. 1988. "Letter to the editor on Utopia." *off our backs* 18, no. 2: 25.

Offaly for Life, at homepage.eircom.net/~offalyprolife/.

Offe, Claus. 1985. "New Social Movements: Challenging the Boundaries of Institutional Politics." *Social Research* 52: 817–68.

OFRA Basel, ed. 1997. *Frauen Machen Geschichte: 20 Jahre OFRA Basel—Ein Rückblick in die Zukunft.* Bern: eFeF-Verlag.

Oliver, Pamela, and Mark Furman. 1989. "Contradictions between National and Local Organizational Strength: The Case of the John Birch Society." In *International Social Movement Research, Organizing for Change: Social Movement Organizations in Europe and the United States,* vol. 2, edited by B. Klandermans, 155–77. Green-wich, CT: JAI Press.

Olson, Mancur. 1965. *The Logic of Collective Action.* Cambridge, MA: Harvard University Press.

Osawa, Mari. 2000. "Government Approaches to Gender Equality in the Mid 1990's." *Social Science Japan Journal* 3, no. 1: 3–19.

"Our Daily Bread." 2001. From WPS Monitoring Agency. *Johnson's Russia List* 5513, October 29, at www.cdi.org/johnson/5513-1.cfm (accessed May 6, 2005).

Oxhorn, Philip. 1995. *Organizing Civil Society: The Popular Sectors and the Struggle for Democracy in Chile.* University Park: Pennsylvania State University Press.

Paintin, David. 1998. "A Medical View of Abortion in the 1960s." In *Abortion Law and Politics Today,* edited by Ellie Lee, 12–19. London: Macmillan.

Papachristou, Judith. 1976. *Women Together.* New York: Alfred A. Knopf.

Papkova, Olga. 2000. "V Rossii Slovo 'Vlast' - Muzhskovo Roda [In Russia the Word for Power Is Masculine]." *Zhenshchina Plius* 4, at www.owl.ru.win/womplus/2000/femina.htm (accessed May 6, 2005).

Pardo, Mary S. 1998. *Mexican American Women Activists: Identity and Resistance in Two Los Angeles Communities.* Philadelphia: Temple University Press.

Park, Maud Wood. 1960. *Front Door Lobby: A Vivid Account of How the 19th Amendment (Woman Suffrage) Became a Reality,* edited by Edna Lamprey Stantial. Boston: Beacon Press.

Patterson, Dennis, and Misa Nishikawa. 2002. "Political Interest or Interest in Politics? Gender and Party Support in Postwar Japan." *Women and Politics* 24, no.2: 1–33.

Patton, Gwen. 1970. "Black People and the Victorian Ethos." In *The Black Woman: An Anthology,* edited by Toni Cade, 143–48. New York: New American Library.

Peers, Jo. 1985. "Workers by Hand and Womb: Soviet Women and the Demographic Crisis." In *Soviet Sisterhood,* edited by Barbara Holland, 116–44. Bloomington: Indiana University Press.

Perlez, Jane. 1984. "Women, Power and Politics." *New York Times,* June 24.

Pharr, Susan. 1981. *Political Women in Japan.* Berkeley: University of California Press.

Pinard, Maurice. 1968. "Mass Society and Political Movements: A New Formulation." *American Journal of Sociology* 73, no. 6 (May): 682–90.

———. 1971. *The Rise of a Third Party: A Study in Crisis Politics.* Englewood Cliffs, NJ: Prentice-Hall.

Pine, Rachael, and Lori Fischler. 1995. "The United States." In *The Right to Know: Human Rights and Access to Reproductive Health Information,* edited by Sandra Coliver, 289–326. London: Article 19, and Philadelphia: The University of Pennsylvania Press.

Piven, Frances Fox, and Richard A. Cloward. 1977. *Poor People's Movements: Why They Success, How They Fail.* New York: Vintage Books.

Polletta, Francesca. 2002. *Freedom Is an Endless Meeting: Democracy in American Social Movements.* Chicago: University of Chicago Press.

Posadskaya, Anastasia, ed. 1994. *Women in Russia.* London: Verso.

Pro-Life Campaign, at www.prolifecampaign.ie.htm.

"Public Opinion Foundation Presents Results of Polls Concerning Women." 2001. Interfax. *Johnson's Russia List* 5141 (March 9), at www.cdi.org/russia/johnson/5141 .html##12 (accessed May 6, 2005).

Radicalesbians. 1987. "The Woman-Identified Woman." In *Radical Feminism*, edited by Anne Koedt. New York: St. Martin's Press.

Randall, Vicky. 1986. "The Politics of Abortion in Ireland." In *The New Politics of Abortion*, edited by Joni Lovenduski and Joyce Outshoorn, 67–85. London: Sage.

Ray, Raka. 1999. *Fields of Protest: Women's Movements in India*. Minneapolis: University of Minnesota Press.

Raymond, Katherine. 1997. "Confessions of a Second Generation . . . Dyke?" In *Pomosexuals*, edited by Carol Queen and Lawrence Schimel, 53–61. San Francisco: Cleis Press.

Read, Melvyn. 1998. "The Pro-Life Movement." *Parliamentary Affairs* 51, no. 3: 445–57.

Redstockings of the Women's Liberation Movement. 1978. *Feminist Revolution: An Abridged Edition with Additional Writings*. New York: Random House.

Reger, Jo. 2001. "Motherhood and the Construction of Feminist Identities: Variations in a Women's Movement Organization." *Sociological Inquiry* 71: 85–110.

———. 2002a. "More than One Feminism: Organizational Structure, Ideology and the Construction of Collective Identity." In *Social Movements: Identity, Culture and the State*, edited by David. S. Meyer, Nancy Whittier, and Belinda Robnett, 171–84. New York: Oxford University Press.

———. 2002b. "Organizational Dynamics and the Construction of Multiple Feminist Identities in the National Organization for Women." *Gender & Society* 16, no.5: 710–27.

———. 2002c. "A Case Study of a Third Wave Organization." Paper presented at Women's Studies Symposium on Third Wave Feminism, Purdue University, April 5–6.

Reid, Madeleine. 1992. "Abortion Law in Ireland after the Maastricht Referendum." In *The Abortion Papers: Ireland*, edited by Ailbhe Smyth, 25–39. Dublin: Attic Press.

Reinelt, Claire. 1995. "Moving onto the Terrain of the State: The Battered Women's Movement and the Politics of Engagement." In *Feminist Organizations: Harvest of the New Women's Movement*, edited by Myra Marx Ferree and Patricia Yancey Martin, 84–104. Philadelphia: Temple University Press.

Remington, Thomas F. 2002. *Politics in Russia*. 2d ed. New York: Longman.

República de Chile. 1991. *Informe Rettig*. Santiago: Comisión Nacional de Verdad y Reconciliación.

"Revolution: Tomorrow Is NOW" 1972–1973[?]. Unpublished manuscript. National Organization for Women Collection. Schlesinger Library, Radcliffe University.

Richter, James. 2001. "All-Russian Sociopolitical Movement of Women of Russia (Obshcherossiiskoe obshestvenno-politicheskoe dvizehnie zhenshchin Rossii, or MWR) (1996–)." In *Encyclopedia of Russian Women's Movements*, edited by Norma Corigliano Noonan and Carol Nechemias, 199–201. Westport, CT: Greenwood Press.

———. 2002. "Promoting Civil Society? Democracy Assistance and Russian Women's Organizations." *Problems of Post-Communism* 49, no. 1: 30–41.

Ries, Paula, and Anne J. Stone, eds. 1992. *The American Woman 1992–93: A Status Report*. New York: W. W. Norton.

Riger, Stephanie. 1984. "Vehicles for Empowerment: The Case of Feminist Movement Organizations." In *Studies in Empowerment: Steps Toward Understanding and Action*, edited by J. Rappaport, C. Smith, and R. Hess. New York: Haworth Press.

248 *References*

Ríos Tobar, Marcela. 2003. "Chilean Feminisms in the 1990s: Paradoxes of an Unfinished Transition." *International Feminist Journal of Politics* 5, no. 2: 256–80.

Risse-Kappen, Thomas. 1995. "Bringing Transnational Relations Back In: Introduction." In *Bringing Transnational Relations Back In: Non-State Actors, Domestic Structures, and International Institutions*, edited by Thomas Risse-Kappen, 3–33. Cambridge: Cambridge University Press.

ROAMS Newsletter, 2000, at www.thirdwavefoundation.org (accessed January 14, 2002).

Robnett, Belinda. 1996. "African American Women in the Civil Rights Movement, 1954–1965: Gender, Leadership, and Micromobilization." *American Journal of Sociology* 101: 1661–93.

———. 1997. *How Long? How Long? African-American Women in the Struggle for Civil Rights*. New York: Oxford University Press.

Rochon, Thomas R. 1998. *Culture Moves: Ideas, Activism, and Changing Values*. Princeton, NJ: Princeton University Press.

Rogers, Everett M. 1962. *Diffusion of Innovations*. New York: Free Press.

Rohlinger, Deana. 2002. "Framing the Abortion Debate: Organizational Resources, Media Strategies, and Movement-Countermovement Dynamics." *The Sociological Quarterly* 43, no. 4: 479–507.

Rosen, Ruth. 2000. *The World Split Open: How the Modern Women's Movement Changed America*. New York: Viking.

Ross, Lorretta J. 1993. "African-American Women and Abortion: 1800–1970." In *Theorizing Black Feminisms: The Visionary Pragmatism of Black Women*, edited by Stanlie M. James and Abena P.A. Busia, 141–59. New York: Routledge.

Rossiter, Ann. 1993. "Bringing the Margins Into the Centre: A Review of Aspects of Irish Women's Emigration." In *Irish Women's Studies Reader*, edited by Ailbhe Smyth, 177–202. Dublin: Attic Press.

Roth, Benita. 2003. *Separate Roads to Feminism*. New York: Cambridge University Press.

Rumph, Suzanne. 2000. "Black and White NOW Members Talk About the Racial Diversification of the National Organization for Women." MA thesis, Department of Sociology, Wayne State University.

Rupp, Leila. 1997. *Worlds of Women: The Making of an International Women's Movement*. Princeton, NJ: Princeton University Press.

Rupp, Leila, and Verta Taylor. 1987. *Survival in the Doldrums: The American Women's Rights Movement, 1945 to the 1960s*. New York: Oxford University Press.

"Russians Not Interested in Political Activity." 2001. Interfax. *Johnson's Russia List* 5332–5333 (July 3), at www.cdi.org/russia/johnson/5332.html##2 (accessed May 13, 2005).

Ruthchild, Rochelle. 1983. "Sisterhood and Socialism: The Soviet Feminist Movement." *Frontiers* 7, no. 2: 4–12.

Ryan, Barbara. 1989. "Ideological Purity and Feminism: The U.S. Women's Movement from 1966 to 1975." *Gender & Society* 3, no. 2: 239–57.

———. 1992. *Feminism and the Women's Movement: Dynamics of Change in Social Movement Ideology and Activism*. New York: Routledge.

———. 1996. *The Women's Movement: References and Resources*. New York: G. K. Hall.

———. 1997. "How Much Can I Divide Thee, Let Me Count the Ways: Identity Politics in the Women's Movement." *Humanity & Society* 21, no. 1: 67–83.

———, ed. 2001a. *Identity Politics in the Women's Movement.* New York: New York University Press.

———. 2001b. "Introduction to Identity Politics: The Past, the Present, and the Future." In *Identity Politics in the Women's Movement,* edited by Barbara Ryan, 1–16. New York: New York University Press.

Ryan, Charlotte. 1991. *Prime Time Activism: Media Strategies for Grassroots Organizing.* Boston: South End Press.

Salisbury, Robert H. 1969. "An Exchange Theory of Interest Groups." *Midwest Journal of Political Science* 13, no. 1 (February): 1–32.

Sapiro, Virginia. 1989. "The Women's Movement and the Creation of Gender Consciousness: Social Movements as Socialization Agents." In *Political Socialization for Democracy,* edited by O. Ichilov. New York: Teacher's College Press.

Sasakura Naoko. 1995. "Aokage Takako: Housewife Turned Political Representative from Seikatsu Club Seikyo." In *Japanese Women,* edited by Kumiko Fujimura Fanselow and Atsuko Kameda, 374–83. New York: Feminist Press.

Sato, Yoko. 1995. "From Home to the Political Arena." In *Japanese Women,* edited by Kumiko Fujimura Fanselow and Atsuko Kameda, 365–72. New York: Feminist Press.

Sawyers, Traci M., and David S. Meyer. 1999. "Missed Opportunities: Social Movement Abeyance and Public Policy." *Social Problems* 46, no. 2: 187–206.

Scanlan, Christopher. 1989. "Buoyed Abortion-Rights Groups Discover New Political Clout." *Philadelphia Inquirer,* October 13, A1.

Scheppele, Kim Lane. 1996. "Constitutionalizing Abortion." In *Abortion Politics: Public Policy in Cross-Cultural Perspective,* edited by Marianne Githens and Dorothy McBride Stetson, 29–54. New York: Routledge.

Schmich, Mary T. 1989. "Women Talk of Past But Look to Future: ERA on Back Burner But Still Warm." *Chicago Tribune,* February 14, A3.

Schneider, Elizabeth. 2000. *Battered Women and Feminist Lawmaking.* New Haven, CT: Yale University Press.

Schulman, Sarah. 1994. *My American Life.* New York: Routledge.

Scott, Anne Firor. 1991. *Natural Allies: Women's Associations in American History.* Urbana and Chicago: University of Illinois.

Sealander, Judith, and Dorothy Smith. 1986. "The Rise and Fall of Feminist Organizations in the 1970s: Dayton as a Case Study." *Feminist Studies* 12, no. 2: 221–39.

Segers, Mary, and Timothy Byrnes. 1995. "Introduction: Abortion Politics in American States." In *Abortion Politics in American States,* edited by Mary Segers and Timothy Byrnes, 1–15. New York: M. E. Sharpe.

Selznick, Philip. 1992. *The Moral Commonwealth: Social Theory and the Promise of Community.* Berkeley: University of California Press.

Shakur, Assata. 1987. *Assata.* Westport, CT: L. Hill.

Sheldon, Sally. 1998. "The Abortion Act 1967: A Critical Perspective." In *Abortion Law and Politics Today,* edited by Ellie Lee, 43–58. London: Macmillan.

Shepard, Benjamin. 2002. "Introductory notes on the Trail from ACT UP to the WTO." In *From ACT UP to the WTO,* edited by Benjamin Shepard and Ronald Hayduk, 11–16. New York: Verso.

Shils, Edward. 1970. "Center and Periphery." In *Selected Essays*. Chicago: Center for Social Organization Studies, Department of Sociology, University of Chicago.

Shukla, Sandyha. 1997. "Feminisms of the Diaspora Both Local and Global: The Politics of South Asian Women against Domestic Violence." In *Women Transforming Politics: An Alternative Reader*, edited by Cathy Cohen, Kathleen B. Jones, and Joan Tronto, 269–83. New York: New York University Press.

Silva, Eduardo. 1996. *The State and Capital in Chile: Business Elites, Technocrats, and Market Economics*. Boulder, CO: Westview, 1996.

Skocpol, Theda. 1992. *Protecting Soldiers and Mothers: The Political Origins of Social Policy in the United States*. Cambridge: Belknap Press of Harvard University Press.

———. 1999. "How Americans Became Civic." In *Civic Engagement in American Democracy*, edited by Theda Skocpol and Morris P. Fiorina. Washington, DC, and New York: Brookings Institution Press and the Russell Sage Foundation.

———. 2003. *Diminished Democracy: From Membership to Management in American Civic Life*. Norman: University of Oklahoma Press.

Slater, Wendy. 1995. " 'Women of Russia' and Women's Representation in Russian Politics." In *Russia in Transition*, edited by David Lane, 76–90. New York: Longman.

Slavin, Sarah. 1982. "The Equal Rights Amendment: The Politics and Process of Ratification of the Twenty-Seventh Amendment to the U.S. Constitution." *Women & Politics* 2, no. 1–2 (Spring/Summer): 66–85.

Smeal, Ellie. 1987. "The ERA: Should We Eat Our Words?" *Ms.* 16, no. 1–2: 170, 218.

Smelser, Neil J. 1963. *Theory of Collective Behavior*. Glencoe, IL: Free Press.

Smith, Barbara. 1982. "Review of *Ain't I a Woman*: Black Women and Feminism by bell hooks." *The New Women's Times Feminist Review* 9: 24.

———. 1998. *The Truth that Never Hurts: Writings on Race, Gender, and Freedom*. New Brunswick, NJ: Rutgers University Press.

Smith, Jackie. 1998. "Global Civil Society? Transnational Social Movement Organizations and Social Capital." *American Behavioral Scientist* 42, no. 1: 93–107.

———. 1999. "Global Politics and Transnational Social Movements Strategies: The Transnational Campaign against International Trade in Toxic Waste." In *Social Movements in a Globalizing World*, edited by Donatella della Porta, Hanspeter Kriesi, and Dieter Rucht, 170–88. London: Macmillan.

Smith, Jackie, Charles Chatfield, and Ron Pagnucco. 1997. *Transnational Social Movements and Global Politics: Solidarity Beyond the State*. Syracuse, NY: Syracuse University Press.

Smith, Jackie, Ron Pagnucco, and Charles Chatfield. 1997. "Social Movements and World Politics: A Theoretical Framework." In *Transnational Social Movements and Global Politics: Solidarity Beyond the State*, edited by Jackie Smith, Charles Chatfield, and Ron Pagnucco, 59–77. Syracuse, NY: Syracuse University Press.

Smith, Jackie, Ron Pagnucco, and George Lopez. 1998. "Globalizing Human Rights: The Work of Transnational Human Rights NGOs in the 1990s." *Human Rights Quarterly* 20, no. 2: 379–412.

Smith, Sharon. 1995. "On the Road Again." *Socialist Review* 191, at pubs.socialistreviewindex.org.uk/sr/sr191/smith.htm.

Smyth, Ailbhe. 1993. "The Women's Movement in the Republic of Ireland 1970–1990." In *Irish Women's Studies Reader*, edited by Ailbhe Smyth, 245–69. Dublin: Attic Press.

Snitow, Ann, Christine Stansell, and Sharon Thompson, eds. 1983. *Powers of Desire*. New York: Monthly Review Press.

Snow, David E. 1992. "Master Frames and Cycles of Protest." In *Frontiers in Social Movement Theory*, edited by Aldon D. Morris and Carol McClurg Mueller, 133–55. New Haven, CT: Yale University Press.

Snow, David, and Robert Benford. 1988. "Ideology, Frame Resonance, and Participant Mobilization." In *International Social Movement Research: A Research Annual Volume I*, edited by Bert Klandermans, Hanspeter Kriesi, and Sidney Tarrow, 197–217. Greenwich, CT: JAI Press.

———. 1992. "Master Frames and Cycles of Protest." In *Frontiers in Social Movement Theory*, edited by Aldon D. Morris and Carol McClurg Mueller, 133–55. New Haven, CT: Yale University Press.

Snow, David, Burke Rochford Jr., Steve Worden, and Robert Benford. 1986. "Frame Alignment Processes, Micromobilization, and Movement Participation." *American Sociological Review* 51: 464–81.

Snow, David, Louis Zurcher, and Sheldon Ekland-Olson. 1980. "Social Networks and Social Movements: A Microstructural Approach to Differential Recruitment." *American Sociological Review* 45: 787–801.

Society for the Protection of Unborn Children, at www.spuc.org.uk.

Spelman, Elizabeth. 1988. *Inessential Woman: Problems of Exclusion in Feminist Thought*. Boston: Beacon Press.

Sperling, Valerie. 1999. *Organizing Women in Contemporary Russia: Engendering Traditions*. Cambridge: Cambridge University Press.

———. 2001. "Consortium of Women's Nongovernmental Associations [Konsortsium zhenskikh nepravitel'stvennykh ob'edinenii] (formerly US-NIS Women's Consortium, 1993–1996) (1993–)." In *Encyclopedia of Russian Women's Movements*, edited by Norma Corigliano Noonan and Carol Nechemias, 221–24. Westport, CT: Greenwood Press.

Sperling, Valerie, Myra Marx Ferree, and Barbara Risman. 2001. "Constructing Global Feminism: Transnational Advocacy Networks and Russian Women's Activism." *Signs: Journal of Women in Culture and Society* 26, no. 4: 1155–86.

Squier, John. 2003. "Henderson on Civil Society." *Johnson's Russia List* 7053 (February 8), at www.cdi.org/russia/johnson/7053.cfm. (accessed May 6, 2005).

Staggenborg, Suzanne. 1989. "Stability and Innovation in the Women's Movement: A Comparison of Two Movement Organizations." *Social Problems* 36: 75–92.

———. 1991. *The Pro-Choice Movement: Organization and Activism in the Abortion Conflict*. New York: Oxford University Press.

———. 1998. "Social Movement Communities and Cycles of Protest: The Emergence and Maintenance of a Local Women's Movement Organization." *Social Problems* 45, no. 2: 180–204.

Steinem, Gloria. 1995. "Foreword." In *To Be Real: Telling the Truth and Changing the Face of Feminism*, edited by Rebecca Edby Walker, xiii–xxviii. New York: Anchor Books.

Sternbach, Nancy Saporta, Marysa Navarro-Aranguren, Patricia Chuchryk, and Sonia E. Alvarez. 1992. "Feminisms in Latin America: From Bogota to Taxco." *Signs* 17, no. 2: 393–434.

Stienstra, Deborah. 1994. *Women's Movements and International Organizations*. London: St. Martin's Press.

Stinchcombe, Arthur L. 1965. "Social Structure and Organizations." In *Handbook of Organizations*, edited by James G. March, 142–93. Chicago: Rand McNally.

Stites, Richard. 1978. *The Women's Liberation Movement in Russia: Feminism, Nihilism, and Bolshevism, 1860–1930*. Princeton, NJ: Princeton University Press.

Strobel, Margaret. 1995. "Consciousness and Action: Historical Agency in the Chicago Women's Liberation Union." In *Provoking Agents*, edited by Judith Kegan Gardiner, 52–68. Urbana: University of Illinois Press.

"Summary of Questionnaire for NOW" 1974[?]. Unpublished manuscript. National Organization for Women Collection, Schlesinger Library, Radcliffe University.

Suneson, Charlene. 1973. Memo to Board of Directors, National Organization for Women, October 12.

Suitters, Beryl. 1973. *Be Brave and Angry: Chronicles of the International Planned Parenthood Federation*. London: International Planned Parenthood Federation.

Swers, Michele L. 2002. *The Difference Women Make: The Policy Impact of Women in Congress*. Chicago: University of Chicago Press.

Swidler, Ann. 1986. "Culture in Action: Symbols and Strategies." *American Sociological Review* 51: 273–86.

Tanaka, Kazuko. 1995. "Work Education and the Family." In *Japanese Women*, edited by Kumiko Fujimura Fanselow and Atsuko Kameda, 295–308. New York: Feminist Press.

Tarrow, Sidney. 1983. "Struggling to Reform: Social Movements and Policy Change During Cycles of Protest." Occasional Paper 15, Center for International Studies. Ithaca, NY: Cornell University Press.

———. 1994. *Power in Movement: Collective Action, Social Movements and Politics*. Cambridge: Cambridge University Press.

———. 1996. "States and Opportunities: The Political Structuring of Social Movements." In *Comparative Perspectives on Social Movements: Political Opportunities, Mobilizing Structures, and Cultural Framings*, edited by Doug McAdam, John D. McCarthy, and Mayer N. Zald, 41–61. Cambridge: Cambridge University Press.

———. 1998. *Power in Movement: Social Movements and Contentious Politics*. 2d ed. Cambridge: Cambridge University Press.

———. 2001. "Transnational Politics: Contention and Institutions in International Politics." *Annual Review of Political Science* 4: 1–20.

Taylor, Verta. 1989a. "Sources of Continuity in Social Movements: The Women's Movement in Abeyance." *American Sociological Review* 54: 761–75.

———. 1989b. "The Future of Feminism in the 1980s: A Social Movement Analysis." In *Feminist Frontiers: Rethinking Sex, Gender, and Society*, edited by Lauren Richardson and Verta Taylor, 434–51. Reading, MA: Addison-Wesley.

———. 1996. *Rock-a-by Baby: Feminism, Self-Help, and Postpartum Depression*. New York: Routledge.

Taylor, Verta, and Leila Rupp. 1993. "Women's Culture and Lesbian Feminist Activism." *Signs* 19: 32–61.

Taylor, Verta, and Nancy Whittier. 1992. "Collective Identity and Lesbian Feminist Mobilization." In *Frontiers of Social Movement Theory*, edited by Aldon Morris and Carol Mueller, 104–29. New Haven, CT: Yale University Press.

———. 1993. "The New Feminist Movement." In *Feminist Frontiers III*, edited by Laurel Richardson and Verta Taylor, 533–48. New York: McGraw-Hill.

Taylor, Verta, Nancy Whittier, and Cynthia Pelak. 2001. "The Women's Movement: Persistence through Transformation." In *Feminist Frontiers*, 5th ed., edited by Laurel Richardson, Verta Taylor, and Nancy Whittier, 559–74. New York: McGraw-Hill.

Third Wave Foundation. 2002a. *"History,"* at www.thirdwavefoundation.org (accessed January 20, 2002).

———. 2002b. *"Grants,"* at www.thirdwavefoundation.org (accessed January 20, 2002).

———. 2002c. *"Board of Directors,"* at www.thirdwavefoundation.org (accessed January 20, 2002).

Threlfall, Monica, ed. 1996. *Mapping the Women's Movement: Feminist Politics and Social Transformation in the North.* London and New York: Verso.

Tilly, Charles. 1978. *From Mobilization to Revolution.* Reading, MA: Addison-Wesley.

Toch, Hans. 1965. *The Social Psychology of Social Movements.* Indianapolis: Bobbs Merrill.

Toner, Robin. 1986. "NOW Marks 20th Year Amid a Strategy Debate." *New York Times*, June 13.

Tornquist Cynthia. 1997. *"Women Gather for Show of Unity."* (October 24), at www.cnn.com/US/9710/24/million.woman.march/index.html.

———. 1997. *"Million Woman March Seen as Step Toward Unity."* (October 25), at www.cnn.com/US/9710/25/million.woman.march/index.html.

Touraine, Alain. 1981. *The Voice and the Eye: An Analysis of Social Movements.* Cambridge: Cambridge University Press.

———. 1988. *Return of the Actor: Social Theory in Postindustrial Society.* Minneapolis: University of Minnesota Press.

Turner, Ralph H. 1964. "Collective Behavior and Conflict: New Theoretical Frameworks." *Sociological Quarterly* 5 (Spring): 122–32.

Turner, Ralph H., and Lewis M. Killian. 1957. *Collective Behavior.* Englewood Cliffs, NJ: Prentice-Hall.

UK Family Planning Association, at www.fpa.org.uk.

UNICEF. 1999. "Women in Transition." Regional Monitoring Reports, No. 6. Florence: UNICEF International Child Development Centre.

United Nations Development Fund for Women (UNIFEM). 2000. *Progress of the World's Women 2000: A Biennial Report.* New York: UNIFEM.

Ustav Programma. 1996. Moscow: Obshcherossiiskoe Obshchestvenno-politicheskoe dvizhenie zhenshchin Rossii.

Valenzuela, María Elena. 1995. "The Evolving Roles of Women under Military Rule." In *The Struggle for Democracy in Chile*, edited by Paul W. Drake and Ivan Jaksic, 161–87. Lincoln: University of Nebraska Press.

———. 1998. "Women and the Democratization Process in Chile." In *Women and Democracy*, edited by Jane S. Jaquette and Sharon L. Wolchik. Baltimore: The Johns Hopkins University Press.

Valiente, Celia. 2003. "The Feminist Movement and the Reconfigured State in Spain (1970s–2000)." In *Women's Movements Facing a Reconfigured State*, edited by Lee Ann Banaszak, Karen Beckwith, and Dieter Rucht, 30–47. Cambridge: Cambridge University Press.

Vance, Carol, ed. 1984. *Pleasure and Danger.* New York: Routledge.

Voss, Kim. 1996. "The Collapse of a Social Movement: The Interplay of Mobilizing Structures, Framing and Political Opportunities in the Knights of Labor." In

Comparative Perspectives on Social Movements: Political Opportunities, Mobilizing Structures, and Cultural Framings, edited by Doug McAdam, John McCarthy, and Mayer Zald, 227–58. New York: Cambridge University Press.

Voss, Kim, and Rachel Sherman. 2000. "Breaking the Iron Law of Oligarchy: Union Revitalization in the American Labor Movement." *American Journal of Sociology* 106, no.2: 303–49.

Walker, Rebecca, ed. 1995a. *To Be Real.* New York: Anchor Books.

———. 1995b. "Being Real: An Introduction." In *To Be Real*, edited by Rebecca Walker, xxix–xl. New York: Anchor Books.

Walters, Suzanna Danuta. 1996. "From Here to Queer." *Signs* 21, no. 4: 830–69.

Wandersee, Winifred D. 1988. *On the Move: American Women in the 1970s.* Old Tappan, NJ: Twayne.

Washington Post, The. 2004. "March One of Largest Mall Events." April 26, Final Edition. Section A: A11.

Washington Representatives. 1997. Washington, DC: Columbia Books.

Weigand, Kate. 2001. *Red Feminism.* Baltimore, MD: The Johns Hopkins University Press.

West, Cornell. 1994. *Race Matters.* New York: Vintage Books.

Westberg, Emily A. 2001. "Madison Members' Meetings." *See It? Tell It. Change It! Third Wave Foundation Newsletter* (Summer): 4.

Whelan, Christopher. 1994. "Values and Psychological Well-Being." In *Values and Social Change in Ireland*, edited by Christopher Whelan, 187–211. Dublin: Gill & Macmillan.

Whisman, Vera. 1993. "Identity Crises: Who Is a Lesbian, Anyway?" In *Sisters, Sexperts, Queers: Beyond the Lesbian Nation*, edited by Arlene Stein, 47–60. New York: Penguin Books.

White, Kendall O. 1985. "A Feminist Challenge: Mormons for ERA as an Internal Social Movement." *Journal of Ethnic Studies* 13 (March): 29–50.

Whittier, Nancy. 1995. *Feminist Generations: The Persistence of the Radical Women's Movement.* Philadelphia: Temple University Press.

———. 1997. "Political Generations, Micro-Cohorts, and the Transformation of Social Movements." *American Sociological Review* 62 (October): 760–78.

———. 2000. "Changing Culture and Policy: Child Sexual Abuse, Collective Identity, and Discourse." Paper presented at the Annual Meetings of the American Sociological Association, Washington, D.C.

———. 2001. "Emotional Strategies." In *Passionate Politics*, edited by Francesca Polletta, Jeff Goodwin, and James Jasper, 233–50. Chicago: University of Chicago.

———. 2002. "Meaning and Structure in Social Movements." In *Social Movements: Identity, Culture, and the State*, edited by David S. Meyer, Nancy Whittier, and Belinda Robnett, 289–307. New York: Oxford University Press.

Wilchins, Riki Anne. 1997. *Read My Lips: Sexual Subversion and the End of Gender.* Ithaca, NY: Firebrand Books.

Wilson, Graham. 1993. "Changing Networks: The Bureaucratic Setting for Government Action." In *The Developing British Political System: The 1990's*, 3d ed., edited by Ian Budge and David McKay, 30–51. London: Longman Group UK Limited.

Wilson, William J. 1978. *The Declining Significance of Race.* Chicago: University of Chicago Press.

———. 1996. *When Work Disappears: The World of the New Urban Poor.* New York: Alfred A. Knopf.

Wolbrecht, Christina. 2000. *The Politics of Women's Rights.* Princeton, NJ: Princeton University Press.

Wolf, Naomi. 1991. *The Beauty Myth.* New York: William Morrow.

Wolfe, Leslie, and Jennifer Tucker. 1995. "Feminism Lives: Building a Mulitcultural Movement in the United States." In *The Challenge of Local Feminisms*, edited by Amrita Basu and C. Elizabeth McCrory, 435–64. Boulder, CO: Westview.

Woliver, Laura. 1998a. "Abortion Interests: From the Usual Suspects to Expanded Coalitions." In *Interest Group Politics*, 2d ed., edited by Allan Cigler and Burdett Loomis, 327–42. Washington, DC: Congressional Quarterly Inc.

———. 1998b. "Social Movements and Abortion Law." In *Social Movements in American Political Institutions*, edited by Anne Costain and Andrew McFarland, 233–47. New York: Rowman & Littlefield.

Women of Color Association. 1991. "Speaking for Ourselves from the Women of Color Association." *Women's Review of Books* 8 (Fall): 27–29.

Wright, Margaret. 1970. "I Want the Right to Be Black and Me." In *Black Women in White America: A Documentary History*, edited by Gerda Lerner, 607–8. New York: Vintage Books.

WWIN Newsletter. 2001, August.

Zald, Mayer N. 1992. "Looking Backward to Look Forward: Reflections on the Past and Future of the Resource Mobilization Research Program." In *Frontiers in Social Movement Theory*, edited by Aldon D. Morris and Carol McClurg Mueller, 326–48. New Haven, CT: Yale University Press.

Zald, Mayer N., and Roberta Ash. 1966. "Social Movement Organizations: Growth, Decay and Change." *Social Forces* 44 (March): 327–40.

Zald, Mayer N., and John D. McCarthy, eds. 1979. *The Dynamics of Social Movements, Resource Mobilization, Social Control and Tactics.* Cambridge, MA: Winthrop.

———. 1987. *Social Movements in an Organizational Society: Collected Essays.* New Brunswick, NJ: Transaction Books.

Zdravomyslova, Elena. 1996. "Opportunities and Framing in the Transition to Democracy: The Case of Russia." In *Comparative Perspectives on Social Movements*, edited by Douglas McAdam, John McCarthy, and Mayer Zald, 122–37. Cambridge: Cambridge University Press.

"*Zhenshchiny i muzhchiny Rossii, 1997 [Women and Men in Russia, 1997].*" 1997. Moscow: Gosudarstvennyi Komitet Rossiiskoi Federatsii Po Statistike.

" 'Zhenshchiny' vyidu—'Otechestvu' legche?" 1999. *Izvestiya*, September 2, 2.

Zhurzhenko, Tatiana. 2004. "Strong Women, Weak State: Family Politics and Nation Building in Post-Soviet Ukraine." In *Post-Soviet Women Encountering Transition: Nation-Building, Economic Survival, and Civic Activism*, edited by Kathleen Kuehnast and Carol Nechemias, 23–43. Baltimore: Woodrow Wilson Press and The Johns Hopkins University Press.

Zollicoffer, Cydney. 2000. *See It? Tell It. Change It! Third Wave Foundation Newsletter.* (Summer): 4, at www.thirdwavefoundation.org (accessed January 14, 2002).

Zurcher, Louis A., and David A. Snow. 1981. "Collective Behavior: Social Movements." In *Social Psychology: Sociological Perspectives*, edited by Morris Rosenberg and Ralph H. Turner, 447–82. New York: Basic.

Index

257

101–4; organizational structure of, 97–100; policymaking of, 86–88; political activism of, 74–77, 83–93; political culture of, 85–86; political opportunities, 84; principles underlying, 85; splits in, 40; third wave feminism and, 56–57, 65–66; and Title VII, 146–47; and Title IX, 219

national organizations, relationship to local organizations, 95–96, 112–13

National Right to Life Committee (NRLC), 12, 199, 201–2, 211–12

National Woman's Party (NWP), 6, 7, 35

National Woman Suffrage Association, 5

National Women's Education Center (NWEC), 188

National Women's Political Caucus (NWPC), 89, 91

National Women's Service (SERNAM, Chile), 143

Nation of Islam, 127

Nelson, Barbara, 180–81

Network (*Netto*) movement, 189

New Conservative Party, 179

New Japan Party, 188

New Left, 29, 33, 34, 41, 48–49

New Sakigake Party, 179

new social movement theory, ERA campaign and, 71

New York City NOW (NYC NOW), 101–4

New York Times Book Review (magazine), 64

Nezavisimaia gazeta (newspaper), 165

Nineteenth Amendment, 6, 133

Nine to Five, 190–91

Nixon, Richard, 11

Nomura Shoken (Japanese court case), 193

Norton, Eleanor Holmes, 91

NOW. *See* National Organization for Women

NRLC. *See* National Right to Life Committee

NWP. *See* National Woman's Party

NWPC. *See* National Women's Political Caucus

off our backs (newspaper), 65

Operation Rescue, 103, 107

opportunities. *See* international opportunities; political opportunities

organizational structure: activities affected by, 85; Chicago NOW, 105; Cleveland NOW, 109; direct action groups, 74–75; mass movement groups, 74–75; NOW, 97–100; NYC NOW, 101–2; second wave feminism and, 29–30, 40–42; significance of, 9

organizers, social movement formation role of, 38–39

O'Sullivan, Mary Kenney, 5

packages: on abortion, 201–12; and framing, 200

Parks, Rosa, 127, 128

Partial Birth Abortion Ban Act (2003), 217

path dependency, 19

Patton, Gwen, 120

Paul, Alice, 6

Payne, Donald, 128

PCSW. *See* Presidential Commission on the Status of Women

Peking JAC (Joint Accountability Coalition), 187

People for the Ethical Treatment of Animals (PETA), 104

Perry, Paticia, 121

Personal Responsibility and Work Opportunity Reconciliation Law (1996), 184

Peterson, Esther, 30, 144–46

Pinard, Maurice, 36, 37

Pinochet, Augusto, 134, 136–37, 140–41

Piven, Frances Fox, 113

Planned Parenthood Federation of America (PPFA), 199, 202–3, 211–12

PLC. *See* Pro-Life Campaign

policy: feminist effect on, 182–84; Japanese feminism and, 192–94; NOW's policymaking, 86–88; policy networks, 219–20

political action committees (PACs): feminist, 181; of NOW, 89, 91–92

women's movement development in, 151–58; WUR, 158–60, 171
Russian Association of Family Planning, 172
Russian Revolution, 13

SAFO (Free Association of Feminist Organizations), 161
Saito Chiyo, 186
Saroyan, Strawberry, 65
Sassy (magazine), 60
Savage, Gus, 128
Schlafly, Phyllis, 12
School of the Americas, 61
SDS. *See* Students for a Democratic Society
Second Independent Women's Forum (Dubna, 1992), 162
second wave feminism: collective identity of, 49–50, 52; generational conflict and, 58, 64–66; grassroots feminism in, 29–35, 41–42, 48–54; growth and institutionalization of, 50–54; older/younger divisions in, 29–35, 40–42; origins of, 28–35, 48–50; political opportunities for, 11; supportive environment for, 53; third wave compared to, 45–46, 56, 57, 60, 61
Seiktatsu (Daily Life) Clubs, 189–90
Seneca Falls Convention (1848), 4, 6, 133, 197
settlement houses, 5
sexism: in Black movements of 1960s, 120–21; third wave feminism campaign against, 59
sexual harassment, 186, 193
sexual identity: queer politics and, 55; third wave feminism and, 54–55, 62
sexuality, in third wave feminism, 55–58
sex wars, 55–56
Shakur, Assata, 120, 121
Sharp Electronics (Japanese court case), 193
Sharpton, Al, 128
Shell, 192
Sheppard-Towner Act (1921), 6

Shiba Shinyo Credit (Japanese court case), 193
Shufuren (Housewives Association), 184
Sikkink, Kathryn, 223
Sister Soulja, 128
Smeal, Eleanor (Ellie), 71, 72, 75–77, 89–91
SNCC. *See* Student Nonviolent Coordinating Committee
"soap movements," 189
Socialist Party, 179, 187
social movement community, 96
social movements: analysis of, 26–27; origins of, 27–28, 35–39, 134–36
social movement scholarship: changes in, 25; on ideas, values, and norms, 15; inadequacies of, 17–20, 117; methodology in, 3; new social movement theory, 71; on political opportunities, 11, 14; on resource mobilization, 8
Society for the Protection of Unborn Children (SPUC), 199, 205–6, 211–12
Soros Foundation, 163
Southern Christian Leadership Conference, 128
Soviet Union. *See* Russia
Soviet Women's Committee (SWC), 159
Spelman, Elizabeth, 78
SPUC. *See* Society for the Protection of Unborn Children
Squier, John, 163
Staggenborg, Suzanne, 217
Stalin, Joseph, 153
Stanton, Elizabeth Cady, 4, 5, 6
State Commissions on the Status of Women, 30–31, 32, 35, 37
Steinem, Gloria, 65, 103
Stinchcombe, Arthur L., 85
Stone, Lucy, 5
Stop ERA (Stop Taking Our Privileges and Extra Responsibilities Amendment), 12, 72
Strike for Women's Equality (1970), 102
structures. *See* organizational structures
Student Nonviolent Coordinating Committee (SNCC), 120

Students for a Democratic Society (SDS), 29, 34, 48
suffragists, 1, 5–6
Sumitomo companies, 192
Suneson, Charlene, 89

tactics, 9–10
Tanaka Sumiko, 185
Tarrow, Sidney, 92, 181
Taskforce on Women's Rights and Responsibilities, 11
Taste of Power, A (Brown), 120
Taylor, Verta, 133
temperance movement, 4, 5
Theorizing Black Feminisms (Ross), 120
Third Wave Direct Action, 58
third wave feminism, 54–64; collective identity of, 63; concept of, 57–58; generational conflict and, 58, 64–66; grassroots of, 59–60, 62–63; and intersectionality, 60–61; lesbians and, 54–55, 62–63; media and, 60; political generation of, 63–64; second wave compared to, 45–46, 56, 57, 60, 61; supportive environment for, 63; transgender issues in, 61
Third Wave Foundation, 58–61, 63, 65, 182
Third World Women's Alliance, 120
Thomas, Clarence, 84, 103
Time (magazine), 216
Title IX, Education Amendments (1972), 219
Title VII, Civil Rights Act (1964), 31–32, 38, 39, 136, 146–49, 182–83
To Be Real (Walker), 65
Tokyo Union, 191
Tokyo Women's Plaza, 189
transgender individuals, 61
transnational feminism. *See* international feminism
Troy Academy for Women, 4
Tucker, Jennifer, 179
Turner, Ralph H., 27

UKFPA. *See* United Kingdom Family Planning Association

uman ribu (women's rib) groups, 185
unions, 5, 190–91
United Auto Workers Women's Committee, 32
United Kingdom Family Planning Association (UKFPA), 199, 206–7, 211–12
United Nations (UN): Conference on Women (Beijing, 1995), 185; Conference on Women (Mexico City, 1975), 139; Convention on the Elimination of All Forms of Discrimination against Women (CEDAW), 172, 185, 186, 196; Development Project (UNDP), 177; IRLF and, 204; women's organization development, 14
United States: abortion in, 200–203; Chile compared to, 134–36, 148–49; Japan compared to, 194–96; political opportunities, 135–36, 148–49, 178–79; Russia compared to, 151–52, 154–55, 166, 173–74
United States Agency for International Development (USAID), 163
United States-Newly Independent States (U.S.-NIS) Women's Consortium, 163
Unity electoral bloc, 169
unity issues, 218–19
University of California v. Bakke (1978), 118
USAID. *See* United States Agency for International Development

Valenzuela, María Elena, 142
Viagra, 193
Violence Against Women Act (VAWA, 1994), 182, 183
voluntary associations, 167
Voss, Kim, 118
Voters for Choice, 181
voting rights, 5–6

Walker, Alice, 58
Walker, Rebecca, 58, 62, 65
Walker, Wyatt T., 128
want ads, sex-segregated, 146–47

Contributors

Lisa Baldez is associate professor of government and Latin American, Latino, and Caribbean studies at Dartmouth College. She received her Ph.D. from the University of California, San Diego. Her book, *Why Women Protest: Women's Movements in Chile* (2002) compares the mobilization of women against the government of Chilean president Salvador Allende in the 1970s with the mobilization of women against Chilean military leader Augusto Pinochet in the 1980s. Her current research focuses on gender quotas and legislative politics in Latin America.

Lee Ann Banaszak, associate professor of political science and women's studies at The Pennsylvania State University, has written on comparative women's movements and the determinants of feminist attitudes among the mass public in the United States and Europe. She is author of *Why Movements Succeed or Fail: Opportunity, Culture and the Struggle for Woman Suffrage* (1996) and editor (along with Karen Beckwith and Dieter Rucht) of *Women's Movements Facing a Reconfigured State* (2003). Her articles have appeared in the *American Political Science Review, Political Research Quarterly,* and *Public Opinion Quarterly.* Her current research examines movement activists within government and their effect on the U.S. women's movement.

Maryann Barakso is assistant professor of government at American University. She is the author of *Governing NOW: Grassroots Activism in the National Organization for Women* (2005), and her article "Civic Engagement and Voluntary Associations: Reconsidering the Role of the Governance Structures of Advocacy Groups" will appear in *Polity* in 2005. Barakso's most recent work considers changes in the levels of internal democracy in women's membership associations.

Jo Freeman is the author of two prize-winning books, *The Politics of Women's Liberation* (1975) and *A Room at a Time: How Women Entered Party Politics* (2002). Her memoir, *At Berkeley in the Sixties: The Education of an Activist, 1961–1965,* was published in 2003. More information is available at www.jofreeman.com.

Joyce Gelb is professor of political science at City College and the Graduate Center, City University of New York. She is director of the Women's Studies Program at City College. She has been a visiting professor in recent years at Yale University and Doshisha and Tokyo Universities in Japan. Her research and publications deal primarily with comparative politics and policy including work on women's political participation, social movements, and policy-making and outcomes in the United States, Europe, and Japan. She has received grants from the Ford, Rockefeller, and National Science Foundations. Her book *Gender Policies in Japan and the United States: Comparing Women's Movements, Rights and Politics* was published in 2003.

David S. Meyer is professor of sociology, political science, and planning, policy, and design at the University of California, Irvine. He is author of *A Winter of Discontent: The Nuclear Freeze and American Politics* and coeditor of four books, most recently *Routing the Opposition: Social Movements, Public Policy, and Democracy* with Valerie Jenness and Helen Ingram. He is most interested in the connections among institutional politics, public policy, and social movements.

Celeste Montoya Kirk is assistant professor at Southern Illinois University in Carbondale. She received her Ph.D. in political science at Washington University in St. Louis. Her current research focuses on the distance between women's rights policy formation and implementation in different countries and how various women's rights advocates (international and national, governmental and nongovernmental) affect the translation of policy into practice.

Carol Nechemias is associate professor of public policy at Penn State, Harrisburg, where she serves as coordinator of the public policy program. Her research focuses on Russian domestic politics and women in politics. In recent years she has published articles and book chapters on Russian women's access to legislative seats, the development of a women's movement in Russia, women's political participation, and women's health. In addition, she is coeditor of two books: the *Encyclopedia of Russian Women's Movements* (2001) and *Post-Soviet Women Encountering Transition* (2004).

Jo Reger is assistant professor of sociology at Oakland University in Michigan. Her area of research examines gender and social movements, in particular social movement organizations and activist identities. She is currently researching a book on the U.S. contemporary women's movement and recently edited a volume entitled *Different Wavelengths: Studies of the Contemporary Women's Movement* (2005).

Belinda Robnett is professor of sociology and former director of African American studies at the University of California, Irvine. She received her Ph.D. from the University of Michigan in 1991. Professor Robnett is the author of *How Long? How Long? African-American Women in the Struggle for Civil Rights* (1997) and the coeditor of *Social Movements: Identity, Culture, and the State* (2002). She has published numerous articles on race, gender, and social movements, and is currently working on a new book project, *Our Struggle for Unity: African Americans in the Age of Identity Politics*.

Deana A. Rohlinger is assistant professor of sociology at Florida State University. She studies mass media, social movements, and gender. She recently completed a doctoral dissertation, "Getting into Mass Media: A Comparative Analysis of Social Movement Organizations and Mass Media Outlets in the Abortion Debate," which examines how pro-choice and pro-life activists have tried to strategically use a range of mass media outlets to affect political outcomes over a twenty-year period.

Barbara Ryan is professor of sociology and director of women's studies at Widener University. She received her Ph.D. from Washington University in St. Louis and in 1998 was a Fulbright Scholar in India. Her specialty areas are sex and gender, social movements, family, and qualitative research methods. She has published numerous articles on gender and women's issues, including three books on the women's movement. Her latest book, *Identity Politics in the Women's Movement*, presents the voices of exclusion based on race, ethnicity, class, age, sexual orientation, disability, and other social characteristics. Her future work includes expanding identity politics into the international arena and a biography of Alice Paul.

Suzanne Staggenborg is professor and chair of the Department of Sociology at McGill University. Her work includes *The Pro-Choice Movement: Organization and Activism in the Abortion Conflict* (1991), *Gender, Family, and Social Movements* (1998), *Methods of Social Movement Research* (coedited with

Bert Klandermans, 2002), and a number of articles about abortion politics and social movements in the United States and Canada. She is currently completing a study of the women's movement in Montreal, examining the ways in which the movement has developed and changed since the 1960s.

Nancy Whittier is associate professor of sociology and a member of the Women's Studies Program Committee at Smith College. Her work focuses on women's movements in the United States since the 1960s, generations, gender and social movements, collective identity, and activism against child sexual abuse. She is the author of *Feminist Generations: The Persistence of the Radical Women's Movement* and articles and chapters on these topics in numerous journals and scholarly collections, including the *American Sociological Review* and *Social Problems*, and is coeditor of *Social Movements: Identities, Culture, and the State*, and *Feminist Frontiers*.